PATHS OF PROGRESS

Strong and true, on its western stages,
Girt by downland and tree-clad hill.
Strong and true as in bygone ages,
The old Bath Road fares onward still.
And strong and true, the young with the older,
Stands the School our youth's abode,
Side by side and shoulder to shoulder,
Guarding the flanks of the old Bath Road.

Paths of progress, links of the parted,
Friends that lighten the toiler's load,
Staunch do they stand, and stalwart-hearted,
Marlborough School and the old Bath Road.

PATHS OF PROGRESS

A History of Marlborough College

Thomas Hinde

JAMES X JAMES

© Marlborough College 1992
ISBN 0 907383 33 5
First published 1992

New photography by Alex Ramsay
Designed by Tom Cabot

Typeset by Action Typesetting Limited, Gloucester
Printed and bound by Hollen Street Press, Berkshire

Published by
James & James (Publishers) Limited
75 Carleton Road
London N7 0ET

Half-title page: The refrain from the School Song,
The Old Bath Road, by C.L.F. Boughey.

Illustration on title page: 'Marlborough College'
from a drawing by John Western.

FOREWORD

by

The Rt Hon Peter Brooke MP

MARLBOROUGH HAS ALWAYS been a magical place, certainly from the days of Merlin and perhaps from the era of the Beaker People, and for the past 150 years the College has been intertwined with its history, conferring something of that magic on generations of Marlburians. For years the largest boarding-school in the nation to be surrounded on all sides save the Town by open country, it is perhaps no surprise that we have produced more than our fair share of poets.

Thomas Hinde's new history of the College is a happy celebration of the school's first century and a half, and wholly engrossing to anyone who has been associated with even the smallest part of that history. All such have their own perspectives, from their particular eras and their particular links. I am confident that anyone who seeks to illuminate their special interest from within these pages will be pleased by the comprehensiveness which the author has attained, but he has also achieved a singular thread of narrative in explaining how the ethos unfolded and the continuity of values evolved.

That pattern of values, derived in no small degree from the founders' original concern for the sons of clergy, has left its own imprint on Marlburians – and now Marlburiennes. Two friends of mine told me, quite separately, that the reason they had sent their children to Marlborough, though they had no prior connection themselves, was because they had never ever met a Marlburian they disliked; and Reginald Jennings, my old housemaster who will be known to thousands of readers, said that in forty years he had known no more than five what he characteristically called 'really bad hats'. This book, enhanced by David West's deft and imaginative deployment of the College archive, is the story of how place and people came together to create a remarkable school.

Peter Brooke

October 1992

ACKNOWLEDGEMENTS

So many people have helped me that I fear I may fail to mention some; to them my apologies. Those I want to thank for special help include John and Michael O'Regan, who let me read and quote from their biography of their father, J.R.H. (Pat) O'Regan (edited by Prof. John Honey); Derek Pelly for letting me use the unpublished memoir of his father, A.R. Pelly, and Miss Oriole Goldsmith for the unpublished memoir of her father, J.H.T. Goldsmith.

I must also thank the many Marlburians who sent memoirs to the college — wherever I have used these I have mentioned my source. Those I have personally met or corresponded with include F.M. (George) Heywood, Thomas Garnett, John Dancy, Roger Ellis and the present Master, David Cope; among other past or present members of staff, Richard Barker, John Byrom, Colin Goldsmith, David Green, Laurence Gunner, Niall Hamilton, Patrick Heffron, John Isaacson, Christopher Joseph, Nicholas Milner-Gulland, Robin Nelson, Maxim Nikolsky, Janet Tanner, Peter Tinniswood, Brian Wallis, David Whiting and Donald Wright; among Old Marlburians, Prof. Cloudsley-Thompson, Dr Alan Del Mar, Sir Henry Fisher, Maurice Hayward, David Hobson, Lord Hunt, Ben Leefield, Norris McWhirter, Dr T.R. (Dick) Maurice, Dr Tim Maurice, Mrs Ann Monk (Willis), David Murison, Richard Russell, Robert Smith, Dr Francis Willis, Steve Willmore; and among others connected with Marlborough, Lady Brooke, Mrs Kempson, today's bursar, Edward Hardman, the lately retired bursar's secretary Hermione Budge, the Master's secretary Elizabeth McKerrow, and Fiona MacCarthy, William Morris's biographer. To all of these my grateful thanks. Finally (more properly first and foremost) I must thank David West, Marlborough's archivist, without whose constant help, wise advice and admirable archives I could not possibly have written this book.

CONTENTS

Foreword   5

Acknowledgements   6

Introduction   11

 1. Plater's Good Idea *1838–1843*   15

 2. Wilkinson Means Well *1843–1851*   25

 3. Rebellion *1851*   41

 4. Cotton to the Rescue *1852–1858*   49

 5. The Great Bradley *1858–1871*   63

 6. Eric's Creator *1871–1876*   76

 7. Bell's Long Reign *1876–1903*   86

 8. One Lay Apple *1903–1911*   109

 9. The Boodle and the Boot *1911–1926*   121

10. Boy, Beak and Master *1926–1939*   146

11. A Different War *1939–1952*   160

12. Bridges and Beagles *1952–1961*   183

13. All Change *1961–1972*   197

14. After the Storm *1972–1986*   213

15. A New Start *1986–1993*   227

Chronology   234

Index   236

'Old Mother of the four grass ways', Sorley's signpost on the
Downs. From a drawing by Christopher Hughes.

And soon, O soon, I do not doubt it,
With the body or without it,
We shall all come tumbling down
To our old wrinkled red-capped town.
Perhaps the road up Ilsley way,
The old ridge-track, will be my way.
High up among the sheep and sky,
Look down on Wantage, passing by,
And see the smoke from Swindon town;
And then full left at Liddington,
Where the four winds of heaven meet
The earth-blest traveller to greet.
And then my face is toward the south,
There is a singing on my mouth:
Away to rightward I descry
My Barbury ensconced in sky,
Far underneath the Ogbourne twins,
And at my feet the thyme and whins,
The grasses with their little crowns
Of gold, the lovely Aldbourne downs,
And that old signpost (well I knew
That crazy signpost, arms askew,
Old mother of the four grass ways).
And then my mouth is dumb with praise,
For past the wood and chalkpit tiny,
A glimpse of Marlborough ἐρατεινή!
So I descend beneath the rail
To warmth and welcome and wassail.

* * * * * *

This from the battered trenches—rough,
Jingling and tedious enough.
And so I sign myself to you:
One, who some crooked pathways knew
Round Bedwyn: who could scarcely leave
The Downs on a December eve:
Was at his happiest in shorts,
And got—not many good reports!
Small skill of rhyming in his hand—
But you'll forgive—you'll understand.

From I have not brought my Odyssey *by Charles Hamilton Sorley. Written in France, 12 July 1915, to J. Bain, an assistant master (and poet) at Marlborough. Sorley was killed in action 13 October 1915.*

INTRODUCTION

A T THE START of the nineteenth century the majority of English middle- and upper-class boys, the only group which received any real education, were either taught at home (often by clergymen who were their fathers); or at private schools, which varied in quality from 'Dotheboys Hall' establishments to passably good schools such as Eagle House, Hammersmith; or at about 100 local grammar schools, these too of very differing quality. But there were also what were commonly called the seven Great Schools – soon to become known as public schools: Winchester, Eton, Westminster, Harrow, Charterhouse, Rugby and Shrewsbury.

These seven had not been created Great. They had been founded at different times, for different purposes, and had different histories. Of them, Harrow, Rugby and Shrewsbury had once been local grammar schools, and occasionally some other grammar school, when it had a particularly ambitious headmaster, would achieve similar status: Richmond Grammar School, Yorkshire, for example, under James Tate. But the seven had maintained a high standard over a long period, and as a result were considered the country's best. They had therefore attracted boys from a distance and this had led to one of their essential features. They were either entirely, or at least partly, boarding-schools. Their other common characteristics were that their boys were upper or upper-middle class; and that, like just about every school in the country, they taught almost exclusively Latin and Greek.

Well considered they may have been, but they were uncivilised places, where the boys lived in prison-like accommodation on disgusting food, where bullying reduced the more sensitive to misery, and where headmasters imposed such order as there was with cane and rod. Dr John Keate, headmaster of Eton from 1809 to 1834, typified such headmasters:

> He was a capital scholar but his ingenuous learning had *not* softened his manners and *had* 'permitted' them to be fierce – tremendously fierce. He had such a complete command over his temper – I mean over his *good* temper that he scarcely ever allowed it to appear; you

could not put him out of humour – that is, out of the *ill* humour which
he thought to be fitting for a headmaster. His red shaggy eyebrows
were so prominent that he habitually used them as arms and hands for
the purpose of pointing out any object towards which he wished to
draw attention; the rest of his features were equally striking.... He
wore a fancy dress partly resembling the costume of Napoleon and
partly that of a widow woman (A. W. Kinglake, *Eothen*).

This was the alarming man who on one occasion personally beat 70
boys in succession for cribbing, and on another, 89 for taking part in a
rebellion. It is not surprising that such schools should have provoked
criticism, indeed the surprising thing is that there was so little. Equally
surprising is that so much of it was directed at the prevalence of swearing
– though prevalent it certainly was. 'When I had gone to bed,' an old
Etonian of Keate's time wrote, 'Trench came into my room and pulled
me about in every sort of way he could think of ... also had broken five
panes of glass in my window and this is chiefly to be attributed to my
not swearing with them.'

Such was the state of affairs when, in 1828, Dr Thomas Arnold was
appointed headmaster of Rugby. There he remained until he retired in
1840. Two years later he died and two years later again Dean Stanley
published the biography which established him as the founder of the
Victorian public school. Since these were precisely the years in which
Marlborough's founders were planning and opening their new school,
it might seem likely that they were influenced by him.

The truth is, however, that any direct influence is improbable, because
it was only after Stanley's biography that Arnold became widely known.
'I don't know what you mean by Arnold's reforms at Rugby,' Samuel
Butler, headmaster of Shrewsbury, wrote in 1835. 'You are probably
better informed that I am, and allude to something with which I am
unacquainted.' And Winchester's second master, Charles Wordsworth,
remembered that 1838 was the year in which he first heard of Arnold.

In any case, modern biographers have stripped Arnold of responsibility
for many of the features of public schools with which he was once
associated. He did not, for example, favour organised games. In *Tom
Brown's Schooldays*, Thomas Hughes's novel in which Arnold appears as
Rugby's headmaster, the School House game is probably the best
remembered passage, but it was a disorganised affair, more like a battle
than a football match, in which the whole school took part on one side
or the other. Organised football developed from such mêlées, and, with
other team games, became a substitute for the roaming of the
countryside, bird's-nesting or poaching in which boys had previously

spent their spare time, but at Rugby, neither in fact nor in fiction, were they organised, let alone compulsory, under Arnold.

Nor did Arnold initiate the rule of prefects or Sixth Form boys over junior boys. This was already one of the characteristics of the seven Great Schools. Nor did he make fundamental changes in the school's curriculum. True, he introduced modern history, and a certain amount of mathematics and modern languages; and he encouraged the study of the modern relevance of classical authors. But the learning of Latin and Greek, together with some divinity, remained the central features of Rugby's academic life.

Arnold's reforms were of another sort. On being appointed he saw the school as a place of 'so much wickedness' that he dreaded going there. Its wickedness consisted in widespread and well-established offences against every aspect of Christian morality, from lying and swearing, at one extreme, to gambling, drinking and dissipation (a euphemism for homosexuality) at the other. Included were idleness and the envy or denigration of boys who showed industry or were successful. His aim was to re-Christianise the school. Learning, as he saw it, was less important for what it taught than because it required the Christian virtue of endeavour. He exploited the rule of the Sixth Form over the school because this was vital to his purpose; he personally could influence its boys and use them to spread Christian behaviour throughout the school. It was the whole tone of life at Rugby that he set out in this way to civilise, and in so far as he succeeded the most important change that this brought about was that he and the boys began to work together. If the traditional hatred of boys for masters did not disappear, it was reduced.

He retained flogging and caning because they instilled the Christian virtue of obedience. Boys should be *made* to be good. The idea that there was anything valuable about self-expression never occurred to him. The 1830s were years of a great Christian revival throughout the country and though this divided the Church into quarrelling factions, all took religion more seriously. If Arnold's reforms today seem limited, they seemed to most of his contemporaries desirable and adequate.

One of his undoubted successes, and the one which was eventually to have an important influence on Marlborough, was to inspire a group of devoted disciples who would spread his message. Among these was George Cotton, the man who was, in a sense, to be Marlborough's real founder. Its original founders, even if they knew about Arnold, were curiously little concerned with the nature of the school they planned. It would be Christian, of course, and no doubt more earnestly so than other schools of the time, but this was merely to conform with contemporary values. To understand their purpose, a more significant event of these years than Arnold's headmastership was the opening in 1841 of Cheltenham College, the country's first new public school.

Cheltenham was to provide for a growing demand from middle-class or would-be middle-class parents for places at public schools. Several explanations for this demand have been suggested. The late 1830s and early 1840s were the years when, all over the country, stagecoaches were being replaced by trains, and as a result local schools were no longer so much more convenient than distant ones. They were also years in which the population of the country was rapidly increasing, and in which the number of children who survived in middle-class families was also increasing. As a result, if sons were educated locally, there would often be several of them permanently resident at home, something which middle-class parents found it difficult to tolerate. Sending some away to boarding-school, especially those who were rowdy, relieved domestic pressures. But the most probable explanation is that parents of the newly rich merchant classes wanted to give their sons a public school education to ensure that they should become gentlemen.

Anglican clergymen would not have had precisely this motive – most of them had been to Oxford or Cambridge and would have considered themselves securely upper-middle class. But they may well have wished to do what more and more of their social equals were now doing. They may also have wanted to make certain of their sons' social status, for many of them were desperately poor. In 1839 the Revd Charles Dodgson wrote, 'The proceeds of all the Benefices in England and Wales, if equally divided among the Incumbents, would furnish an income of barely £300 a year. But the actual distribution of these revenues is still more worthy of remark.... While the Income of 1,451 exceeds £500, those of nearly 5,000 are below £200 and those of nearly 200 are below £100 a year.'

While Dodgson himself was at Daresbury with an income of about £190 he sent none of his children to school, but educated them at home. Only when he moved to Croft, a richer living, could he send his eldest son, the future Lewis Carroll, first to board at Richmond Grammar School, then to Rugby. The predicament of a curate like Thomas Teasdale of Luckington, Wiltshire, was more extreme. On a stipend of £80 he had to bring up five children. He is remembered because he laboured for ten years to improve his condition by compiling a Greek lexicon, before hearing that Liddell and Scott's famous lexicon was about to appear – as it did in 1843, the very year that Marlborough School opened. It was for the children of such poor clerics that it had been planned.

1

PLATER'S GOOD IDEA

1838–1843

O N 5 NOVEMBER 1851 a rocket fired into the night sky above the buildings of Marlborough College signalled not just the start of normal Guy Fawkes Day celebrations, but of a school rebellion.

For the whole of that evening [wrote A. G. Bradley, author of the 1893 history of the school] despite every effort of the authorities, the entire Court, was ablaze with fireworks. Not content with this, the boys carried them into school, let them off under desks, tossed them into the fires, hissing, stamping, and shouting down the futile efforts of the form-masters to quell the disorder. All that night the row continued, and the echoing corridors of B House rang with the continual detonations. The whole College for the next two days reeked of gunpowder. Authority was paralysed.

How could such an event have occurred? It would need explaining whatever its date, but it was more remarkable at a time when school rebellions had become rare; and at Marlborough of all places, which was the creation of a group of worthy churchmen, had the blessing of W. E. Gladstone and the Archbishop of Canterbury and was specifically intended to educate the sons of the Anglican clergy.

To answer the question it is necessary to go back 13 years, to the moment when the idea of the school which became Marlborough first occurred to an obscure English parson, the Revd Charles Plater, Vicar of River, near Dover.

Charles Eaton Plater's family came from Canterbury, where his grandfather had been a grocer. His father, however, took holy orders and throughout Plater's childhood held the Kent livings of Whitstable and Seasalter. It was then that Plater was sent back to his family town to attend the King's School, Canterbury, where he was a scholar from 1809 to 1815. Marlborough's founder thus had direct experience of the problems his father had had as an Anglican clergyman who wished to give his son a middle-class education. He had also experienced the deficient education offered by a typical country grammar school. At this time the King's School was in decline, reduced by 1815 to a mere 26 boys, and though the lower master, Francis, seems to have been enlightened, Naylor, the flogging headmaster taught only the classics. One story survives about Plater during his time at the King's School. His contemporary, George Gilbert, remembered that 'For Mathematics I enjoyed the instruction of that benevolent man Rev. Henry Hutchesson who was well able to teach Euclid, Algebra, Trigonometry etc.... With him Bishop Broughton and Charles Plater and myself read successively for several months by the advice of Rev. John Francis, our Under Master but without Rev. C. Naylor's knowledge.'

Plater's connection with William Broughton is of much interest. Broughton, who was to become the first Anglican bishop of Australia, founded there in 1831 the King's School, Parramatta. In 1834 Broughton visited Canterbury and attended a meeting of the King's School's Feast Society (its old boys' association), at which he described his Australian school. Whether Plater was present is not known, but it seems quite likely that he would have come to hear his old school friend. He was then probably acting as his father's curate at Whitstable, and within easy reach of Canterbury. If he did come, Broughton's account of his Australian foundation could well have given Plater the idea of doing something similar in England.

The date would fit subsequent events. Documents have now been found, many of them by the Old Marlburian, Leonard Warwick James, which give a fuller picture of the school's founding than Bradley was able to give. James made his luckiest discovery in 1943 when, in the 'boiler area' of the old Music School, he found the boys of the City of London School (then evacuated to Marlborough) keeping themselves warm by feeding into a tortoise-stove the pages of the leather-bound volumes which recorded the minutes of the school's founding committees. One of the documents he recovered was a letter addressed to Plater, commenting on a proposal for a school for the sons of the clergy, dated 10 August 1838. Plater's first scheme must therefore have existed four years at most after Bishop Broughton's visit to Canterbury.

This letter was from the Revd Stephen Cattley, who gave his address as River, Dover. Perhaps he was Plater's curate, or perhaps a retired clerical friend. Fifteen months later, however, Plater's proposal had been more widely circulated, for a letter addressed to him on 23 November 1839 was signed by 24 clergymen. They approved the general principle of the scheme and asked to be invited to a public meeting to discuss the idea. Several gave the number of sons they might send to such a school. In a covering letter, however, the Revd Samuel Sheen wrote that the general opinion of the 24 was that 'even the Prospectus of such an Institution ... should either emanate from, or be accompanied by the openly expressed sanction of some leading Bishops of our Church'.

Plater acted quickly on this advice. Within two months he had obtained the support of the Archbishop of Canterbury, and in January 1840 was able to send out a new proposal headed:

SCHOOL

for the

SONS AND ORPHANS OF THE CLERGY

* * *

PATRON: THE ARCHBISHOP OF CANTERBURY
PRESIDENT: THE BISHOP OF THE DIOCESE
VICE-PRESIDENTS: ALL THE BISHOPS IN THE KINGDOM
AND ITS COLONIES, AND OTHER DIGNITARIES

The school, Plater suggested, would only charge clergymen's sons 'the sum of £30 per annum, Books, etc., excepted'. He continued, 'The need of such an Institution for the Sons of the Clergy will be apparent to all who consider that the average net professional Income of the Clergy is not more than £200 per annum, while the known average expense of Education for a Boy does not fall below £60 per annum.'

The school's curriculum was to include, besides the classics and religious instruction, Hebrew, arithmetic and geometry, history, the French and German languages, geography, drawing, mechanics, engineering, surveying, experimental philosophy, architecture ecclesiastical and civil, practical agriculture and horticulture. If the school prospered, orphans of the clergy were to be admitted free. An accompanying letter requested answers 'signifying your approbation of the Principles [of the scheme] or your wish to send one or more Sons to the Institution contemplated'. A reply form was enclosed.

Finally, Plater proposed the establishment of a sinking fund. That July he received the following letter from Mr Gladstone (at this time out of office).

London, July 27, 1840.

Dear Sir,

I have had the pleasure to receive your recent circular, which seems to prove that you are making real progress. I give you full permission to make use, if it be worth your while, of my name, thinking it better however that it should not be as a Trustee: and I beg you will put me down for a donation of (£50) fifty pounds.

I remain dear Sir,
Your very faithful servant,
W. E. Gladstone.

Two years later Gladstone, by then Vice-President of the Board of Trade, sent a second donation, describing it as 'his subscription'.

During 1841 a committee was formed to further Plater's scheme, and this committee produced revised proposals which, on 6 September, the Revd George Bowers sent to the Archbishop of Canterbury. After Plater, Bowers, described by Bradley as 'ever-active', was the most important of Marlborough's founders. At this time Rector of St Paul's, Covent Garden, he subsequently (1847) became Dean of Manchester. It was he who later suggested the foundation of Rossall and of Haileybury. 'The latter', says the *Dictionary of National Biography*, 'gained much on its establishment from Bowers's personal help and experience', much of this undoubtedly gained when establishing Marlborough.

To the Archbishop Bowers wrote that he hoped the new proposals would be as acceptable as the earlier ones and that 'the provisional Committee to whom the work of forming some plan for the establishment of a School for the Sons of Clergymen has been entrusted, may be encouraged by the honour and advantage of your Grace's approbation'. These new proposals must in essence have been the 22 which were printed on 11 January 1842, introduced by a letter addressed to the Archbishop. They suggested that parents who wished to send boys to the planned school should acquire the right to do so by paying £100 to become life governors, or £50 to become governors. Life governors would be entitled to have one boy at the school throughout their lives, governors to a place for one boy only. The life governors were to elect a council to manage the affairs of the school. There were to be 300 boys, rising to 500, two-thirds of whom were to be sons of clergymen, paying £35 a year, one-third sons of laymen paying £60 a year.

In his letter Bowers admitted, however, that out of 300 replies received showing interest in the school, the writers of only 28 had said they could afford to become life governors. He therefore suggested that payments should be made by instalments, 'and that parties so subscribing should have the right to nominate immediately after payment of one-half the sum required'.

He went on to deal with objections to the charging of different fees for the sons of clerics and those of laymen. 'In answer to which,' he wrote, 'it may be said, that the school is instituted primarily for the sons of clergymen; it is in fact *their* school, and it is for them to say on what conditions others shall be admitted into it.'

On 1 July of that year the committee called a public meeting at 79 Pall Mall, premises of the Society for the Propagation of the Gospel in Foreign Parts. It must have been an impressive occasion. In the chair was the Archbishop of Canterbury, and others attending included five bishops and three peers of the realm, not to mention Gladstone. Trustees were appointed and a comprehensive prospectus of 24 clauses agreed.

Though these were similar to the 22 of Bowers's January leaflet, there were differences. The school was initially to have only 200 pupils, the fees were to be only 30 guineas and 50 guineas respectively, and Bowers's suggestion for the buying of governorships by instalment was incorporated. So was his reduction of Plater's original ambitious curriculum, which was now merely to include classics, mathematics, modern languages and 'sound Theological teaching'. The Council of 18 which Bowers had proposed was to have as its president the bishop of the diocese in which the school was situated, and as its vice-presidents the bishops of England and Wales, but its proportion of clerics was reduced from two-thirds to a half. Unwisely, as it turned out, the proposals not only stipulated that the boys should be aged between eight and 18, but added that when first admitted they should be under 14.

The new proposals were incorporated in a fresh prospectus, and 3,500 of these were sent out by Christopher Hodgson. Hodgson, another active member of the committee, whose portrait hangs today in the Master's Lodge, was secretary to Queen Anne's Bounty, a body set up in 1704 to assist the poorer clergy. It was as a result of his work that he claimed to know this number of clergymen personally. In an introductory letter to them he wrote:

> I have taken a great interest in the establishment of the undermentioned School from a deep conviction of the usefulness and the extensive benefits it is likely to afford, and I take the present opportunity of enclosing a prospectus and strongly recommending it to the attention of the clergy, and through them to the notice of gentlemen of property with whom they may be acquainted.

How, it may be asked, did the committee expect to be able to charge fees so much lower than those of other schools? The answer lay in the different boarding arrangements it planned. At other schools, public and grammar, boys who boarded had in early times lived with the headmaster or with some other master. By this time, however, they usually lived in town houses – the Dames' Houses of Eton were typical – and there was general agreement that those who kept such houses found them highly profitable. If the school provided its own boarding accommodation *it* would make these profits. The committee had therefore been busily looking for a building large enough to be used in this way.

It had received various general suggestions: 'an hotel establishment at the end of a country town', 'some foundation Grammar School which is doing nothing, of which there are several in the Midland Counties', 'one of the many Mansions in Yorkshire or Westmorland'. It had also considered particular buildings. As early as 1 February 1840 Plater had written to Gladstone asking for his help in the puchase or renting of Worksop Manor from the Duke of Newcastle. A month later he had given up the idea because the Archbishop of Canterbury thought the building would be too expensive to repair and heat. By April 1842 Filkins Hall near Lechlade had also been considered but rejected because of the high price the owner wanted.

On the 29th of that month, however, one Richard Rice wrote to Bowers, 'I expect to be in Marlborough shortly and will inquire if there is any prospect of engaging the Place for the school.' He referred to Marlborough's Castle Inn, a formidable building, splendidly set in the countryside immediately to the west of Marlborough town. The same month committee member F. P. B. Martin told Bowers, 'I have thought of your suggestion respecting the Castle Inn at Marlborough. I wish you would permit me to sound out Lord Bruce on the subject.' Lord Bruce was the eldest son of the Marquis of Ailesbury, Warden of Savernake Forest, owner of the Castle Inn.

Charles Halcomb, whose grandfather had kept the Castle, whose father had had charge of the posting arrangements on one side of Marlborough town, and who himself was a boy at Marlborough in its earliest years, explained in old age how Bowers had discovered the inn. In about 1840 he had come to live at Preshute to undertake the duties of the vicar who was ill. At that time he was so 'full of a scheme to found a school for the "sons of clergy and others"' that he would 'start the subject whenever anyone was in his society', and as a result it became 'a constant topic of conversation' between Bowers and Halcomb's father whose good friend he had become. It was Halcomb's father who pressed the idea of the Castle Inn on Bowers, an idea supported by another committee member, Robert Few, who had been at Marlborough Grammar School and therefore knew it well.

In the summer of 1841 Halcomb's father gave a dinner party at the White House (which stood on the site of the present Book Office) for Bowers, Few and another committee member, Foster McGeachy. After dinner Halcomb followed the party to the Castle Inn and through it, on to the bowling-green. Here his father told his guests to turn and look back. 'It was then one of the gentlemen, in a tone expressive of both admiration and surprise, said, "What a place for a school". I did not notice who made this remark, but I have always thought it must have been Mr McGeachy ... because he was the only stranger present and all the others were too familiar with the scene to have made it.'

A year later negotiations were advancing well. On 27 May 1842 the Revd John Ward was able to write, 'It gives me great pleasure to hear that you have made some progress towards securing the Castle at Marlborough'. Ward was the Vicar of Great Bedwyn and East Grafton, on the other side of Savernake Forest from Marlborough, and another active clergyman, though a less lucky one. At this time he was giving his East Grafton church a new Norman barrel roof. By December 1842 it was complete, though still supported by scaffolding, when he was visited by Sydney Herbert, Secretary for the Admiralty, and a cousin of Herbert named Montgomery. Ward was unable to resist the temptation to remove the scaffolding and show off his fine new roof. Briefly it held, then entirely collapsed, a large stone hitting Montgomery and instantly killing him.

A pencil drawing *c.* 1844 showing (right) the White House where Matthew Wilkinson lived until the Lodge was built. To the left are the brew-house and laundry of the Castle Inn, demolished 1846 to make room for B House.

Meanwhile, on 20 July the formal decision had been taken and soon afterwards this was announced in the press:

The Castle Hotel, Marlborough, with ten acres of land in the county of Wilts ... will (it is expected) be ready for the reception of pupils at Lady Day 1843.

The committee had good reason for choosing the Castle Inn. It was no mere coaching-inn of the sort which had thrived for the previous hundred years along most of the country's main roads, but a grand mansion, built early in the eighteenth century in Queen Anne style by the 'proud' Duke of Somerset. When Celia Fiennes, the well-known lady traveller, rode through Marlborough, probably in about 1710, work was still in progress. The Duke's previous house, she reported, which had been 'a greate Rambling building', was now 'most pulled down', and its successor was 'newly building'. Only one wing had so far been completed, with 'drawing dineing roomes and bed Chambers with Closets and dressing-roomes and two Stair Casees', but they were still being painted and were unfurnished. Another wing was planned, the two to be 'Joyn'd with a Greate Hall'.

In its grounds she noted the bowling-green, from which you went down many steps to reach the foot of the Mound. This could be climbed 'by an Easye ascent bounded by ... quick sett hedges Cut Low, and soe you rise by degrees in 4 rounds bounded by the Low Cutt hedge, and on the top ... you have a prospect of ye town and Country round, and two parishes two mile off in view ... and this mount is Encompass'd about with ... a cannal which Emptys itself into a ffish pond then it Empts itself into the river.' Celia Fiennes makes no attempt to explain the Mound, nor has it been satisfactorily explained since. It is not as high as Silbury Hill but, like Silbury, was probably man-made in late-Neolithic times – though for what purpose remains a mystery.

A print published in 1723 shows the two wings of the house complete, with single-storey loggias reaching north from the outer ends of each, but the central hall still only partly built and no portico, which was only added when it became an inn. Near by is the Mound, with its helter-skelter hedges, exactly as Celia Fiennes described them, while stretching south stands the wood known as the Wilderness. South of the house itself, hedges surround an area which became the bowling-green, this in turn surrounded by the sort of formal garden of pathways and parterres which surrounded every English country mansion until some 25–30 years later Capability Brown set the fashion for replacing them with ha-has, lawns and clumps of trees.

That this did not happen at Marlborough, though the site would have

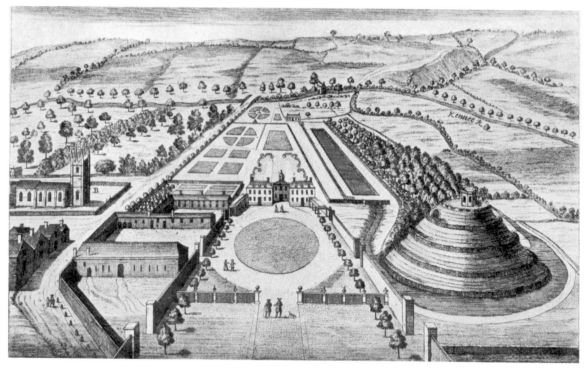

View of the Mansion by Stukeley, 1723. Note, on the left of the Mansion, two stable courtyards, the nearer of which still exists as New Court.

suited it well, may be explained by the fact that, in 1748, the Duke of Somerset died and three years later the family abandoned their new house (they had several others) letting it to one George Smith. It had been open as an inn for a fortnight when, on 19 October, Lady Vere stayed there, reporting that it drew multitudes and was 'overflowing with company continually'. It was 'furnished inn-like, two beds in each room' with furniture that was mostly new, and looked 'spruce and clean'. On 17 August the following year Smith advertised in the *Salisbury Journal and Devizes Mercury*:

I beg leave to inform the Publick that I have fitted up the Castle at Marlborough in the most genteel and commodious manner, and opened it as an Inn, where the Nobility, Gentry, etc., may depend on the best accommodation and treatment: the favour of whose company will be always gratefully acknowledged by their most obedient Servant, George Smith, late of the Artillery Ground, London. – Neat Post Chaises.

The Castle Inn continued to flourish, especially in early coaching-days when coaches took three days to make the journey from London to Bath, and Marlborough was the most convenient second-night's stop. In 1767 William Pitt, the elder, travelling in the opposite direction after a visit

to Bath for his gout, was forced by a new bout to stay there for a fortnight. According to Horace Walpole he was 'surrounded by a crowd of domestics that occupied the whole inn and wore the appearance of a little court'. Even after 1784, when John Palmer's first mail coach made the London to Bath journey non-stop in 16 hours, it continued to be used by more leisurely travellers. Finally, however, the railways came, and by April 1842 the landlord had been allowed to pay a reduced rent.

It may seem surprising that such a famous coaching-inn should have stood so far back from the main road, but in coaching days light traffic used a private drive which entered the present school's grounds by the gate opposite St Peter's Church, ran across the site of B House and along the front of the inn, then turned north and crossed the site of the Chapel before rejoining today's Bath Road. To the north of this route, as soon as it entered today's school grounds, stood the inn's extensive stables. It was these stables which, along with the mansion itself, convinced the committee that the Castle Inn could accommodate the 200 boys it was now busily recruiting.

2

WILKINSON MEANS WELL

1843–1851

MARLBOROUGH SCHOOL, as it was at first called, failed to open on Lady Day (25 March) 1843. The last tenant of the Castle Inn did not leave until January, and there were then arguments with the Marquis of Ailesbury about the school's lease. As a result the architect's plans for the alterations were only finally agreed on 18 May, and the Council set a new opening date of 23 August. At its meeting of 2 August it doubted whether even this could be met and gave Bowers and two other Council members power to announce another postponement. But on 19 August, with 400 men now working on the conversion, it decided that, because of 'the great disappointment that must result to the parents and guardians of pupils if the school were not opened' this must take place without waiting for the rebuilding to be completed.

Four months later it reported, 'By great perseverance and decision, your Committee were enabled to effect their object, and the pupils were received on the appointed days, and although considerable inconvenience was experienced, yet by the cheerful co-operation of the Masters, Matron and other persons connected with the institution, all difficulties were overcome.'

It was a day of 'brilliant and auspicious sunshine', Bradley wrote, and confidently named it as 20 August, a Sunday. But the Council's report speaks of days, rather than a single day, and in fact the boys arrived throughout the week, while the opening was not formally celebrated till the evening of Saturday the 26th, when the Mayor of Marlborough entertained the Master and Council to a banquet.

MARLBOROUGH COLLEGIATE SCHOOL.

MARLBOROUGH COLLEGIATE SCHOOL.

This institution, for the education of the sons of clergymen and others, originated in a letter addressed to the Archbishop of Canterbury; the committee first appointed to carry out the plan having been materially assisted by the co-operation of the noblemen, clergy, and gentry connected with the county of Wilts and the adjoining counties, as also with the counties of Oxford, Devon, and Cornwall. The distinctive features of the plan are:—Providing the best possible education and maintenance at cost price; constant superintendence and sound theological teaching, according to the doctrines and formularies of the Established Church; watchful care over the morals of the boys, as well as over their education; and admission to the privileges of the school by means of nomination only. The establishment has been planned for 200 boys (to be increased hereafter, if required, to a number not exceeding 500), of whom two-thirds shall be the sons of clergymen; and one-third, the sons of laymen. The right of nomination is acquired by donations towards the general fund, to be appropriated to the providing and maintaining of buildings and accommodations, furniture, and articles of outfits; and the residue to the foundation of exhibitions at the universities, or for annual allowances for fixed periods, upon entering either of the professions of law or medicine, to be open to the whole school, and distributed according to merit. The institution is managed by a council, consisting of the Lord Bishop of Salisbury, as president; the bishops of England and Wales, as vice-presidents; together with trustees, treasurers, and life governors, of whom one-half are clergymen: the Archbishop of Canterbury is visitor.

The preliminary arrangements being completed, the institution have located themselves in the noble mansion represented in our engraving; and which, in the early part of the last century, was the residence of the Marquis of Hertford; in later times, it has been better known as the Castle Hotel; and has just been fitted up to accommodate 200 scholars. The situation, immediately adjoining the town of Marlborough, is very desirable, especially to the south-western counties. The mansion, of which the engraving shows the south front, with St. Peter's Church to the right, is a massive red brick edifice, consisting of a centre and two wings, with a terrace walk, and very fine trees and shrubs. In the rear, or north front, are spacious grass-plots, and a covered play-ground; and the extensive offices have been converted into a school and class rooms.

We are happy to add that the school was opened on the 26th ult., with 200 scholars, the full number intended to be received at first. As became the importance of the occasion, the president, the Bishop of the diocese, accompanied by the Marquis of Aylesbury, the Mayor and Corporation of Marlborough, the Rev. Sir Erasmus Williams, Bart., Rector of St. Peter's, several members of the school council, viz.: the Earl of Eldon, the Venerable Archdeacon Berens, the Rev. G. H. Bowers, the Rev. J. G. Brett, Robert Few, Esq., Sir Stephen Glynne, Bart., M.P., the Rev. R. Gorton, Christopher Hodgson, Esq., the Rev. B. Harrison, F. A. M'Geachy, Esq., M.P., Joseph Neeld, Esq., M.P., the Rev. C. E. Plater, T. H. S. Sotheron, Esq., M.P., the Rev. John Ward; the auditors, John Shepherd, Esq., William Pott, Esq.; and the masters and scholars of the foundation, went in procession to St. Peter's Church, where, after divine service, the Bishop of Salisbury preached a most eloquent and admirable sermon, explanatory of the great and important objects such an institution is calculated to attain, if based, as all education must be to ensure success in its results, on the sure foundation of the Christian religion.

A more important movement in the cause of education has scarcely occurred in these times; it will give to that large and influential body of men, the clergy of the country, the means of providing for their children that measure of classical instruction which he be n could only be obtained in our great public schools; but at a expense which entailed upon them far greater sacrifices than in many instances their limited incomes rendered prudent or even justifiable. The same education is also offered to the sons of laymen at a comparatively small expense.

The establishment consists of a master and five assistants (besides masters for modern languages and drawing), who are to instruct the scholars in classical and mathematical literature, so as to qualify them either for admission into the universities, or for any profession their parents might design.

The arrangements for the domestic comforts of the boys, and for discipline and superintendence on the part of the masters, have been carried out to the admiration and satisfaction of those parents and friends who accompanied the pupils on the days of their admission; as well as of those noblemen and gentlemen who visited every part of the buildings and grounds on the day of opening.

The good feeling of the inhabitants of Marlborough was testified by inviting the council to a public dinner on that day, at which the mayor presided. The speeches delivered on the occasion by the Bishop of Salisbury, the Earl of Eldon, and F. A. M'Geachy, Esq., M.P., were listened to with the greatest attention.

BOROUGH OF MARLBOROUGH

Having received a requisition calling on me to convene a Meeting of the Inhabitants "For the purpose of considering" "the proper way of expressing the good feelings of the" "Town on the occasion of the opening of the New School" "established in the Buildings lately known as the Castle" "Inn," I do hereby appoint such MEETING to be holden at the GUILDHALL, on TUESDAY the 15th Instant, at 3 o'Clock in the afternoon.

T. B. MERRIMAN, MAYOR.

August, 1843.

High-Street, Marlborough.—Printed at the Office of Emberlin & Harold.

Facing page: *Illustrated London News* feature announcing the opening of the School, 1843.

A welcoming notice from the Mayor of Marlborough.

Did the arrival of 199 new boys at a school with no traditions and still incomplete buildings, cause confusion? Forty-three years later Dean Farrar spoke, somewhat obscurely of 'that memorable morning when some 200 pairs of boots were dancing about in the wildest confusion without any registered owners'. Certainly Clement Cobb, a boy who came from Kent where his father held the living of Nettlestead, reported crowds, but no confusion – and rain.

Matthew Wilkinson. From a lithograph by Fleuss.

> My dearest parents ... we arrived at Swindon about ten minutes past 3 and I never saw such a splendid station before, there was a silver steam engine ... We went ... in a fly with another gentleman and his boy, and when we arrived at the school, there was such a number of boys standing under the entrances as it was raining, we then went to see Mr Bowers and Mrs Corfield [the matron] and then went into tea. There was such a crowd of boys such long tables, we soon found out some friends.

His second letter added:

> I was first introduced to Mr. Bowers who most kindly welcomed me and said kind things ... We next saw Mr. Wilkinson ... He is rather young about 38 or 40 I should think, pale and short ...

27

Our bedroom is splendid – 8 windows and 24 panes in each. 35 boys all little except myself – dearest W[illiam, his brother] sleeps within a foot and a half of me by Mr. Bower's kind arrangement. I am to be a sort of 'monitor' in my room.

Other boys came via Reading, where the railway still ended, and others in their fathers' coaches, 'the country parson of that day, being ... a simple, untravelled man, and many of them having a great fear and dislike of the newly invented railways'. Edward Lockwood and his brothers, sons of the Rector of Kingham in the Evenlode valley, came in their father's carriage and pair. He found many of the boys roaming the Wilderness and Mound where one party was hunting frogs. Already there were 'great heaps of the slain ... prominently exposed to view'. Presently they were led off to tea consisting of such a small quantity of bread and butter that one boy, who knew that the school butler was named Rogers, started a shrill shouting for him. 'No Rogers came, but in his place a master with a formidable cane appeared, and then we learned our first lesson, that in future we must remain content with what the gods provided.'

On one of the days of his first week another boy remembered an equally educational experience. His first friend had 'brought a very dirty little black pipe with him, of which he kindly proposed to allow me the benefit. Accordingly one dark night we slipped over the rails, and getting close under a wall, commenced operations. I need not say that I was soon very uncomfortable, but my pride would not allow me to confess it, so I declared the tobacco was delicious – smoked the pipe out – was very sick – moreover, being detected by a master, got severely punished for

Nelson's plan for the conversion of the Castle Inn to accommodate 200 boys. The beds appear to be about nine inches apart. C House now sleeps about 65 boys.

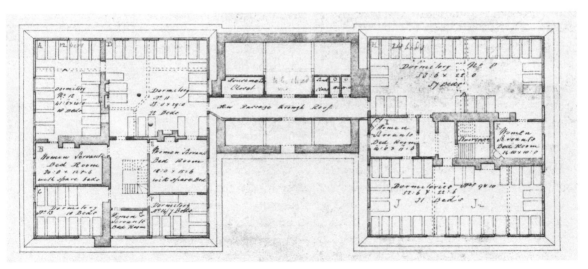

breaking the rules.'

Most of the 199 were put to sleep in dormitories in the old Castle Inn, then usually described as the Mansion, but later as C House, because it was given this letter on architects' plans. Satisfactory as Cobb found his dormitory, the Mansion must have been crowded to say the least. It also provided the boys' dining-room, rooms for masters, a sickroom, a dormitory for maids and a room for the housekeeper. There was probably a library in its basement.

The most important of the other buildings which had been – more or less – prepared for the great opening was a large new schoolroom. Those who do not know Marlborough can best picture the layout of its buildings by relating them to the large court which lay (and still lies) immediately in front of the Mansion, approximately to its north, between it and the Bath Road.

The Mansion's stables stood to the east of Court where they had formed an irregular E, the ends of the cross-strokes facing the court. The range which formed the E's centre stroke, however, had been found to be infested with dry rot and pulled down (the gable-end where it joined the rest of the stables can still be seen) leaving a U-shaped block. The new schoolroom, later known as Lower School, was built across the mouth of the U, on the site now occupied by the Museum Block. Thus it faced west towards Court. Attached to its rear were three classrooms which faced east towards a new courtyard, surrounded by the remaining stables.

These stables themselves became known as New Court, or alternatively the Covered Playground. Here boys played at marbles, peg-top, fly-the-garter, hicockolorum (leap-frog) and other games of the time.

South-east of the stable block, between it and the Bath Road (which here runs north–south) stood the only other important building on opening day: the White House (where the Halcomb family had lived). Originally this was to have been the Second Master's house, but by June 1843 the Master himself had moved into it, and here he boarded nine of the original boys.

Marbles in the covered playground. Vestiges of the archway can still be seen on the outside wall of New Court House.

Applications for the position of Master had first been invited by the Council in November 1842. One of those who had shown interest was a young master at Rugby, George Cotton. In December Cotton had written to Bowers asking, among other things, 'Will the whole internal discipline of arrangements of the School be under his authority?'

Cotton already foresaw one of the problems he was to face ten years later. In 1842, however, he made no formal application and on 22 February 1843 the Council chose, from 16 who did apply, the Revd Matthew Wilkinson.

Wilkinson was 35 years old, even younger than Cobb had guessed. Teaching had been his life, and he had made a success of it, first becoming headmaster of Huddersfield School, then in 1840 of Kensington Grammar School. True, he had had no experience of a boarding-school, but the Council was no doubt persuaded by his Kensington Grammar School record, where, at its 1843 prize-giving, its directors had spoken of the headmaster's 'active and watchful superintendence ... calculated to diffuse spirit and exertion through every department of the school'.

Wilkinson was not only pale and short but, according to Lockwood, usually wore a cassock, tied round the waist with a cummerbund or scarf, which 'gave him a very effeminate appearance'. In a contemporary lithograph his long hair, falling in smooth curves on either side of his somewhat chinless face, adds to this impression. Nevertheless, under his supervision the school seemed at first to prosper. The number of boys rose steadily, and in some years dramatically. By the end of 1845 there were 250, the following summer 293 and at Christmas 400.

A year after its opening it received a good report from two inspectors, the Revd J. A. Hessey and the Revd W. S. Wood. They were particularly impressed with the boys' divinity, which they attributed to the 'judicious catechising of the Head Master'. In August 1844 this report was sent to parents by the Council, which used it as justification for their decision to 'extend the school to the number of 500 as soon as accommodation can be provided'.

The proposal was set out in detail by Hodgson for Bowers. In a sketch he showed where another schoolroom and a dining-hall could be built, but suggested no site for the extra dormitories which would be needed. The new buildings, as they eventually appeared, consisted first of the new schoolroom, to become known as Upper School, attached to the back of the three classrooms which were themselves attached to the back of Lower School. Further south, closer to the Mansion, the southern range of stables was demolished and B House was built. B House survives, with its bleak internal courtyard surrounded by tiers of galleries. 'Utilitarian' is the kindest description that can be applied to it.

Across Court, approximately opposite Lower School, the new dining-hall was built on the site of the present one; and immediately north of this, A House. About A House even Bradley, usually a loyal Marlburian, was cool. It had, he wrote in 1893, 'repelled the mellowing hand of time with exasperating success'.

North of A House came the school's first Chapel, completed in 1848. Until then the boys had used St Peter's Church in the town. When the Council had appealed to parents and friends for contributions to a chapel

it had received a little over £2,000, but the building cost £6–7,000, and the balance was paid by the school. It was an impressive building, in fashionable neo-Gothic style, and many Marlburians were sorry when, less than 40 years later, it was judged to be too small and demolished.

North again stood the Porter's Lodge, 'a mean little one-storied building, very like the wretched little huts which serve as dwellings to those in charge of level crossings along the South-Western railway'. Here lived that important college servant, the Gate-Sergeant. At first he was Sergeant Bompas, a man of formidable build and reputation; the gash in his chin was supposed to have been made by a French soldier at Waterloo, whose head he had then chopped off. But Bompas had a soft heart, would close his eyes to boys he should have seen climbing trees, and at term-end would buy for them small bottles of rum disguised as medicine to drink on their icy coach drives home.

One day an Irish drunk arrived at the college gates, claiming to be a Frenchman come to revenge himself on the sergeant. Instead of standing and fighting, Bompas hurried off to fetch the town Beadle. Left, as it were, victorious, the Irishman entertained the school with mock boxing matches up and down the Bath Road, until the aged Beadle appeared,

An early photograph of Court *c.* 1860. An avenue of lime trees was planted in 1864 (and removed in 1960). Left to right: rudimentary fives courts up against the wall of the old stables (now New Court House), the old school room (Lower School), B House and C House. Upper School stood in New Court behind Lower School.

31

followed by most of the town's down-and-outs, when he fled towards
Bath. Back in his lodge, Bompas sat up all night, afraid that he might
be murdered in his bed, but the Irishman never returned.

East from the Lodge, iron railings with an iron gate closed off Court's
northern end. They were embedded in 'a strong iron framework resting
on a low wall', but this was not strong enough to save them when, in
September 1853, a freak wind ripped them from their framework.

Away from Court, the present Master's Lodge was the most
important new building, begun in 1845 and completed by the middle of
1848. Of other improvements to the school's premises, the most
significant was the creation of the Adderley Library, given by Council
member McGeachy, and named after his first wife. It was established in
the large ground-floor room of the Mansion which had previously been
the school's dining-hall.

The architect of most of the new buildings, including A House, B
House, the Chapel and the Master's Lodge was Edward Blore. Blore, one
of the country's most distinguished architects and a pioneer of the Gothic
Revival movement, was then in his late fifties and near the end of a long
career. He had built or restored 49 churches and numerous domestic
buildings. Because he had the reputation of being 'the cheap architect'
he had been employed to complete Buckingham Palace, after Nash had
been dismissed for extravagance. Cheapness was also what
Marlborough's Council wanted, and the need to design cheaply perhaps
excused the buildings he produced for the school.

Not, however, to the *Ecclesiologist*, a paper with a special interest in
Gothic Revival architecture, which in April 1849 wrote that Blore had
'stuck down his buildings anyhow, or rather, nohow'. He had 'repeated
the original pile twice to its right and left ... but it is the original pile
shorn and starved – with its deeply cut cornice dwarfed, and its dormers
pinched, with staring blue slates instead of the richly tinted tiles of the
original. Deal serves, where oak ruled – and instead of the chateau we
think of the factory.'

The dining-hall was redeemed by its size 'from absolute meanness; it
is a wonder, that being the work of Mr Blore it is not worse'. As for
the chapel, it was 'hitched into a corner of the playground, standing at
right angles to nothing, and at wrong angles to everything'.
Furthermore it had a 'miserably insufficient bell-turret, with a bell so
ridiculous, that it cannot be heard within the college walls', and its
unnecessary west door had been added, 'we suppose, for the very purpose
of welcoming the cutting winds from every quarter of the bleak downs'.
As for its internal arrangements, the altar was 'of a most preposterous
size – we should think nine feet long' and fitted into a 'strange recess

Plate 1.
The Castle Inn in the hey-day of the London to Bath coach route.

Plate 2.
The whole range of Blore's buildings. To the right of the Mansion: kitchen and dining-hall (replaced 1960), A House (now Morris House), Chapel replaced (1886) and the Porter's Lodge (replaced 1887). To the left: B House (only chimneys visible), Lower School (replaced 1883) and a wing of the old stables (now part of New Court).

compounded of a fireplace and an Easter sepulchre'.

The *Ecclesiologist* objected to the positioning of the Chapel because it 'failed in that lesson which college chapels ought to convey, that religion is part and parcel, not an isolated element of the work carried on within it'. The paper's concept of the premises suitable for a college was an Oxbridge one and it recommended at Marlborough the building across the north end of the court of 'a good seventeenth-century red-brick solid screen, for masters' houses etc. to complete the quadrangle'.

Despite its many criticisms, the article admitted that there was 'something about the whole mass of the domestic buildings, perhaps its disjointed and broken outline ... perhaps the old mansion itself ... which Mr Blore could not entirely escape from, though he has done his best' that made Marlborough College 'a very striking whole indeed ... a place by no means to be forgotten'.

Marlborough College (as it had officially been named by its charter of 1846) soon began to develop in other ways. From the start it had had its own medical officer, one of the first to be appointed by any school. Music was taught, there was a choir, and both in 1849 and 1850 there were Christmas concerts. Senior Prefect Cobb sang and played the piano. Between 24 April 1848 and 14 March 1849 five issues of *The Marlborough Magazine* appeared. They varied between 32 and 40 pages and contained learned essays and original stories and poems. And in 1851 there were four issues of the first *Marlburian*, a slimmer affair of eight pages, with reports of such school societies as the Cricket Club and the Music Society, and on the back page, two chess problems. Numbers also continued to grow, bringing the total in autumn 1848 to 521, the highest the Council would allow. There were now 14 assistant masters instead of the original six.

All in all, the college seemed to be fulfilling the hopes of its founders, and of most of its parents. Not of every one of them, however. Already in 1845 some had complained to the Council. 'There appeared a prevailing feeling', Lockwood's father wrote, 'that the food at Marlborough was not good, that the meat was of late only half-roasted, the potatoes badly boiled, the bread often mouldy, and the beer sour.' Lockwood himself, looking back on his eight years at the school (1843–51) attributed his unhappiness to two causes: 'not having been properly "grounded" [in the classics] before I went to school; and ... suffering from almost chronic hunger'. And J. S. Thomas, the future Bursar who devoted 37 years of his life to the school, remembered as a boy that the carving 'was done by the two biggest fellows at the head of the table. Think what the mangled meat was like when our turn came at the remote end of the table! Though that was the only meal of the three at which we had anything beyond bread and butter, it was often impossible to eat it. It was a rare event to go to bed without feeling a positive craving for food.'

In 1848, at the dinner which followed the opening of the school Chapel, Wilkinson admitted that all was not well. He regretted earlier extravagant forecasts that within five years Marlborough would be able to 'achieve all the good and avoid all the evil of the old public school system'. As he himself had never had such hopes he did not 'share the disappointment which he believed existed in some quarters'.

The state of the school during the next four years has been fiercely debated. On the one hand Bradley in his 1893 history described them as its low point, about which 'nothing much that is good can be said', clearly implying that Wilkinson should be held responsible. The opposite view was first presented by Canon William Gildea in 1918 in his booklet, *Recollections of School Days at Marlborough College 1848–1851*.

Bradley's basic complaint was that Wilkinson failed to give the school prefects responsibility. If so, he would have had some excuse. At first only Cobb and a few other boys were 16 or over, while the rest were young, many of them very young. There were just four prefects, and at the end of the second term (there were only two terms a year) the Sixth Form still had only ten boys. The prefects had privileges, Bradley claimed. They could visit the Mound and take their friends with them. But they had only such formal duties as reading out the names of delinquents in the schoolrooms, or announcing the start and finish of work periods. They could not punish and did not have fags. Gildea claimed that this was not true. 'I myself, as a prefect, have stopped a boy in a course of mischief, by warning him that, if the thing occurred again, I would without question bring him up before a *prefects' court*.'

There were dormitory Captains, Bradley admitted, but they merely called the roll of their boys in the schoolrooms after evening prayers and led them off to bed. Gildea, however, described an occasion when he was Captain of a dormitory. One night, as soon as the duty master, Henry Tweed, arrived, a boy burst out laughing. Tweed gave Gildea 400 lines of Virgil to write out for failing to control his dormitory.

If Gildea was right about prefects' powers, he was unconvincing about a range of other matters. About corporal punishment he wrote, 'Its frequency and severity, and the nature of the cane itself [described by Bradley as 'of hideous length and terrible circumference'] is enormously exaggerated.' About the notorious fights of the time by which boys established seniority among themselves he wrote that he 'could not remember these fierce and frequent fights'. And about poaching by boys of the school, 'I loved Savernake Forest and with my friends spent many and many a half-holiday there, but I can say with perfect truth that neither I myself, nor any friend with me, nor anyone within my knowledge, ever hurt fur or feather there.'

J. S. Thomas, Gildea's exact contemporary, gave a different picture. In the two schoolrooms the masters' desks were placed around the walls, with, in front of each of them, his two forms. While one form sat at its desks, preparing (there was no preparation out of school) he taught the other, standing round him in a circle. The Master himself taught the Sixth Form in the same way.

> Probably no one of us [Thomas continued] could hear that peculiar sound which is made by a heavy oak chair when pushed back over a hollow wooden stand, without involuntarily looking around. It always betokened the rising of a master to inflict corporal punishment. The familiar sound produced an instantaneous silence, and a concentration of all eyes on the spot indicated. There stood the victim and the executioner. If the latter was notorious for the strength of his right arm, it was a matter of no small interest to us to see whether the victim's pluck would suffice to bring him victorious through the limited number of strokes which custom and decency enjoined. If he never flinched or uttered cry, we regarded him as a hero who had scored one against the redoubtable wielder of the rod of justice. There was one awful occasion on which a master lost control of himself, because his victim stood as immovable as though he had been a pillar of stone, instead of a being of flesh and warm blood. Again and again the strong cane descended till 30 strokes had been passed, and yet that boy never flinched. Exhausted at last, the master desisted, and an hour later that resolute boy was having his sliced shirt extracted from his wounds by the gentle hands of dear, tender-hearted Dr. Fergus.

Lockwood remembered that 'occasionally two masters would be caning at the same time', setting up a rhythm which suggested blacksmiths hammering on their anvils.

Beside caning there was the more severe punishment of flogging, which Thomas associated with another sound: the jingling of a bunch of keys.

> Why these were carried by the Master on this particular occasion I do not know, but almost invariably as he advanced to his seat of state . . . he held his bunch of keys in his hand. Attracted by the sound we looked up. The Master was advancing followed by the culprit. He took his stand on his raised dais, the culprit before him.

Two prefects, who were to act as assessors, placed themselves on his right and left. Then the Master, in a short speech, explained the character of the offence for which retribution was to be exacted and a few words of warning were added to point the moral. He descended, and the melancholy procession of Master, culprit, and prefects proceeded to the Sixth class-room. The door closed, and the sound of the birch rod, not seldom accompanied by cries of distress, brought home to our minds the severity of this – the utmost penalty of the law.

Alongside caning and flogging went a punishment which was more resented: gating. Sometimes a whole class was gated. Thomas remembered that his class was gated for five weeks because a member was seen making paper calculations during a lesson and it was assumed that he was running a lottery, though in fact he was adding up contributions for the buying of cricket equipment. Forty years later, Thomas was still indignant, less at the mass punishment than at the way, when it was found to be unjust, it was rescinded without apology.

'Confinement to grounds' was a less severe form of gating, since grounds included the school's field. A whole class would be confined to grounds if one of its boys ran away, and remain confined until he was recaptured. Fines were also imposed for many offences. A guinea was the fine for carving a school desk, a shilling for throwing stones in Court, climbing trees or possessing lucifers. Since the approved pocket money was about 3*d*. a week, many boys were penniless for weeks in succession, their only relief the occasional coins which friends or relatives sent them concealed in letters.

About fighting Thomas wrote:

Fights might take place anywhere in the court, the field, the school-room, the dormitory; but for more formally arranged encounters Fleuss' Arch [which projected from New Court near Fleuss, the drawing-master's classroom] was recognised as the appropriate spot, unless the principals were leading fellows in the school. In that case the Upper Fifth was sometimes selected. All arrangements would have been made beforehand; a plentiful supply of water and towels would have been brought in; after breakfast the combatants and their personal friends would adjourn to the class-room, and, with the doors securely barricaded, there was no danger of interruption until the school-bell necessitated dispersion. Not a few old Marlburians will recall that famous fight of the early years of the fifties, in which two fellows, strong in limb and of indomitable pluck, met in the Upper Fifth immediately after breakfast until the

A fight at Fleuss's Arch. Upper School on the left, New Court beyond (from a sketch by P. Chenevix Trench).

bell rang for ten o'clock school. One of the combatants was severely punished, but at the close neither was nearer to yielding than in the first round. These two fellows afterwards entered the army, and one died in India. The other is still living, a humble-minded, earnest, Christian man; yet even now, after the lapse of so many years, it is not without a feeling of pride that he hears reference to that famous fight.

Seventy years later D. G. Compton named the two antagonists as Hodgson and Study. He and other small boys were excluded, but stood grouped outside. 'From time to time news of the fight came through. One item from a special courier, if I remember rightly, was "they are drinking each other's blood".'

Thomas also remembered notorious cases of bullying. In the new houses, with their deep interior courtyards, 'thoughtless fellows by way of amusement used to tie sheets together, and with these drop small boys over the balustrade at the top ... to the basement. One that suffered in this way experienced such silent agony, as he descended the thirty or forty feet, that he has never forgotten it, and that terrible experience has made the memory of Marlborough hateful to him.'

For mutual protection the boys would organise themselves in groups, known as tribes, which took their names from their leaders. It was not

37

surprising, Bradley wrote, that various Marlburians became distinguished soldiers, and named four distinguished but now forgotten military men.

About poaching Bradley claimed that boys would regularly spend their free time roaming south of the Kennet or in Savernake Forest where they would birds' nest or poach, using traps, snares or a weapon known as a squaler, consisting of a lead head the shape of a pear, fixed to an 18-inch cane handle. With this rabbits, squirrels and even deer could be killed at a distance.

Lockwood's account of his free-time activities supports Bradley. He remembered catching and roasting Kennet trout, fighting the miller who guarded the most convenient way across the river and snaring a large tom cat – which he believed, after its confiscation, to have been incorporated in the Saturday stew.

The diary of Boscawen Somerset (1847–52) shows him day after day raiding the local birds' nests.

> Ap. 11 [1851] Went to Region with S.1., B.1. and B.3. took 4 robins and 1 blackbird. S.1. took a thrush, 2 robins were broken in the nest ... Kept in ½ hr. for being late in chap ...
>
> Ap. 18 ... Went out from 12–1 with B.3. to Gundry's bridge. Got caught by his keeper ...
>
> Ap. 21 ... Went out 1st to sweet briar pit with M. and B.3. Only got 6 black-birds. After 4–6 with Hutch. to Ash. rookery and got 5 rooks from S.I's tree, one of which fell from tree, neither being broken ...
>
> May 2 Went out from 1.45–4 with B.3. to Ash. Rookery and Gales. Got 2 rooks and 4 starlings. Bought jackdaws.
>
> May 3 Got some Dabchicks, House sparrows, mavis's, Tree-climbers, Redstarts and Linnets.

From the start occasional boys who found the harsh conditions unbearable ran away, and after a few years escapes became so common that Council member Few said he dreaded meeting the parents of Marlburians in the streets of London, in case they would furiously 'demand from him their lost sons'. Two boys, Thomas remembered, spent a month touring Scotland before they returned and surrendered. To avoid 'a public thrashing' one of them ran away again a few days later, but was caught ten miles along the Bath Road. Thereafter he was permanently escorted by members of his form during non-school hours and put in a lock-up for an hour a day between 12 and 1 by the gate-sergeant – no longer the obliging Bompas but a man named Peviar, 'peculiarly obnoxious to us boys'.

For Thomas the harsh and uncaring regime was epitomised by his first meeting with the Master, brought there on arrival by his parents. Wilkinson asked him just one question: did he suffer from chilblains?

Among the many new boys of 1848 who raised the school's numbers to over 500 was the most influential of all Marlburians, William Morris. When Morris revisited the school in his thirties he found his old room in A House 'such a dismal place ... a troublous life I led of it there for two years, after which I became a dignified person comparatively and was Captain of the room ...'.

> Alas I did not fight enough in my time, from want of hope let us say, not want of courage, or else I should have been more respected in my earlier days: in the few fights I had I was rather successful, for a little, and thin (yes) boy as I was: for the rest I had a hardish time of it as chaps who have brains and feelings generally do at school ...
>
> I was watching two little boys fighting in the street and it refreshed my memory of what used to go on at school: for each seemed afraid of the other and held his head down and hit round; and certainly the one who had stood up straight and hit out well from the shoulder would have got the best of it.

The only memory which one of Morris's contemporaries had of him was of his sitting for hours on end on his desk in Upper School, 'netting', but for what the nets were meant is not clear. In letters to his sister Morris described being much moved by the singing of the choir; and on another occasion crossing water meadows to climb Silbury Hill. Summing up his memories of Marlborough he wrote in 1883,

> As far as my school instruction went, I think I may fairly say I learned nothing there, for indeed next to nothing was taught; but the place is in a very beautiful country, thickly scattered over with prehistoric monuments, and I set myself eagerly to studying these and everything else that had any history in it, and so perhaps learned a good deal, especially as there was a good library at the school to which I sometimes had access.

Wilkinson cannot entirely be blamed for the harsh conditions of these years. He could fairly claim that the way in which he had to run the school was forced on him by the Council's mismanagement of its finances. In order to pay for the new buildings needed when the school expanded it had raised £10,000 in 1844 by the issue of bonds and two further sums of £15,000 each in 1846 and 1847 in the same way. One result of having to service these loans was that it had had to increase fees in November 1848 to £36 and £60 respectively. A more severe consequence from the boys' point of view was the deteriorating quality of the food.

Almost as fundamental was the Council's insistence on managing the school from London. As a result Wilkinson had to write to it for every sort of decision. In one term of 1844 at least 129 letters were sent from Marlborough to London, 47 personally by Wilkinson. They concerned such trivial matters as the amounts to be paid to the organist and bellows-pumper of St Peter's Church.

In June 1850 Wilkinson succeeded in having the administration transferred to Marlborough, and Albert Gill, the School Secretary, moved there, but the following June, without telling Wilkinson, the Council called Gill back to London, on the grounds that a London office was a better advertisement for the school, and that it enabled the Council to control affairs more firmly.

Underlying Wilkinson's differences with the Council may have been the fact that certain members of the Council considered him High Church. His customary soutane suggests that they were right. Marlborough's High Church reputation probably explained the founding of Rossall in 1844, a north-country school meant mainly, like Marlborough, for the sons of the clergy but with a Low Church slant.

In Wilkinson's defence it must also be said that, before the end of his time, he made one important reform. On 31 May 1850 he wrote to the Bishop of Salisbury, President of the Council:

> I am sometimes afraid my own dislike of corporal punishment may have influenced my judgement – but I confess myself so far unable to have thought out any adequate substitute for the use of the cane by assistants save that of the wholesale flogging which I dare say your Lordship recollects was the use at Eton.

On 19 August of the same year, probably after the sadistic caning incident which Thomas remembered, he told the Bishop that he had 'after very long consideration resolved to abolish the use of the cane by the Assistant Masters and to leave no discretion as to corporal punishment in any hands but my own'.

In September 1851 Wilkinson expelled two boys for insubordination. He was allowed by the school's by-laws to do this, though the parents were entitled to appeal to the Council. Not only did the Council reinstate the boys without consulting him, but it failed to inform him of what it had done, so that he first heard of it through a prefect. Wilkinson wrote to the Council that such an action 'struck at the root of discipline and control'. This was the incident which set the scene for the dramatic events of the following three months.

3

REBELLION

1851

SCHOOL REBELLIONS WERE not new – Marlborough's has been described as the last, though there were in fact later ones, including the rebellion of 1873 at the King's School, Canterbury. At the seven Great Schools they had been frequent during the eighteenth and early nineteenth centuries, most frequent at the oldest, Winchester, where there were four within 22 years. The last of these, the Great Rebellion, occurred in 1793, during the French Revolution, and the rebels hoisted the Red Cap of Liberty, but the cause was less fundamental: the forbidding by the headmaster of the boys' right to listen to the playing of the Bucks Militia band in the Cathedral Close.

Rugby's Great Rebellion occurred three years later and was precipitated by the flogging by Henry Ingles ('the Black Tiger') of a boy for firing cork bullets in the yard of his house. Among several rebellions at Harrow, those of 1771 and 1805 were the result of depriving the boys of a right they believed to be theirs to have a say in the appointment of a new headmaster. Eton had its Great Rebellion in 1768, when the headmaster took away the prefects' right to patrol areas out of bounds to the rest of the school. Under Dr Keate there were a number of rebellions, the most famous in 1818 (a year in which the boys of several other schools rebelled). Again their grievance was that senior boys were forbidden to 'extend their excursions beyond those bounds which the prudence of their superiors thought proper'. There were also rebellions at Shrewsbury and Charterhouse. With few exceptions, they all were caused, not by the brutal regimes of headmasters like Keate, nor by demands for 'freedom', but by the deprivation of the boys of some traditional right.

Marlborough's rebellion in 1851 had more complex origins. As J. S. Thomas saw it, the immediate provocation was a curfew imposed by Wilkinson, who ordered the gates of the school to be shut at dusk each night, so penning up all 500 boys in Court for many evening hours with nothing to do. The author of *Marlborough Thirty Years Ago* described the events which led to this mass gating:

An old man, who gained his livelihood by the sale of chips, appeared one day before the college authorities, and asserted that on the previous afternoon he was returning from the village of Ogbourn St Mary to Marlborough with his donkey, when he met three boys, who asked leave to ride, and being refused, took forcible possession of the animal, rode it rapidly to and fro, and at last drove it into the river, whence he extricated it with great difficulty. The leader in the outrage said his name was Lamb (this was only a stupid joke, there being no boy of that name).

The doctor [Dr Wilkinson] summoned us all to the great school-room, repeated the peasant's story in a speech from the throne, and in peremptory tones called on the culprits to surrender themselves on pain of heavier punishment if they delayed.

We had been in so much awe of him that this course had generally proved successful.

But now his voice lost its spell: no one came forward. He renewed his demand more sternly; still no one stirred; then, after waiting a few minutes, during which all continued motionless and silent, he 'gated' the whole school until the offenders should be discovered.

Gate-Sergeant Peviar became the focus for the anger this gating provoked. According to Bradley he had recently made himself more than usually unpopular by getting flogged a number of boys he had reported for dancing in the moonlight on the roof of the Mansion. The same article continued:

One morning two men entered the school-room, carrying a large and heavy hamper, which they deposited at the foot of the central dias.

One of them was the porter of the college, who had also to check and report all offenders against the law, and to manufacture the birches with which we were flogged. He was a little bumptious man, with a prying nose, small sharp black eyes, and eyebrows habitually elevated. We hated him ...

On the previous evening, which was dark and stormy, he was having tea with his wife and infant, when they were startled by a

The Porter's Lodge where Peviar experienced the rebellion. This photograph was taken probably shortly afterwards, in the late 1850s, and shows Voss and his family.

heavy crash against the door. He looked out, but was driven back by a shower of stones and brickbats, and thinking there was some design on his life, retreated with his wife and boy into the wash-house at the rear of the premises. Meanwhile the hurricane of missiles continued, and did not cease until the door, windows, and many of the tiles were smashed, and his solitary chimney pot smashed to atoms.

When, at last, he ventured forth, all was quiet, and he had not been able to detect any of his besiegers, but had picked up most of the brickbats, and put them in a hamper which he now produced.

There had been previous attacks on Peviar's lodge, but Wilkinson apparently considered this more serious than any before because on 1 November he dismissed Samuel Pigott, son of the Revd S. R. Pigott of Bredgar, Kent. 'Your son', he wrote to Pigott's father, 'is regarded by Masters and Prefects as a ring leader. I think I might say *the* ring leader.'

During the days that followed the boys began to collect the fireworks they used in the outbreak of 5 o'clock on 5 November which Bradley described so vividly (see page 15), and which is usually considered to have been the real outbreak of the rebellion.

Wilkinson clearly saw it as such. On 11 November he wrote to the uncle of one boy, 'the 5th of November unfortunately being close at hand the cowardly assailants got up a larger conspiracy and a combined assault was made in all the Houses – with large quantities of squibs, crackers, etc.' In his diary for 5 November, Somerset wrote, 'Fireworks in the schoolroom after tea and out of doors from 5½–6½.' And for 6 November, 'Fireworks in the schoolroom after tea and out of doors from 5½–6½. Lots of windows broken after chapel and some at 3.'

Meanwhile Wilkinson, according to Thomas, had assembled the boys in Upper School, where he addressed them 'in grave and angry language'. Thomas then watched a boy sitting in front of him, while leaning his head on his desk as if suffering from a severe headache, extract a fire-cracker from his pocket, light it with a lucifer, and throw it up the aisle between two rows of desks towards the Master's rostrum.

> You know how a cracker jumps about and explodes ... until its twelve or fourteen detonations have exhausted themselves ... The Master awaited the end, and then began again. But other boys had crackers.... The example was contagious. Here, there and everywhere crackers began to explode, so that he had to abandon the attempt and retire.... That night crackers were ever exploding. It was not difficult to open a dormitory door and throw one over a balustrade or on to the landing, and for many days and nights the stock seemed inexhaustible.

After this the sequence of events becomes uncertain. According to Bradley there was general disorder and disobedience, with more attacks on the Gate-Sergeant's lodge – 35 years later the dents in its lead drain-pipe could still be seen – and more attempts by the masters to restore order. Several, including the Master, were standing together near one of Upper School's fires when a device described by Thomas as a bundle of crackers, by Lockwood as a bottle of gunpowder, was thrown into the flames where it exploded 'with a fearful bang'. The Master, Thomas claimed, remained calm and dignified. But he now dismissed four more boys, after discovering from a shopkeeper in the town the names of those who had bought the fireworks. When he learned that an escort was being prepared for Augustus Twyford, one of the dismissed and a popular boy, he arranged for him to leave directly into the town from the Master's Lodge, so avoiding Court, but the plan was discovered and several hundred boys were waiting outside.

Tramp, tramp, tramp, [Lockwood wrote] eight abreast we doubled along the road leading to the town, and woe to any obnoxious person whom we met, and who found no method of escape.

My old antagonist, the Miller, unfortunately for him, was enjoying a morning's outing on his donkey at the time, and sniffing danger in the air, turned round and did his best to fly.... Bending his body almost double, he struck his heels into the donkey's sides, working his legs and arms as the winner of the Derby does when he approaches the winning-post. But it availed him little, for a dozen stalwart youths flew after him, and dragged him from his seat, rolled him over and over in the gutter; whilst his long-eared steed delighted to be free, tore down the road exulting, amid the uproarious laughter of the crowd.

The miller complained to the Master, saying that the boys had insulted him by calling him 'treacle bolly'. From then onwards these words became (*a*) the name of the riverside path where the miller had suffered, (*b*) the name for treacle suet-pudding and by extension for other suet puddings, e.g. speckled bolly. Immediately after the procession, unknown boys smashed 30 of the 36 windows of the Master's Sixth Form classroom. The boys were ordered to their classes, but when their masters arrived, Bradley wrote, 'the uproar broke out again, and all authority was defied with groans, slamming of desks, and stamping of feet. Windows were smashed, desks were broken, and anarchy reigned everywhere throughout the week.'

During the following days flogging went on continually. At one stage Thomas claimed that 28 boys were flogged in a batch. The story of the flogging of a particular boy, the future Field Marshal, H. Evelyn Wood, suggests that Wilkinson, a kindly and conscientious man, had been reduced to a state of desperation in which he lost his sense of justice. Wood had already been once flogged for an offence he had not committed when he was summoned for a second time.

Spy cartoon of Field Marshal Sir Evelyn Wood VC who was a boy at the College at the time of the rebellion and later hero of the Zulu War.

I urged my flogging on the Monday should cancel that now ordered, but the Head dissented, adding, 'I apologised for that; and you are such a bad boy, I'll flog you before your Form.' My twenty-two classmates were marched in to the Sixth Form classroom, and I was ordered to get up. The culprit knelt on a bench, his elbows on a desk. Two prefects held his wrists ... with one hand, and the tail of his shirt with the other. When the Master was about to strike, a noise made him look round: he saw all my classmates looking at the wall. He raged, vowed he would flog them all, but in vain; for when the top boys of the class were forcibly turned about by the prefects they faced around again, and my punishment was inflicted without the additional indignity intended. My class gave me £5.

At the same time Wilkinson tried to pacify the boys, asking them to explain their grievances. 'They demanded back', Bradley wrote, 'all the privileges (relating chiefly to liberty) which during the past four years had been taken from them.' To this Wilkinson agreed on condition that they contributed £10 to the damage they had caused.

For a time peace returned, but on the last day of November came the rebellion's climax.

> I was in the upper school-room [Thomas remembered] when a gang of young rascals entered, headed by a clever fellow who afterwards joined the Civil Service in India. He appeared to have found some means of picking locks, for he went the round of the masters' desks in the room and opened them. His followers immediately laid their hands on the contents and threw them into the two large fires. Most masters kept their registers here, and as a consequence in the school list of that half-year many forms will be found to have been printed in alphabetical order.

The writer of *Marlborough Thirty Years Ago* added other details:

> Down went the doctor's crimson throne, forms, chairs, and desks were overturned and smashed, and the floor was soon strewn with grammars and dictionaries, and Latin and Greek classics. Emboldened by impunity the marauders flew at higher game. Adjoining the school-room was the head-master's class-room, a sacred chamber.... In it the doctor kept his papers, including the manuscript of Sophocles which he was preparing for the press; it was the scene of the daily tribunal for the trial of all grave offences; it likewise contained the stock of birches ...
>
> The door was broken open, the detested twigs were scattered to the winds, the furniture was smashed, the records torn up, the large inkstand flung through the window, and Sophocles dragged forth and burnt.

Soon after this Lockwood was called to see the Master and asked whether he knew if skeleton keys were being used by the rebels. 'The interview, which made a great impression on me at the time, soon came to an end. When I entered the room I saw one whom hitherto I had regarded almost as a god, but now when I came out, he had henceforth, in my estimation, to take his place with other mortal men.'

Canon Gildea among others believed that such accounts of Marlborough's rebellion were exaggerated, but a letter of the following February from William Saumarez Smith (future Archbishop of Australia) confirms its main events.

> The origin was I believe that 'the Doctor' kept in the whole school and this incited various boys to do a good deal of mischief: and then in the middle unfortunately came Novr. 5th and as we are *not* allowed fireworks, 4£ worth *were* got. Well after various expulsions and changes of schooltimes etc. the boys sent a petition to the Master wh. was granted. The petition was for some old privileges. The second was a more wanton outrage than the first I believe; and some notes, wh. the Doctor had been compiling for 4 years were burnt. Doors were broken open, desks and registers burnt etc.

Wilkinson's letters not only provide further confirmation, but reveal matters which made his position even more difficult. Throughout November and December he was engaged in a parallel struggle with the Council which was again undermining his authority. On 15 November he wrote to the Revd T. B. Cornish that the Council had passed a resolution suggesting that the five dismissed boys should be readmitted after Christmas. This was 'a wretched "blowing hot and cold",' and so upset him that he told Cornish he was ready to accept the first church living of £300 a year which he was offered.

More distressingly, the boys of the school once again heard of the Council's resolution before he did. To McGeachy he wrote, 'This becomes a very momentous question, how the School is to be ruled. It is now continually the case that the Council, before investigation, *shows* a different opinion from my own and the most ruinous indiscretion as to publishing this difference.'

Two days later he told one of the dismissed boys' parents that 'Some of our Council wish to make it rustication only and so undo the wholesome terror'; and on 20 November he wrote again to McGeachy, 'All the Masters without one exception supporting me, asking me *not* to defeat all efforts to maintain authority by restoring any of the dismissed.' He had his way, and despite a petition from the boys for a reprieve for Twyford, none was readmitted.

Wilkinson regarded Robert Few as particularly hostile to him. In February the following year he wrote to Few, 'Your letter is certainly not likely to inspire or promote that vigorous confidence in one's own exertions which is so necessary for the successful Schoolmaster.... I was to hear in two totally different quarters lately an opinion expressed that *you* were doing us harm.... You are so determined to regard me as distrustful and mean that I must despair of appearing to you ever otherwise.' Few had two sons in the school at this time, aged 17 and 13. It seems likely that it was through them that boys heard of Council decisions before Wilkinson.

Meanwhile Wilkinson had told the Bishop of Salisbury on 17 November that although there were bound to be 'occasional collisions' between the Council and the Master, 'of late this seemed rather the rule than the exception'. He had been attending Council meetings since 1848 (though not before), but 'At these meetings my presence has often been, I conceive, useless, and certainly matters appertaining to the management and discipline of the school have been much more fully opened and resolved at Meetings at which I was not present.'

Looking back on the rebellion, Wilkinson admitted that his most serious error had been, because of his personal dislike of caning, to abandon it without providing an appropriate substitute. To a correspondent he wrote in January 1852, 'A short time ago I (contrary to the judgement of my Assistant Masters or of many of them) determined to do away with the use of the cane and all corporal punishment except from my own hands. The result of this for a while has been as I foresaw it would be, that many boys ... became insubordinate impudent etc.' Gating, as it turned out, was counter-productive, and he personally was forced to resort to more and more flogging.

The rebellion's consequences for the school were catastrophic. News of it spread among the school's parents and when the boys reassembled for the following term, instead of 500 of them there were 'not many more than 400'. All the Council's financial calculations had been based on receiving fees from 500.

4

COTTON TO THE RESCUE

1852–1858

THE CHRISTMAS HOLIDAYS of 1851 brought an end to Marlborough's rebellion, but Wilkinson remained Master for the first half of 1852. During his last term he proposed an important change for the school: the separation of the younger boys from the older. On 29 December he wrote to McGeachy:

> In one respect Marlborough has been a failure I mean in the management of little boys ... the plan I propose will I think shield the inexperienced from vice and oppression.... At the same time it will restrain those (worst ingredient of all schools!) who are well-grown animals and animals in disposition but ill grown in all intellectual matters. I wish each of our six House masters to have in his House a Class-room to be occupied by those members of each House who are below the 4th Form.

The diary of an older boy, Robert Nunns, for the year 1852 gives a picture of school life during Wilkinson's last term. Nunns was the son of a Leeds clergyman and had been at the school since 1848. Though now 16, this did not save him from punishments like the writing out of 100 lines of Greek every day until further notice, for singing in his dormitory.

His journey to school was exhausting. Starting from Leeds at 7 a.m. on 4 February he missed his connection at Gloucester and did not reach Marlborough till 5 a.m. next morning. He brought with him provisions consisting of a pot of jam, a dozen biscuits, three packets of Scotch[?] and 5 lbs of cheese. By 8 February he had 'finished all the grub but the cheese'.

Plate 4 (Facing page).
Bodley and Garner's Chapel refurbished and relit for the Centenary in 1986.

The diary for 1852 kept by R. A. L. Nunns (MC 1848–1854).

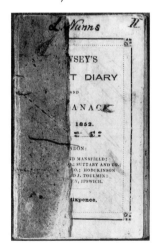

49

Soon after term started he reported 'Bulldogs' at the school (one of whom was sent away for smoking). There were to be two in each house and they were presumably disciplinary officers appointed to prevent fresh disorder. But in general Nunns confirms that school life continued much as before.

He studied Homer, Horace's *Epistles*, Thucydides and Tacitus, but also French, mathematics, drawing and English classics like *Paradise Lost* and Macaulay's *Horatius*. It was easy for him to spend long periods – sometimes a whole day – out of school. Often he breakfasted in the town at Norris's. His chief amusements were hiring a velocipede (sometimes a double one with a friend) or, in summer, swimming and rafting on the Kennet. On 13 March he took part in a paper-chase during which 'a lot of boys jumped at a stream and got in'. A certain amount of poaching, or at least trespassing, continued. Once he saw two boys fishing, and on another occasion all the Fifth Form were called to see the Master 'about the Forest etc.'.

The diary of Nunns's contemporary, Somerset, shows him continuing to make regular excursions into the countryside or into the forest to climb trees, but he makes no mention of poaching and, unlike the previous spring, only three of bird's-nesting. On 12 February he took his first organ lesson and from then onwards practised regularly. On 2 March he had his first haircut since the previous November. On 13 April he was made a prefect. One morning in February he reported 'A's sponge frozen, and . . . mine also . . . and ice on the floor from the water A. had thrown about'. On 3 March both he and Nunns heard the rumour that Wilkinson was to leave.

Wilkinson had in fact been offered the living of West Lavington some 12 days earlier and had been deciding whether to accept it. Money was one problem. As he explained to the Bishop of Salisbury, with a wife, eight children and an old mother to support, he would need to take pupils. He was also unsure whether he should 'desert the school in its present condition'. When eventually he made up his mind he wrote to the Revd J. B. Hughes, one of the original assistant masters, '*Confidentially* I may add that one of my reasons is the difference of opinion betwixt some few members of the Council and myself.' But he did not depart in disgrace. Early the following term he and his wife were welcomed on a visit to the school, which did indeed send him pupils. And on 20 October Nunns and a friend walked the 12 miles to West Lavington to dine with him.

Meanwhile the great event of the new term had been the arrival of a new Master. On Friday 13 August Nunns, after first noting that he had been put into the Sixth Form, added, 'Cotton has a wife and child'. Next day he wrote, 'Bathed twice. Went off spring board ... brought a lock for my locker. Had to go to Cotton to receive a jaw, etc.'

George Edward Lynch Cotton was the young man who had written to the Council showing interest in the Mastership in 1842. Ever since he had been a master at Rugby, brought there by Arnold at the age of 23 direct from Trinity College, Cambridge. There he is generally agreed to have been the unnamed young master admired by Tom and his friends in *Tom Brown's Schooldays*. He had became a housemaster and taken holy orders. 'Tall, gaunt, rather awkward, gravely kind' as one boy described him, Cotton was the man who was to rescue Marlborough.

He began at once to make changes. It seemed to him that Marlborough's prefects led 'a life of privilege without duty or responsibility'. He planned to give them both. He called the boys together and told them:

George Edward Lynch Cotton.

> The Council informed me on my appointment that its School was in a bad state of discipline, and they hoped I would allow no boys to go out except in pairs with a master. I told them I could not accept office upon such terms, that the School I hoped to govern was a public school not a private one, and I would try and make it govern itself by means of prefects. The School knows now how matters stand. They must either submit to the prefects, or be reduced to the level of a private school, and have their freedom ignominiously curtailed. The prefects are and shall be, so long as I am head, the governors of this School. As soon as I see this impracticable I will resign.

Cotton's speeches to the assembled school were, according to Thomas, models of school addresses. They 'were not great displays of oratory, but they were so reasonable, so earnest, and so resolute, that their influence in moulding the school was quite remarkable.... I never remember his failing to create a deep impression.' Almost the only comments on Marlborough's staff in Nunns's usually factual diary refer to Cotton: 'Capital speech from Cotton. The VI Form are to govern the school,' he wrote on 22 September.

Cotton could be a disciplinarian himself when necessary. On Guy Fawkes Day, anniversary of the rebellion, he ordered that no fireworks of any kind should be set off, and was obeyed. When the school choir threatened to strike he told them he would flog every one of them – and they decided to sing. But it was through the prefects that he mainly ruled and he defended three of them when they captured and hanged a dog which other boys were using for poaching, remarking in his explanation to the assembled school, 'At any rate the dog is dead; and

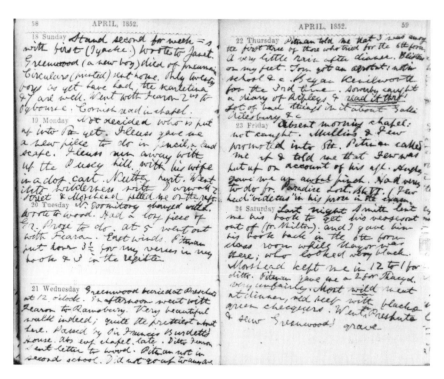

Pages from Nunns's diary.

I am inclined to think it died through excess of zeal,' words considered so witty that they were scrawled as graffiti on school walls.

Nunns, as a prefect, soon became involved in Cotton's new arrangements. On Tuesday 21 September he wrote 'Court of Prefects, Everest going to be licked. He got off', and on Sunday 20 November, 'In the afternoon took my afternoon of public-house duty. Caught Woodward etc., out of bounds. Caught Talmadge smoking. Mullins, like a fool, told Morshead. Court of Prefects. He got a fortnight's gates and Bath Road out of bounds.'

Cotton also abolished fines on the grounds that they were merely paid by parents, and substituted detention and impositions. But he never found the boys easy to control. During his final year he reprimanded them in a single circular for damage to gas-burners, the destruction of chairs in the school and classrooms, and the stealing of cutlery from the dining-hall. A week later he imposed extra afternoon lessons on the school for 'hissing, groaning and otherwise manifesting their disapprobation of a step which the Master thought necessary'. A week later again he forbade the Prefects' Court to discuss any of the Master's proceedings.

He did not at once sack Wilkinson's staff, retaining in particular two who were already well-established characters. One of these was Dr Walter Fergus. The school had had two previous medical offers, neither of whom stayed long. John Gardiner (Assistant Surgeon to the 1st Foot Guards at Waterloo) had been succeeded in 1848 by Robert Buchanan, the first doctor to be resident at the school. By August, however, the Council had received so many letters of complaint about Buchanan that it gave him notice. During these early years various sickrooms and infirmaries had been abandoned and instead Blore had been told to convert D House (the old White House) into an infirmary. When Fergus succeeded Buchanan in December 1848 it was here (and after 1860 in the new sanatorium) that he attended the sick of the school for 37 years, and became one of the best loved of early Marlburians. A quaint figure he must have been; bespectacled, in a velvet cap, he would be heard praying aloud as he approached boys who were seriously ill. But he was a well-considered doctor, who wrote for the *Lancet*. Letters and diaries of the time are full of evidence of his concern for the boys, even if his notions of hygiene were primitive. He would arrive 'before breakfast with a jug full of stuff to keep off the Scarlet Fever in one hand and in the other a wine glass which is fated to be within one hour the medicine glass of all the upper school without once being washed'.

A page from the substantial volume which was a leaving testimonial to Dr Walter Fergus.

Typically, on 19 February 1850 he wrote to Wilkinson complaining about the dirtiness of the clothes of the servants, and the smallness of the allowance of butter for the boys at breakfast and tea. On 27 September 1852 he ordered 'Edward 3 . . . to have a glass of ale at dinner daily for 10 days'. On 14 October he wrote, 'Nihill would be benefited by having a mutton chop for Breakfast for a fortnight,' and on 1 November, 'I think Nihill would be benefited by continuing his mutton

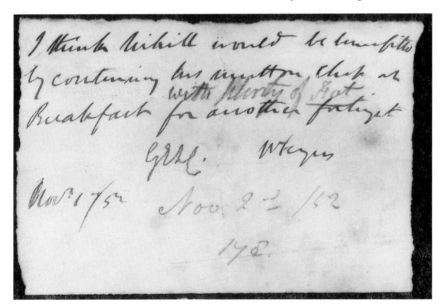

A note about H. D. Nihill in 1852, written by Dr Fergus and countersigned by the Master, Cotton.

53

chop with plenty of fat at Breakfast for another fortnight'. Fergus was also well liked in the town. His obituary in *The Marlburian* reported that on the day of his funeral 'every shop was partially closed and every house had blinds drawn, from the humblest to the highest'.

W. P. Sellick, an equally well-known character from early days, had arrived at Marlborough two years before Fergus as one of the writing-masters. He was a short, portly man, who wore large spectacles and had a broad Devonshire accent, in which he would give the sort of sharp answers to cheeky boys which suppressed them but they did not resent. His other gift was for organisation, and as a result he had put upon him a huge range of school duties, from the issuing of textbooks to the conducting of the school bank and the despatch of termly reports. But the function for which he was best remembered was organising the great end-of-term exodus. Before Marlborough had a railway station this was effected largely by coach, and it was Sellick who hired the coaches (known collectively as Jerry 'ammond's 'bus), marshalled the boys in the Mansion from 2 a.m. onwards and sent them out in groups to the coaches.

The journeys to Swindon (13 miles) or Hungerford (11 miles) were slow, uncomfortable, and in winter icy cold, especially for the nine out of 15 of an average coach load who had to ride on top. Clever boys

Jerry 'ammond's 'bus, presumably crossing the Downs to Swindon station via the old coach road.

54

would slip out with the previous group so that they could get inside places when their own coach arrived. When he caught one of these escapers, Sellick told him that next term-end he would put him in the last coach. The boy replied that he wouldn't be there next term. 'Nevertheless, sir,' said Sellick, 'I will do as I say.'

There were usually a few boys who chose to walk rather than ride, calling on the way at well-known inns like the Plough at Badbury for pipes and ale. One boy who walked the 18 miles to Chippenham remembered passing Silbury Hill in the early June morning where 'the mowers were cutting in the meadows by the roadside and the larks filling the air with song'.

But to supplement men like Sellick and Fergus, Cotton soon brought a group of dedicated young masters, several of them from Rugby. They were not easy to recruit. In November 1855 he wrote to James Bright reassuring him about his duties. He would only have to take prep twice a week and would have four prefects who would take it instead if he had an engagement. By this time new by-laws, had been passed, and the only salary Cotton could offer was '100 shares, lodging and subsistence'. He continued, 'I am sure that you would think that you had chosen rightly, if you knew the transports which your approach causes in the bosoms of Bull and Scott. "There are good days in store for Marlborough yet, if *he* is coming," exclaimed one of them.' When the ex-headboy, Tom Burn, graduated, Cotton wrote to him, 'I hasten to invite you to Marlborough,' but he could still only offer him 'a certain part of the profits, undoubtedly not less than £100 a year'.

One of those who came from Rugby was Charles Bere. When Cotton received his acceptance, he made one request. 'This has reference', he wrote, 'to the use of the pipe, now ... thoroughly adopted with other Mahometan practices.... I do hope you will not practise it. Considering the past ... propensities of the boys, I cannot fancy a much greater evil than a master encouraging smoking by his example.' Whether Bere obliged is not known, but, according to Thomas, 'No man in so short a time ever left his mark so conspicuously on Marlborough College.' When Bere resigned after only a year, Henry Palmer wrote in his diary, 'Mar. 6, Mon ... Bere made his fellows a very affecting speech this morning, it being his last time of coming into school and sent them all away blubbing and he himself rushed out of school in the same predicament'; and four days later, 'Bere was heartily cheered as this is his last game with us.' The game which Bere had been playing and which he had brought to Marlborough was Rugby football.

Football of a sort had been played at Marlborough almost from the start. In 1843 a boy became ill from drinking cold water 'when coming in from football'. At this time the sides were of no precise number and piles of coats were used for goal-posts. The ball in general had to be kicked, though a player who caught it was allowed a free kick. But until 1860 the Captain of Cricket was also the Captain of Football and cricket was the more prestigious game.

It had an equally haphazard early history. The author of *Marlborough Thirty Years Ago* remembered that,

> Our cricket-club slowly emerged from a chaos of discordant elements: our first chief was a broad-shouldered, good-humoured boy ... but he had no ... undisputed throne.... An Irish boy opened a sort of Cave of Adullam, and gathered about him all the discontented spirits. Another boy, a native of Devonshire, was so loquacious and argumentative, and had so little notion of subordination, that no one could act with him. He also drew aside, and revolved in his private orbit, forming a club for himself of such boys as were willing to render him implicit and unquestioning obedience. For some years there were several rival clubs in the school.

Nevertheless, in 1847 Sharpe, the Second Master, asked the Council for a roller for 'the boys' cricket pitch'. That year the levelling of the Eleven began. In 1848 the Master gave a small silver bat as a challenge trophy to be awarded to the best batsman of the year, and by 1851 there was also a bat for bowling. In April that year *The Marlburian*, excusing the school for its poor cricket, explained that only three years ago the best ground the club possessed was 'a steep slope on the side of a hill'.

The same issue reported a house match. Twyford (to be sacked in November) was the highest scorer for his side. Nunns, the diarist, batted last, was run out for 2 in the first innings and bowled for a duck in the second. That afternoon (7 May) Somerset, his fellow diarist, had other amusements. 'Went from 2–4 with B.3. to Martinsall and got 1 wood-pigeon. From 4–6 with Harvey to Hawk copse and took 5 sparrow hawks.'

The match against Purton, a village near Swindon, soon became as important an occasion as the later Cheltenham and Rugby matches, and the school's 1893 history illustrated it with a picture of the great Purton player, E. H. Budd, bowling in short white jacket and top hat.

Alongside proper cricket the game of Snob flourished, a Marlborough peculiarity in which playboxes were used for stumps, the bat was a stick or a weapon like a baseball bat and the ball of roughly cricket-ball size with an outer net of string. Until the 1860s it was played in Court, but when too many windows were broken it was removed to the Field

Old-fashioned Cricket

The Purton Match, from a sketch by G. F. Glennie.

where, 'reduced to a single-wicket game', it ceased to be 'a first-class amusement' (A. G. Bradley), but nevertheless lasted till the 1920s.

As early as 1844 Wilkinson had seen the need for an estate of some 55 acres, almost certainly for playing-fields. He was not, however, in favour of compulsory games. In October 1849 he wrote to a parent, 'There are very few boys here I think who do not get abundant exercise and those few would not like being put on what they would probably consider a *private school* system.' Thomas estimated that no more than a fifth of the school played formal games. And there was no strong feeling that these should be more important. Of the two to three thousand letters written by parents, boys and masters between 1843 and 1858 which Warwick James collected, only two mention games.

Cotton's abolition of fines had caused a further problem, since these had been used to support games. In a long letter he told parents that at most public schools 'the subscriptions, necessary for keeping them [games] up, are levied as a matter of course on every member of the School'. But Marlborough's charter did not allow compulsory extra charges. He therefore proposed that boys should subscribe voluntarily to the Cricket Club and suggested payments each term, starting at 1s. for boys of the Lower School, rising to 5s. for Sixth Form boys.

All boys now became members of the school's games club, and at

Marlborough, as elsewhere, organised games were soon a central feature of school life. They were encouraged for the qualities they promoted – bravery, endurance, the team spirit. In Cotton's words they were 'healthy and manly', providing 'constant and wholesome recreation'. In the pulpit he went further. To develop the body as well as the mind was to fulfil the will of God: 'All our powers and faculties, the limbs which are strong and healthy, the understanding which is strengthened and developed by our daily studies, are equally the workmanship of Him who has also reunited us to Himself in Jesus Christ. And, therefore, in giving wisdom and knowledge and bodily strength, we are carrying out His gracious purposes.'

But he had another motive. He wanted to introduce 'gradually the feeling that they [the boys] should keep as much as possible together as one body in the College itself and in the play-ground'. Till now boys had spent their half-holidays 'wandering about the country – some in bird's-nesting, or in destroying the property of neighbours'. In other words, games were a way of imposing good behaviour on the school.

Cotton like Wilkinson was fighting on two fronts. While he struggled at Marlborough to reform the school, he also struggled with the Council in London. In part the issue was straightforward: his right to run the school in the way he chose. There was an early confrontation when the Council told him that he was to do as other schools did and, in honour of a new headmaster, give the boys an extra week's holiday at Christmas. Cotton refused to do this unconditionally and told the boys that they would only get it as a reward for good behaviour.

Like Wilkinson, Cotton suffered from the necessity of referring tiny problems to London. Typically, in April 1853 he wrote to the Council asking to be allowed to give the boys of the choir a supper of bread and cheese after they had been kept up late at practice. But, as this suggests, it was the school's financial situation which was the real problem. In April 1853 the Council tried to set things right by raising fees for all *new* sons of clergymen to £45, and by reducing the amount life governors would have to pay to £50 and governors to £20.

That August it also discussed appealing to its bond-holders to accept reduced interest and appealing to clerical parents still paying £36, voluntarily to increase their payments to the new level. Far from supporting these proposals, Cotton wrote at length to the Council objecting to the second of them. 'If £30 was once raised to £36', he wrote, 'and if now parents are requested to make it £45, what security is there, it will be asked, that the £45 may not soon become £50 ... the public announcement, that it [Marlborough] cannot pay its way, must

deter parents from sending their sons to a place where it seems doubtful
whether their Education will be completed.'

The superstitious might have seen the hurricane of that autumn as an
ill omen.

Now for a description of an *ear*-witness [Saumarez Smith wrote].
In the first place it came with a fell swoop down into our
wilderness, making it a *wilderness* indeed, and destroyed *twenty or
thirty* large trees, maiming and stripping as many others ... It then
proceeded to ruffle the equanimity or rather the stability of the leads
on the top of the chapel, then pulled some tiles off the covered play
ground, then knocked down one of the fives court walls, uprooted
several trees in the field, took a gable off a new built national school
in the town, and went on its way *raging*.

When, on 20 January the following year, the Council finally decided
to send appeals to *all* parents and to bond-holders, and at the same time
proposed to reduce the salaries of masters by 10 per cent, Cotton told
the school secretary in London, 'It appears to me that the resolutions
about the laymen's sons, and the masters' salaries, are simply suicidal.'

Every sort of disappointment is happening at once, and I am at my
wits' end [he wrote three days later]. Congreve resigns from ill
health. Scott has bad eyes and cannot continue the work of the
Sixth. I have given him a Lower form ... and am now looking
about for a man for the Sixth, wherein I am greatly embarrassed
by the 3rd Resolution. Packe leaves at Easter because there is no
modern department. But how can a modern department be founded
under present circumstances? Clayton, on reading the resolutions,
has sent me in a (confidential) resignation.

A week later the Council postponed both appeals but agreed instead
to consider a far more radical reform: the 'transference of the
management of the College to the Master'. The minutes credit a Council
member, T. H. S. Sotheron, with this suggestion. On 8 February the
Council authorised Sotheron, Christopher Hodgson and the Master to
work out the proposal in detail. It was at this meeting that it noted 'the
severe loss which they and the College had sustained' by the sudden
death of Charles Plater, 'the Originator of Marlborough College'. Only
a week before, Plater had attended a Council meeting, and his death at
the age of 55 may well have had a connection with the crisis in
Marlborough's affairs.

The Council also now sent out its appeals and by 28 April holders of

£30,000 of the outstanding £40,000 bonds had agreed to receive reduced interest. Parents had been less responsive, only 141 out of 250 agreeing to increase their fee payments. Nevertheless, the total benefit to the college amounted to £1,844 a year.

More importantly, at this meeting, the Council agreed the full schedule of changes which turned over to the Master the management of the college. Cotton had continued to have doubts about the reduction of the assistant masters' salaries. On 7 March he had written to the Council, arguing that these 'should not be so reduced as to prevent the continuance of men of standing and distinction'. The final schedule ordered that a fifth of the school's profits were to go to the Council for repaying its debts, but the rest was to be divided between the Master and the assistant masters, as he thought fit.

A bursar at Marlborough was now appointed and Cotton chose the same Jonathan Clayton who had provisionally resigned five months earlier. But he did not stay long and the following year was replaced by Mrs Cotton's brother, Henry Tomkinson. From this time onwards the school began to prosper once more. Though its numbers were at their lowest (340) in 1855, they had risen to nearly 400 by 1858, and by then all temporary bank loans had been repaid as well as another £7,000 of bonds.

In 1852 Cotton put into practice a more radical version of Wilkinson's suggestion about the younger boys of the school by giving them A House (an arrangement which persisted until 1989). Here they were to 'live and say their lessons, being kept *generally* separate from the rest of the school'. The Lower School was to have Mr Tayler as its housemaster

MODERN SCHOOL.

	DIVINITY.	LATIN.	FRENCH.	GERMAN.	HISTORY & GEOGRAPHY.
FIFTH FORM.	Kings. St. Matthew in German.	Sallust, Cataline.	Molière Villemain's Essays. La France Littéraire.	Goethe: Ballads and "Aus Meinem Leben."	Keightley's England. England and Ireland.
UPPER FOURTH.	Kings. Acts of the Apostles.	Livy.	Guizot. Voltaire's Charles xii.	Hoffmann.	Keightley's England. The British Colonies.
LOWER FOURTH.	1st & 2nd Samuel. St. John	Cæsar.	La Grande Charte.	Grimm's Hausmärchen.	Yonge's England. Physical Geography.

The Grammars are Wordsworth's Greek, Kennedy's Latin, Brasseur's French, and a small French Grammar drawn up for the use of the School, and a small German Grammar abridged from Becker.

The Mathematical Books used are Barnard Smith's Arithmetic; Pott's Euclid; Colenso's and Todhunter's Algebras; Todhunter's Trigonometry, and Conic Sections, Galbraith's Trigonometry is used in the Modern School.

Lectures in Chemistry are given by DR. FERGUS: subject for next half-year :—Frictional Electricity—Chemistry of Gasses and other Non-Metallic bodies—Heat.

The curriculum as published in 1860. The upper part refers to the classical side and required no explanation. The lower part shown here has the heading 'Modern School'.

(Tayler and Mrs Tayler were to live there) and three other masters. Also allotted to it would be three Sixth Form boys, to be called Prefects of the Lower School. It would consist of about 100 boys who would constitute the school's lowest three forms.

The Revd Charles Tayler was a good choice for the Lower School. John Harrison, who arrived as a boy a few years later, described him as 'one of the dearest of men'. He 'rather fancied himself as a sportsman' and was 'certainly fairly good at archery', but also played the flute. He once saved Harrison from punishment for getting drunk on port and sherry at a celebration dinner in hall by saying the wine was bad. Because of his habit of 'exercising his jaw after the manner of a cow chewing the cud' he was known as 'Chump'.

An equally important change came two years later with the establishment of a Modern School. On 10 March 1854 Cotton wrote to parents:

> I receive an increasing number of requests from parents that I will permit their sons to give up some part of the regular Classical work, in order that they may devote themselves to special subjects connected with their future professions. I have, therefore, resolved to place this matter on something of a systematic basis, by establishing a Class in which such subjects shall be more regularly, and thoroughly taught.... The regular course of instruction will, if possible, comprise Religious Knowledge, Latin, French, History, Geography (with Physical Geography and the Elements of Geology), Euclid, Arithmetic, Algebra and English Composition. Besides these – German, Natural Science, and Military Drawing will be added as extra subjects, of which every boy must select one.

Since the Lower School now had its own classrooms in A House, the Modern School was to use the old Lower School, and the building soon acquired that name. By 1860 it had three classes with about 20 boys in each.

A number of schools had by this time begun to teach modern languages and such modern subjects as history, but Marlborough was one of the first to establish a separate Modern Side. Rossall did so the same year, and Clifton had one from its foundation in 1862. Manchester Grammar School and Haileybury followed in the mid-1860s, but Eton not until 1886 and Winchester had no so-called 'B ladder' until 1930.

Conditions at Marlborough remained rugged. On 2 March 1854 Palmer 'watched a mouse for at least an hour quietly getting into my bed and grubbing my bread and cheese – set a trap for same'. Next day he 'Caught the rascally mouse and gave him to the boy P[o]le who was delighted and executed him in a basin'. The same February Edward Mosley, who gave his address as 'The Cellar, Marlborough College', told his mother, 'I am almost frozen and the night I got here the bed clothes felt as if they had been dragged through a river'. When the frosts ceased he was grateful, 'although this cellar suffers by it, for the melting snow makes the wall as damp as possible'. That March he had chilblains. 'I have about three or four times a day awful pains in my heels and fingers ... heat generally brings it on even the warmth of bed.... I am awfully glad it does not last all day or else I should not know what to do with myself.'

During Cotton's time at Marlborough, Britain was involved in the Crimean War, the first it had fought since the defeat of Napoleon 40 years earlier at Waterloo. The boys were keenly interested. On 8 September 1854 they debated who was the best man to 'stand at the head of affairs' and voted for Lord Palmerston. On 30 September Palmer wrote that a friend, George, was 'now going to the Siberian coast to nab the Russian vessels'. And on 2 October, the day he left Marlborough for Cambridge, he heard that Sebastopol had fallen (a rumour – Sebastopol did not fall for another year).

The following February several boys were allowed two or three extra weeks' holiday to see relatives who were going to the front. Meanwhile the government had told Cotton that it would give two or three boys aged between 17 and 19 commissions in the artillery. In May a troop of the Sixth Dragoon Guards stayed a night in the town on their way to the Crimea. Cotton had a special interest in the war. His wife's elder brother, Colonel H. Tomkinson, was serving there. At Balaclava he survived the Charge of the Light Brigade, though his horse was killed under him.

Early in 1858, after less than six years at Marlborough, Cotton was offered the position of Bishop of Calcutta. He did not hesitate long, and was consecrated at Westminster on 13 May. Any differences he may have had with the Council were now in the past and he was appointed a life governor.

Eight years later Bishop Cotton, travelling by river-boat on the Hooghly and suffering from fever, went ashore at the small station of Kooshtea to consecrate the cemetery. Returning in the dark, he set off along a narrow gangway towards his boat, slipped, fell into the water and was never seen again. There is no evidence to support the school rumour that he was eaten by an alligator.

5

THE GREAT BRADLEY

1858–1871

ONE AFTERNOON IN early August 1858, on a bleak part of Salisbury plain not far from Stonehenge, a gentleman, his family and servants could have been seen sitting by the roadside in the pouring rain beside a shattered horse-drawn bus. The bus had been taking them the 28 miles from Salisbury to Marlborough. The gentleman was the Revd George Granville Bradley, the new Master of Marlborough College. Bradley had chosen to approach Marlborough this way because he had been holidaying in the Isle of Wight. The bus had crashed because it had been driven downhill 'in too hilarious a fashion'. But no one had been hurt, and Bradley's party completed the journey in two Amersham flies.

Cotton had known Bradley for many years. They had taught together at Rugby from the time Bradley arrived there in 1846 till Cotton left in 1852. Since then Bradley had visited Cotton at Marlborough. At Rugby he had become housemaster of one of the school's largest houses. His decision to come to Marlborough was therefore not an easy one because it meant a considerably lower income, but Cotton had persuaded him that the job of sustaining Marlborough's recovery would make this loss worth while.

And Cotton had manipulated the Council in order to get Bradley chosen without the issuing of a public advertisement. At its meeting in mid-March he had managed to get the 13 members present (who constituted a majority) to vote for Bradley. Bradley had still to have printed 25 copies of his testimonials and send one copy to each Council member so that they could confirm him. 'Preface them', Cotton told

George Granville Bradley and family outside the drawing-room of the Master's Lodge.

him, 'by a brief letter, offering yourself in the ordinary way, and promising orders if you are elected.' On 14 April Bradley was duly elected and before coming to Marlborough he duly took holy orders.

Towards the end of Cotton's time, Edward White Benson (who became Wellington's first Master in January 1859) visited Marlborough. The notes he made give an outside view of the school Bradley inherited.

> One very great difference between Marlborough and Rugby or any other school where the *House System* properly so called prevails is in the oneness of interest throughout the school – and if there is any good in this, there is very great evil also. Rows and discontent of all kinds are smothered within one of the houses at Rugby, for all the members of the House have a pride in keeping their affairs to themselves and not exposing either their own set of boys or their own master to the animadversion of the rest. But at Marlborough disaffection spreads like fire. The boys all meet in Chapel twice, in Hall 3 times every day. Formerly also they used to be taught in the same schoolroom, but great good has been done in eradicating this particular evil by building class rooms which facilitate very much the breaking up of the boys.

Bradley's experience as a Rugby housemaster had taught him about the handling of boys. His son, Marlborough's first historian, told the story of an early confrontation at Marlborough, where, to test him, a number of boys staged a large poaching expedition in the forest, killing 'some twenty or thirty rabbits', then selling them in the town. The figure sounds improbable – it is hard enough for adults with guns to collect such a bag, let alone boys with sticks and catapults – but the story was no doubt based on a real event and continued with Bradley addressing the assembled school, demanding within an hour the names of all who had taken part, and sending a cheque for the money the boys had made by selling the animals, to the Marquis of Ailesbury. It was those 'mercenary transactions upon which the lash of the Head Master's tongue fell with such scathing force'.

The new Master could also pen a scathing notice. As part of his anti-poaching campaign he posted on the school notice-board: 'Boys who are afraid to face squirrels in the forest without "squalers" and catapults are requested to leave these weapons of offence behind them before re-entering the college.' His son came close to admitting that he was not liked for his sharp tongue, but claimed that 'somehow or other, under the soothing hand of time', his sarcasms had 'been unanimously transferred to the credit account of their author'.

'The Last of the Squirrel Hunters.' The weapons are, from left to right, peashooter, squaler and catapult. (F. S. Baden-Powell)

In other ways, too, Bradley was unlike Cotton. Courtenay Ilbert, who was in the sick-house when Cotton showed Bradley round, remembered that nothing could have been 'more striking' than the contrast between the 'gravely kind' Cotton and the 'bright, keen, vivacious little man who was so soon to take his place.... If reserved strength was the note of the one, vitality ... exuberant, irrepressible, contagious, stimulating, was the note of the other.'

Under Bradley's stimulating influence the school, within two years, achieved a remarkable academic triumph: the winning of both the open scholarships to Balliol. At a time when there were relatively few open scholarships to Oxford or Cambridge, the two offered by Balliol were considered the most prestigious. Ilbert was one of the successful candidates. The other was Thomas Papillon, son of the Revd John Papillon, a member of Council. When the father heard the news he is said to have burst into a Council meeting, 'pale and almost speechless with excitement'. At Marlborough the news was taken from class to class by the Senior Prefect and heard with 'wild shrieks of delight'. That October when the two boys left Marlborough for Oxford (they had returned to the school for the first weeks of the term) much of the school followed them in procession through the town up Kingsbury Street, across the Common and down into the Og Valley. Ilbert became Clerk to the House of Commons, after a distinguished career as a civil servant in India. In 1908 he was knighted, and for 37 years he was a member of Council. Papillon remained an academic, winning the Chancellor's Prize for Latin Verse and becoming Dean of New College, before taking the living of Writtle, Essex. He served on the Council for 43 years.

'The Balliol Scholars Going to Oxford.' Ilbert and Papillon being seen on their way in 1859.

Adderley Library as it was in the 1860s when Bradley took 'Review'.

About Bradley's teaching, another of his pupils, Samuel Butcher, wrote:

> To small boys he was an object of fear. They knew him as presiding over a very formidable ceremony called 'Review', when once in the half-year he examined each form in the School. He was known to say sharp things on these occasions; and one can remember standing at the [Adderley] Library door as a new boy, trembling as the dreadful moment approached; and then, when the hour was over, wondering that we had come out alive from the ordeal. Even in the fifth form the feeling towards the Master was one of awe and distant admiration. In the Sixth we came to know him personally.

The Sixth Form boys' translations into Latin prose would come 'back to us black with pencil marks; no corrections were made, there was no attempt at rewriting what was wrong'. Bradley then 'took our Latin, held it up to the light, turned it inside out, translated it back into its true English equivalent, producing a medley of incongruous phrases. He revelled, as it seemed, in our absurdities, and we ourselves shared the enjoyment. But in another moment he spoke with trenchant irony and all the force of moral denunciation; we felt as guilty as criminals.'

Butcher and his contemporaries 'felt as schoolboys, and still feel, after the lapse of many years, that, intellectually speaking, Marlborough was

Bradley'. Ilbert considered that 'the period during which Bradley ruled Marlborough was the most brilliant period of Marlborough's history'. And though another boy of the time, John Harrison, remembered that bullying was widespread and the food meagre and disgusting, he also noted the most important of Cotton's legacies: that there was no longer chronic enmity between boys and masters. On the contrary, their relationships were 'of the friendliest nature'. Most of them 'gave little tea parties in their rooms from time to time'.

In 1862 Bradley described Marlborough to the Parliamentary Commission, generally known as the Clarendon Commission, which was preparing a report on the seven Great Schools, plus the two day-schools, St Paul's and the Merchant Taylors'. For comparison it approached five less ancient schools, one of them Marlborough. Like Benson, Bradley picked out its centralised arrangement as the feature which distinguished it from most other schools, but unlike Benson, he saw this as an advantage. The boys could be housed and fed more cheaply, the 25 assistant masters had to be young and unmarried and could therefore be paid less. As a result their ratio to the boys could be greater. Furthermore 'The general work of the school' could be 'more systematised', a 'natural effect ... of so large a number of masters being in constant communication with each other'.

Bradley described how Marlborough's 'Review' worked.

> At a certain hour, each form in its turn comes before the Head Master; a list is placed before him of the names of the boys in the Form, ... opposite each boy's name is entered ... a short, but sufficient account of his regularity, industry, and conduct. The Head Master with this by his side, examines every boy before him in the subject of the Review ... recording on the same sheet of paper his impression of the performance of every boy. The time consumed in the inspection of a form is about two hours.

The school now consisted of 450 boys: 62 in the Lower School, 315 in the Upper School and 73 in the Modern School. Though the Modern School was eight years old, Bradley still considered it an experiment in whether it was possible 'to give a really good public school education, on any other basis than that of instruction in the dead languages'. Its other purpose was 'to prepare boys for definite examinations in which they would not succeed if they competed direct from the classical school'. Previously such boys had had to be removed to be tutored privately, and thus been deprived of 'the outdoor organization and amusements' of a public school.

Though his personal preference was for an education based on 'the language and substance of the great writers of antiquity', he believed it would be possible to give 'a thoroughly good education' consisting largely of 'mathematics and a thorough study of German and French'. The problem was to find satisfactory modern language teachers. Should they be foreigners? Bradley asked, and wrote, 'the answer is decisive and final. A foreigner, in the vast majority of cases, cannot control, understand, or stimulate a large class of English boys.' But competent English teachers of foreign languages were *at present extremely rare*. Ten years later (June 1872) when Charles Bull became the master in charge of the Modern School the Council gave him 50 guineas to go to Germany to learn German.

James Bright, its master in 1862, reported a different problem. The Modern School was too small. As a result the three teachers allotted to it found themselves teaching in a single class boys of too diverse abilities. Their difficulties were exacerbated by 'the great variety of objects which induce boys to enter the Modern in preference to the Classical school. Some are intended for Woolwich, some for the public offices, some for commercial life, some for any opening which may offer itself.'

At Freshwater on the Isle of Wight, where Bradley regularly holidayed, and where his children would be photographed by the famous and eccentric Julia Margaret Cameron, he befriended an even more eminent neighbour, the Poet Laureate, Alfred Tennyson. When Tennyson sent his son, Hallam, to boarding-school he explained that 'I sent him to Marlborough because Bradley was a friend of mine, and [Dean] Stanley has told me that it is the best school in England'. In January 1866 Tennyson himself brought Hallam to Marlborough, stayed four days with Bradley at the Master's Lodge and gave poetry readings to the masters and the Upper Sixth.

Hallam, who became unpoetically portly later in life, was remembered by his contemporary, Henry Simpkinson, as slim, sallow and long-legged, a good sprinter. But his school-fellows considered that a poem which won second prize for School English Verse would not have done so if his name had not been Tennyson. A set of English hexameters which he published in *The Marlburian* and signed T, were parodied by another boy who signed himself 'Coffee'. (Hallam's hexameters were in fact part composed by the Poet Laureate.) But boys agreed that he deserved the Colbeck Reading Prize. 'Tennyson chose the scene in *Henry IV*, where Falstaff describes how he was set upon by countless men in buckram. He gave it magnificently, and was unanimously adjudged the winner. The only criticism was, that his was a dramatic declamation rather than a reading.' Simpkinson went up to Cambridge with Hallam, and remembered an early meeting with him and two other Marlburians, when the four of them lamented their loneliness as the only freshmen from the school that year. Later Hallam became Governor-General of Australia, and for 37 years was a member of Marlborough's Council.

Throughout Bradley's time there was a steady improvement in the school's finances. This was achieved partly by persuading the bond-holders to continue to receive reduced interest, partly by increasing the fees to £52.10s and £70 respectively (December 1860), but most importantly by attracting more boys. In 1867, for the first time since Wilkinson's days, numbers rose to the full 500, an impressive achievement against new competition from Wellington (1859), Haileybury (1860) and Clifton (1862). By 1867 the whole of Marlborough's debt had been repaid.

In the same years there were important additions to the school's premises. From early in the 1860s some boys had begun to board in the town — Dr Fergus had taken a few of 'the less hardy sort' at his home, the Hermitage. Then in 1861 Preshute House was established across the river. To distinguish it from the older in-college houses around Court, it — and those which followed — was known as an out-college house. It took 30 to 40 boys and its first housemaster was Bright, head of the Modern School, future Master of University College, Oxford.

Preshute, however, was a rented house and the first building to be newly erected by the school since the 1840s was a sanatorium. Appeals ultimately collected £600, but another £1,000 was needed, and Bradley asked parents to pay an extra 10s. per boy per term for three years to raise this amount. In 1860 the sanatorium was built, across the Bath Road at the south-east corner of the school's field.

Another improvement of Bradley's time was the conversion of New Court, the old Covered Playground, into a gymnasium (1869). It remained, however, a place where 'Grub-boxes ... packing-cases, and hampers appeared on every side, piled on the crazy shelves round the walls or littered over the floor' (A. G. Bradley), and the school had to wait another 40 years, until 1908, for a purpose-built gymnasium.

But the change which most effectively separated old from new Marlborough was the arrival at the town of the railway. The keenest promoter of this was Bursar Thomas. It was Thomas who gathered the support of important citizens including the mayor, Jonah Reeve. And in July 1861, once the railway's Parliamentary Bill had received the Queen's signature, it was Thomas who told a public meeting that the cheapest way to build it would be to start at once, while the contractor who had built the Berks and Hants Extension still had his equipment in the area.

The five-and-a-half-mile branch ran from Savernake, where the Great

Western Railway had a station, north-west for most of its length before turning north-east to arrive at Marlborough's High Level Station, some 200 yards south of today's town centre. Three years later (March 1864), when the great opening day arrived, the *Marlborough Times* reported that 'shops were rigidly closed, the church bells also rang merrily at intervals, the drum and fife band paraded the streets'.

That day the train made three runs, none of them exactly a technical triumph. On the first from Marlborough to Savernake, 'owing to the unfitness of the engine which positively refused to take the train up the incline to Granham and had to be backed to obtain impetus, a delay of ten minutes occurred and half an hour was occupied in the journey'. It then made a slow return to Marlborough, where it took on board a load of local dignitaries, including the Master, and carried them back to Savernake for a festive lunch. A fortnight later on 14 April, a regular service began, with five trains a day in each direction, the journey taking 15 minutes.

Eleven years later, in 1875, Marlborough's second railway opened and the town was at last connected with Swindon. Its two railways ran for almost exactly 100 years, the High Level station closing in 1961 and the Low Level in 1966.

The year after the railway first reached Marlborough *The Marlburian* reappeared. The editor of the first edition mentioned in his editorial 'the

'Going Home by Train.' High Level station (terminus) in the foreground, Low Level station (Southampton to Cheltenham) is on the right in the distance. (The cricket bag carries the initials of the artist P. Chenevix-Trench.)

THE
MARLBOROUGH MAGAZINE.

"Est quaedam prodire tenus, si non datur ultra."—HORACE.

APRIL 24th, 1848.

INTRODUCTION.

FEW books come before the public now-a-days without a Preface or Introduction of some kind or other, and it is not to be expected, that in ushering a Magazine into the small world of a Public School, we should make it an exception to the general rule. Those to whom we address ourselves have certainly a right to inquire, what were our motives in starting this publication—what will be our plan in proceeding with it —and on what reasonable grounds we found our hopes of success; and on all and each of these points we will endeavour to satisfy our Readers.

In the first place, then, we confess that the novelty of the undertaking went some little way in recommending it to our favour, when it was once proposed. Every one who has learnt his Latin Grammar is, or ought to be, familiar with the saying ("Est natura hominum novitatis avida")—and certainly the truth of the remark is not diminished by time. There was something pleasant and exciting in the idea of establishing a Magazine among ourselves, and we were perhaps rather too much inclined to seize on any plan, which might have the effect of varying the even and somewhat

The *Marlborough Magazine*, published from 1848 to 1861.

The *Marlburian* of 1851; only four issues, and then abandoned. The present *Marlburian* has been continuously published since 1865.

former' *Marlborough Magazine*, but seemed not to know that there had also been a former *Marlburian*. Just the same, the new *Marlburian* was very like its 1851 predecessor. Though slightly larger in format and without chess problems, it was again an eight-page paper and again contained a mixture of poems, articles, letters to the editor, cricket scores and reports on school societies.

The editor warned contributors that 'no personalities whatever, no reflections on the conduct of any particular person, and also no religious discussion' could be printed, but told them that political questions could be debated, and that on these he would give 'a free hand and no favour'. He was keen to encourage 'literary energy, especially as we are here too apt to care little beyond the actual sphere of our work, and to find our sole recreation in often worthless novels'. News of the paper must already have spread for its final page added that the number of contributions had 'rather exceeded our expectations' and asked for more prose and less poetry. Would contributors write legibly, as otherwise the trouble of correcting proofs became 'something enormous'.

Within a few years *The Marlburian* experienced a crisis. On 9 April 1875 Charles Bull, by then the best-paid assistant master, wrote a note to Bursar Thomas headed 'In the train near Newbury, jolting'. *The Marlburian* should be stopped, Bull wrote. 'No apology ought to prevent this necessary measure.... It is not at all unlikely that the thing was written in the merest thoughtlessness, and published by the editor in the same blind ignorance of what they were doing ... But this is no reason for letting the *Marlburian* go on any longer.'

A search of the previous issue suggests that Bull had been shocked by favourable comments on a poem describing an old man's memories of his love for a 'youthful playmate' (male). *The Marlburian* survived and has been published regularly ever since. Year after year its pages reflect the flavour of the school at the time. Occasionally they have wider interest. In its second issue there was an earnest and disapproving article on Muscular Christianity.

Bradley's regime ended with the most serious crisis since the financial one of 1853–4. Epidemics were a problem at most nineteenth-century boarding-schools. The best known of these was Uppingham's typhoid epidemic of 1875, when the school had to move for a year to Cardigan Bay while its drains and water supply were rebuilt. Wellington's epidemic 'sore throat', diagnosed as malaria, was almost as notorious in its time. Scarlet fever epidemics were also common; Rossall had no fewer than five between 1845 and 1873. Marlborough had had scarlet fever outbreaks from its early days. In 1848 the Master ended the summer term early because of the prevalence of scarlet fever. There were other outbreaks in the 1850s, but it was only in 1865 that the series began which culminated in the major epidemic of 1870.

By March that year it had become too serious to conceal, and Bradley posted a notice reading 'It is of the utmost importance that any boy who feels unwell, above all who has any rash, should without a moment's delay report himself to the Doctor. Lying on the grass with or without rugs, is the most dangerous thing, at present, which a boy can do.' The same day he wrote to parents admitting that a boy had died. He continued, 'There is no intention of dispersing the school; but if you have special cause for anxiety, you can, of course, procure for your son leave of absence.' The parents of all except 150 boys did so, and by 15 April Bradley had changed his mind, closing the school for the first time for a three-week Easter holiday.

Meanwhile, on 6 April the Council had considered the crisis and recommended the placing of boys in separate houses of 80 to 100, and a light additional evening meal of 'bread and cheese and beer or bread and cocoa'. Three days later a public meeting in London attended by 20 parents resolved that 'larger house accommodation than is now afforded by the college buildings, better ventilation in the existing classrooms and dormitories, and a more liberal diet, are necessary for the maintenance of vigorous health and due resistance to the inroads of Epidemic disease'.

Eventually the epidemic subsided and later that year parents presented Fergus with 'a very beautiful and valuable gold watch and chain, together with Quain and Wilson's Anatomical Plates in 2 volumes' in gratitude for 'the great ability he displayed during that trying time'.

Meanwhile on 14 April Dr Stalland, described as 'the Sanitary Commissioner to the *Lancet*', had inspected the school and come to conclusions similar to those reached by Council and parents. Overcrowding and insufficient ventilation were particularly serious in the first floor of the old house, the upper floor of 'the new house' (B House), the dining-hall and all the rooms of the sick-house.

The idea of more accommodation was not new. Both in 1867 and 1869 the Council had employed their architect, William White, to draw up plans for a house to be built where the old Lower School (by then the Modern School) stood. White's elegant coloured plans survive, but were never used, and the Council now adopted a different idea: the building of two new out-college houses.

For the designing of these it dropped White (who was about to become involved in a five-year court case about an Irish house he had designed, which he eventually lost) and went instead to the distinguished architect, George Edmund Street. By 16 August 1870, when the new idea was finally approved, James Gilmore and Francis Thompson had

G. E. Street's two new houses (1872). Cotton House on the left (much the same today) and Littlefield on the right; an early view, long before Littlefield was burnt down and rebuilt.

already been chosen as housemasters of the new houses. They were each to contribute about half the cost of their houses (£3,000 and £2,500 respectively), an arrangement showing clearly that setting up a boarding-house was considered a financial investment. By 16 November work was in progress and the Council agreed to pay Street an extra £400 for having to buy material for his concrete instead of using 'that which might be found on the ground'.

The most serious consequence of the epidemics of 1865–70 was that Marlborough became known as the place to which to send your boy if you wanted him to catch scarlet fever. Not surprisingly, fewer parents did so, and the school began again to lose money. In 1870 the Council decided that it must once more raise fees and proposed a radical change: future parents, whether lay or clerical, would pay £80. In compensation there would be 70 Foundation Scholarships open only to sons of clergymen, the fees for the winners to be £50 a year. Though this seemed to some parents inconsistent with the principles on which Marlborough had been founded, the new arrangements were agreed at a special meeting of life governors on 2 June 1870.

In 1871 Bradley accepted the Mastership of University College, Oxford. By then he had done all that Cotton had hoped from him and Marlborough was recognised as one of the country's major public schools. Nor did this end his contribution. For many years he was an active member of Council, often chairing its meetings.

His ready tongue may have made a first meeting with Bradley 'a little paralysing' and 'produced the effect of an intellectual torpedo' (Butcher); and his astringent teaching may have been alarming even to the Sixth Form, but he became a friend to many boys, and would take them riding with him on the downs or in the forest. He had a more unexpected hobby: homing pigeons. Boys would co-operate with him by accompanying cages of these to distant stations and releasing them. The Master can be pictured on early summer mornings in the garden of the Lodge, half his mind on the precise translation of a phrase from Virgil while at the same time he fed barley to his flock, or looked anxiously into the sky for some missing bird.

Spy cartoon of Bradley as Dean of Westminster.

6

ERIC'S CREATOR

1871–1876

WHEN BRADLEY WAS replaced by the Harrow master, Frederick William Farrar, author of the best-selling school story, *Eric or Little by Little* (1858), one of Bradley's Marlborough pupils sent him a postcard reading

> Dear Dr Bradley
> We miss you sadly
> And we wish Dr Farra
> Would go back to Harra.

Frederic William Farrar as a young man.

Farrar was the son of an Indian missionary, brought up in England by maiden aunts. At various schools he had soon distinguished himself, and by the time his parents finally returned to London when he was 15 he was winning enough prizes and scholarships for the rest of his education to cost them nothing. While at Trinity College, Cambridge, he was appointed an assistant master at Marlborough before even taking his degree.

From Marlborough Farrar had gone to Harrow, where he had remained ever since, and become a housemaster. But teaching had been far from his only occupation there. During those 16 years as well as *Eric* (which he dedicated to Bishop Cotton) and other school stories, he had written pioneering works on philology and grammar. Because his views on these subjects were evolutionary, he had been befriended by Charles Darwin, who had successfully nominated him in 1860 for a Fellowship of the Royal Society. Ultimately it was Farrar who persuaded the authorities that Darwin should be buried in Westminster Abbey. And in 1869 Farrar had published a volume of sermons, soon afterwards being appointed chaplain to Queen Victoria.

Farrar had also made public his advanced views on contemporary teaching. In February 1867 he had addressed the Royal Institution on the subject, and in firm if florid terms deplored, not only the almost exclusive teaching of the classics but the way these were taught.

> Imagine, ladies and gentlemen, that at this moment you yourselves were desirous to learn Arabic; imagine an Arabic grammar, with rules in Arabic, put into your hands; imagine these Arabic rules clothed in a scholastic terminology, and bristling with philosophical abstractions, interspersed here and there with the castanet music of an abhorrent doggrel; imagine that the Arabic verb, like the Greek verb, had twelve hundred synthetic forms, and that you had to learn them every one by heart before proceeding a step; imagine that this amzing sum-total were forced on you in a solid and amorphous form, perhaps by a wholly incompetent teacher who repressed all questions at the point of a ferule; imagine this, and you have the very photograph of what in very many cases is being done with your little sons in Greek and Latin.

A small boy of eight or nine, Farrar continued, would be 'terrified ... with such incubi and succubi as "quid-quale verbs", "gerundive attractions", "suboblique clauses", "spirants", "receptive complements", "relations circumstantive and prolative", "quasi-passives", "demi-passives", "semi-deponents" and I know not what.'

A public school curriculum was exclusively designed to fit boys for an academic future at the university, where some 25 per cent might go. Even these boys had been taught in ways which produced 'parrot-like repetition and sing-song knowledge, to the abeyance and destruction of the intellectual powers.... But, if this be so with the successful, what are the results with the unsuccessful? ... Ask our parents and they will sigh over the vacant hours spent in lounging in the billiard-room and the stable-yard.'

The classics were already under attack. The earliest *Marlburian* (April 1851) carried a long article defending the teaching of them. But if opinions like Farrar's were not uncommon by 1867, and the members of the Royal Institution would have enjoyed hearing them, it was less common for a senior housemaster at a leading public school to express them so forcefully. That year Farrar applied for the headmastership of Haileybury and was probably rejected because of his views on education.

Farrar did not advocate the abolition of the teaching of the classics, but alongside them he wanted boys to learn science. Science would seem to most boys more real, and as a result they would be happier in their school work. 'The theory which strove to make teaching unpleasant was an odious heresy.' Furthermore learning science would be useful to future clergymen, who now often found themselves 'actually inferior in these great fields of knowledge to many clerks and artisans in their own congregations, before whom they cannot venture to speak of them without the danger of raising a contemptuous smile'. In spite of his opinions, and though his rival candidates included three headmasters of other schools, Marlborough's Council chose Farrar, who had the advantage of being proposed by Bradley and seconded by Dean Stanley.

But Bradley was not an easy man to succeed. Thirty years later John Rogers contrasted him with his successor.

> Bradley was a schoolmaster to his fingertips, with clear, exact mind: an excellent teacher of scholarship . . . very thorough; quick and merciless in searching out weak spots; diligent in the use of probe and microscope; armed at all points, and without a single weak spot himself; invulnerable, firm, business-like.
>
> Farrar was the antithesis of all this. He was not only something more, but he was also something less than a schoolmaster.

He had 'the grand manner'. Aristotle's description of 'the grand man' suited him exactly: 'His gait is slow, his voice deep, and he speaks . . . in measured cadences.' It was typical of Farrar that he preferred Milton to Shakespeare. Like Bradley, he was perpetually enthusiastic, and 'his industry was positively tireless', but 'all the characteristic stories about Farrar reveal a lofty strain of enthusiasm, just tinged with the ridiculous'.

One day Farrar took some guests to visit a Sixth Form study and found the boys not working but eating roast potatoes and drinking cocoa. Next day he told his class that he had expected to find them 'immersed in the study of some Attic masterpiece. . . . But what was my indignation, vexation, and shame when I discovered them greedily engaged in ravenously devouring the semese fragments of a barbaric repast.'

'Our first impression', Rogers wrote, 'was, how odd it was that he should have felt disappointed. Our second, Could he really expect to crush cocoa and roast potatoes with those furious blows of his Nasmyth hammer? Our third, What Gargantuan humour. . . . True, it was at first unconscious, then semi-conscious, and only at last (if then) wholly conscious; but this only made the humour more humorous.' Farrar's grand manner 'cast on everything he did . . . an intermixture of serious and farcical which used to strike us as so whimsical that we could not laugh at it, we could only quote it'.

Nevertheless Farrar was an inspiring teacher. His boys appreciated the fact that he did not 'take a drill sergeant's view of his profession' and still more that he 'made up for want of firmness by excess of kindness'. They were infected by his enthusiasm for beauty of all sorts. A Harrow pupil remembered how he would 'endeavour to make us see the loveliness of common things – sunsets and wild flowers and fresh grass and autumn leaves'. He would decorate his classroom with 'antique casts, as models of form, and Fra Angelico's blue Madonnas and rose coloured angels on golden backgrounds as models of colour'. Against Philistinism he campaigned relentlessly, and once told some dull boy not to sit there 'gorgonizing me with your stony British stare'.

At Marlborough his Sixth Form boys found his enthusiasm for modern writers equally exhilarating. He would describe contemporary giants like Ruskin, Browning and Matthew Arnold as his 'eminent friends'. They would feel in touch with that world when Farrar might say, 'I have just been staying with Tennyson, who read me his new poem'. Rogers concluded that, among the half-dozen headmasters he had known, Farrar was 'the most interesting of the lot'.

One of the first things Farrar did at Marlborough was formally to introduce science. At once he set up a Science Committee, which reported on 24 June 1871 that the 'Shell' and the Upper Fourth Form should have at least one hour a week of science, that in other forms it should be a voluntary subject, and that in the Modern School it should be a regular part of the work. The following term he appointed George Rodwell as science master, poaching him from Clifton, one of the few schools ahead of Marlborough in science, after he had been there only a year.

Rodwell was among the most distinguished of the country's early science masters, the publisher of many papers and several books on scientific subjects, an authority on volcanoes. In his inaugural lecture at Marlborough, which was of great length and well above the heads of most of his audience, he explained why he thought science should be taught: not for practical purposes, but 'to cultivate a certain set of mental faculties, to induce a mode of thought'. Its only practical use was to enable boys to secure science scholarships which were 'much on the increase', and to pass examinations for Woolwich or the Civil Service.

Rodwell had, according to his pupil A. E. Garrod, who himself became a distinguished medical scientist, 'peculiarities of voice and gesture which lent themselves readily to schoolboy ridicule and caricature'. But his enthusiasm for his subject was infectious and made him popular. To some boys, Garrod wrote, 'the scanty hours devoted to science were like oases in the desert'.

Common room in 1876 showing, in the back row, Farrar (centre), Fergus (fourth from the right) and Rodwell (third from the right).

When Rodwell began to travel widely, visiting Iceland, Vesuvius, the Lipari Islands, Etna and Algiers, he would lecture on his journeys to the Natural History Society. His book on Etna (1878) was an important contribution to volcanology. But at Marlborough he worked under difficulties. These he described in his 'almost Pepysian' (Garrod) correspondence with Bursar Thomas. He was desperately short of apparatus, which he considered 'more essential to lecturing on experimental science than scenery and dresses to a stage play'. When Thomas cut his first request from £50 to £30, he offered to contribute the difference himself.

Gradually the Council became more generous and in 1877 allowed him a spectroscope. In June 1881 he told Thomas, that 'the spectroscope which you allowed us to purchase some years ago is doing good work.... The instrument ... can only be ... used ... by those well acquainted with its working, but for such fellows as Elder and Callendar it is satisfactory to have it ... Callendar is a very brilliant fellow in the matter of science.' Hugh Callendar became Professor of Physics at the Imperial College of Science, and Harry Elder Honorary Secretary of the Physical Society.

Rodwell's other need was for a laboratory or at least an adequate classroom. On 14 May 1872 he wrote 'Please let me have a fire in my classroom on damp or wet Wednesdays or Thursdays, otherwise I fear my electrical experiments will all fail.' On another occasion he explained that it was because he had been doing experiments in his classroom that he had had to refuse to allow Sellick to conduct detention there. Farrar's attempts to provide Rodwell with a laboratory were not successful, but eventually, in 1879, one was built and Rodwell invited Thomas to 'come and see us at work.... There are now 14 fellows and one other who has already promised for next term.' He remained dissatisfied. 'Three hours a week are such a little time for such a study; an hour goes so quickly in preparing one gas, or testing one metal; the work and subject are now so perfectly new and unknown to most of the fellows.'

Rodwell had been 12 years at Marlborough when, working abroad on one of Murray's travel guides, he suffered a stroke which incapacitated him for the rest of his life. Friends supported him, the Council made him regular payments, usually of £50 a year, and he married a kindly Miss Davidson who looked after him at Palermo until he died in 1905. Meanwhile, in 1890, Charles Boys had dedicated his paper, 'Soap Bubbles and the Forces which Mould them', to Rodwell, 'in gratitude for the interest and enthusiasm which his ... lectures awakened in the author, upon whom the light of science then shone for the first time'.

In Farrar's second year Littlefield and Cotton Houses, built as a response to the 1870 scarlet fever epidemic, finally opened. They stood a short distance to the west of the school, north of the Bath Road, and provided, at somewhat higher fees, a less spartan life, which included breakfast, suppers and studies for all. This was not the end of the matter. On 24 June 1872 the Council regretted 'to have to express their dissatisfaction at the incomplete manner in which the two houses have been delivered up to their masters – the drainage especially ... having been so badly carried out as to require entire reconstruction even while the Pupils were in residence'. In September the following year it instructed solicitors to recover damages from G. E. Street, the architect.

Surprisingly, at the same time the Council was employing Street to build a hall in memory of Bradley, to become known as the Bradleian. At the same meeting at which it instructed solicitors to act against Street, it agreed to a celebration dinner on 22 December 1873 for the Bradleian's opening. And the Council continued to employ Street. Fourteen months later (17 February 1875) it agreed to his plans for new buildings around Court, including the laboratory Farrar wanted for Rodwell with a museum above, on the site of the old Lower School. There was also to be a new porter's lodge and a range of buildings across Court from the

The Bradleian, 1873, soon after completion. Across the end of the Stable Block (right) is the start of the Bradleian Arches, not completed until the Museum Block replaced the old Schoolroom in 1883.

Bradleian to A House, completing a university-style quadrangle (but leaving the Chapel outside).

On 25 May, however, Farrar wrote to the Council urging it to change its mind. He reminded it that the whole project had originated with his desire for a science laboratory, and that he had then persuaded the Council to add a museum on top. But when Street had visited Marlborough he 'took us all by surprise by his elaborate and splendid plan for buildings wh. wd. involve a great clock-tower etc and wh. wd. complete a regular Quadrangle'. Though Farrar had supported Street's splendid plan he claimed that he had never imagined the college could afford to build it all at once. For financial reasons he considered it now essential to postpone the whole scheme for a year or two – adding that he 'knew enough of Mr Street to be quite ready to undertake this business' of explaining the delay to him.

The compromise which Thomas, as Bursar, suggested and which the Council accepted was to ask Street to build the porter's lodge at once and postpone the rest of his plan. Street was not pleased. He wrote, 'I was disappointed to hear of your altered plans. I had made the most careful drawing of every part of the building and had put other work on one side in order to do it.' In compensation the Council offered to pay him for work done so far and he charged it 2½ per cent of the estimated full cost of £10,000. He also built the porter's lodge, so at least satisfying Thomas by providing 'something more befitting the Approach and Entrance to the School buildings'.

On 28 August the same year (1875) the *Lancet* began to publish the reports of its 'Commissioners on the Sanitary Conditions of our Public Schools'. To Marlborough it could hardly have been more complimentary.

> Of the schools as yet visited, Marlborough decidedly takes the lead with regard to the excellence of its sanitary arrangements. We have therefore selected this school for our first report, as it so nearly approaches the standard we laid down in our introductory articles as to what a school should be. The excellence of Marlborough in this respect is chiefly owing to the medical officer, Dr Fergus.

Overcrowding had been reduced by the new boarding-houses. Besides Littlefield and Cotton, The Green (comprising three houses in Silverless St) and Summerfield had been acquired and opened as two town houses. Though the *Lancet* admitted that *large* dormitories were 'a protection against immoral practices being carried on there' it nevertheless advised that none should have more than 14 beds. The school's general care of its boys' health remained 'in every respect ... perfect'. Dr Fergus, the

Bradleian interior as first used. Note the desks, the tops of which could be swung back to form seats with backs for concerts and lectures. (There was no other hall for this purpose until the Memorial Hall was built in 1925.)

To the left of Blore's Chapel can be seen G. E. Street's Entrance Gates, Porter's Lodge and, beyond, the Bradleian, about 1877.

article explained, would attend the gymnasium where, if he saw a boy 'taking too much out of himself', he would caution him. In Lent Term, 'a time trying to the health of all schools', he would allow delicate boys to stay at home, keeping only the summer and winter terms.

Farrar remained anxious, and when Uppingham in 1875 had its outbreak of typhoid, with 'utterly disastrous effects in endangering the prosperity of a flourishing school', he wrote to Dr Maurice, a landowner in the Preshute area and member of the well-known Marlborough medical family: 'I may tell you (in confidence) that . . . for some reason or other, the health of the boys of that house [Preshute] . . . is . . . most decidely below the average health of every other house.' He strongly suspected that the cause was the nearby farmyard 'in which there is frequently rotting manure, and in which at least one pig is kept . . . *most* of the dormitories look out immediately on this yard, the smell is often not only perceptible, but very strong and indeed a decided nuisance.' He asked Maurice 'either firstly to reduce or . . . largely to modify the tenure of the yard'.

The poet, Algernon Swinburne, accused Farrar of being a sadistic flogger – he called him 'Mr Thwackham of Marlborough'. But descriptions of Farrar by boys make the charge seem improbable. Swinburne was addicted to being caned (a taste he claimed to have acquired at Eton) and was no doubt alert to masochism or sadism in others, but none of the memoirs or diaries of the time suggests that Farrar flogged more frequently or enthusiastically than other headmasters. On the contrary, one after another speaks of his kindness. His daughter remembered that convalescent boys would be taken for drives by Farrar, 'he as often as not perched on the box, correcting papers'. At the Lodge 'he would pace up and down his garden, with his arm on a boy's shoulder, or sit with him on the lawn correcting his "prose". Perhaps the happiest times in our young lives were when starting out in brakes and carriages, crowded with happy boys, to picnics to Martinsell or the forest, and on these occasions my father was not the least happy of the party.'

Charges of homosexuality at Marlborough in Farrar's time are no easier to prove. The fact that an old Marlburian, Alfred Taylor, was tried alongside Oscar Wilde, does not mean a great deal. True, it was common at Harrow, where pretty boys were given girls' names, and there is much evidence of perverse practices. Vaughan, the headmaster, who had employed Farrar there, was forced to resign and later to refuse a bishopric at Rochester by a parent who threatened to reveal his passion for a boy. And there are veiled references to such goings on in *Eric*. The expelled boy, Ball, for instance, 'had tasted more deeply of the tree of knowledge of good and evil than any other boy'. But this does not mean that Farrar found, let alone would have tolerated, similar practices at Marlborough, and while it would be naïve to suggest that they did not exist, there is no reason to believe that it was a special feature of the school.

Farrar had been at Marlborough only five and a half years when he was offered a canonry at Westminster and a London parish. While at Marlborough he had continued to write on religious subjects, publishing his *Life of Christ* in 1874, a retelling of the Gospel story which soon became a best seller. But he did not willingly abandon Marlborough for advancement in the Church and only agreed to do so because he considered it his Christian duty. He and his family looked back on their time at the school as the happiest of his life.

'I remember', his daughter wrote, 'the melancholy journey to London and how one of the party was unable to restrain her tears at the last glimpse of well-known landmarks. My father, putting aside his own regret, said tenderly, "Never mind – you will come back to Marlborough one day".' This daughter did indeed return to Marlborough, where she became Bursar Thomas's second wife.

Spy cartoon of Farrar as Chaplain to Queen Victoria and to the House of Commons.

7

BELL'S LONG REIGN

1876–1903

Part I

FARRAR'S RESIGNATION CAUSED dismay. 'I suppose there are good and clever Head Masters to be found in England,' Clara McGeachy wrote to Bursar Thomas (her founder husband was seriously ill) 'but when I think how few stood for Rugby I cannot help feeling rather uneasy.'

Bradley, as a member of Council, took an almost obsessive interest in finding a successor. To Thomas he wrote on 21 April 1876, 'Farrar's going is really a very serious matter ... if he is to be a Bishop, 2 or 3 years in London next door to [Dean] Stanley will be a gain to him.... For the present it will be no gain in position, rather the reverse.' At first his three candidates were Edward Young, a master at Harrow, H. L. Thompson, a tutor at Christ Church and W. Fearon who 'towers above the Winch[este]r masters'.

Nine days later he wrote (with characteristic abbreviations) that he had

> thought a great deal about RBS [Reginald Bosworth Smith – also called Bos]. I am not sanguine. The laymanship is a tremendous obstacle, and there is not time eno. to have him ordained before Sept. unless by a Bp. keenly interested on his side.... Wd. Bos like to be ordained if possible at once? Wd. it be possible? ... His Harrow openings have been sufficient to impress the public and the rest of the Council eno. Butler I know thinks *very* highly of him – but could he produce sufficient Harrovian backing and evidence?

86

'I don't intend myself to rush into a candidate, Young or other,' he wrote on 2 May. 'I don't object to Bos standing; but I will not vote for a layman unless there is a real dearth ... Bell – Fearon – Robertson are spoken of besides Young and Thompson. T. will be prepared – he is universally liked; but his experience is 0.'

Six days later, to Thomas again, he wrote, 'If Bos could *happily* take orders I think I could have rallied round him a good gathering, but to get him ordained wd. have required *pressure* on himself which no one ought to apply.... Young, Thompson, and for aught I know Fearon are *pleasant* people. Everyone likes Thompson and, I fancy, the others – but we want more.'

By May 12 he had found fresh candidates. 'I have written to Abbott – I decline to promise a vote to anyone ... I *am* afraid of anti-broad Church cries about Abbott, but I must hear more about A's influence on boys and Bell's.... If Robinson were in orders!'

Four days later he told Farrar, 'I have done my best with Abbott. He will not stand. Bell I think may yet. If he does I have no doubt as to his being better than E. Young.... With Bell it is very different – a general and strong impression of weightiness and power ... tho. of course Christ's Hospital may be against him.'

By 16 July Bell had still not made up his mind, but two days later Bradley was at last able to tell Thomas, 'Bell stands'. Eventually there were five candidates, including the headmaster of Cheltenham, but when the Council voted in secret he got no supporters, Thompson got one, Young got two and Bell 17.

The Revd George Charles Bell, aged 44, had been eight years a mathematics lecturer at Oxford, three years deputy master at Dulwich, then for the last eight years headmaster of Christ's Hospital. Four years after his arrival at Marlborough the anonymous author of an article in the *New Quarterly Review* wrote, 'It is unlikely that he [Bell] will ever commit a rash or ill-considered action; and perhaps equally unlikely that he will ever care to originate any very startling improvement', a judgement which the remaining 23 years of Bell's regime were to confirm.

Bell, the article continued, believed in delegation. He had committed 'much of the teaching, even of the sixth form, to others, while he devotes himself to the details, great and small, of the general management of the school, and thus strives to make himself the pivot on which the whole machine turns'.

It is therefore not surprising that the most important developments during Bell's time were to the school's building. Anyone who knew Court when he arrived, in 1876, and revisited it in 1903, when he left,

George Charles Bell as a young man.

Blore's Chapel after
refurbishment by
G. F. Bodley.

would have found it hugely changed: the Mansion, A House, B House, the dining-hall, the Porter's Lodge and the Bradleian remained, but virtually everything else was new. Anyone who visits Court today will notice at once the new dining-hall, but see it otherwise much as it was when Bell left.

Most impressive of the new buildings was the Chapel. By 1880 there were 600 boys in the school and 30 masters. Blore's Chapel of 1848 had been meant for only 500 boys and 15 masters, and was now so crowded and ill-ventilated that boys, according to one of them, Frederick Poynton, would faint and have to 'crawl or be conducted out'. There was also a growing feeling that Blore's Chapel, built in thirteenth-century style in an earlier Gothic Revival period, was not a beautiful building.

Even in Bradley's time there had been plans for redecorating its interior. At the height of the school's most serious scarlet fever epidemic the Council deferred discussion of these. Two years later, however (February 1872), Pattison, the college auditor, offered to produce a scheme at his own expense. He went to the well-known firm of Bodley and Garner, and that April George Bodley produced a plan for the Chapel's east end and recommended painting the ceiling. During 1873 these first stages were completed.

Two years later Bodley designed and installed a carved wooden reredos, flanked with painted angels. The painter of these was John Roddam Spencer-Stanhope, a well-to-do Pre-Raphaelite, whose work is once more admired (he painted the murals in the Oxford Union). The following year Bodley commissioned Stanhope to paint a dozen large Biblical scenes, six from the Old Testament, six from the New. Stanhope lived in Italy, and was, furthermore a perfectionist. It took him several years to complete the paintings but they were eventually hung above the rows of seats along the walls of the Chapel.

No refurbishing, however, could alter the size or proportions of the old Chapel (which was too wide and low for its length) and the Council decided to ask Bodley and Garner to lengthen it, to raise its roof by nine feet and to enlarge its windows. Now the full consequences of having employed Blore, 'the cheap architect', became apparent. To the Council Garner reported that 'the bricking [was] of inferior quality, not properly bedded, carelessly laid, in some cases without any mortar; the mortar worthless. The walls themselves had been built on a thin layer of concrete, never more than 9 inches and frequently only 3 inches in thickness; whilst the concrete was of so poor a character that it was nothing better than loose gravel.' Such a structure would never support the extra weight of taller walls, and the only thing to do was to start again.

The apse of the new chapel.

Demolition began in 1884, and for the next two years services were held in Upper School, where for the first time lay masters were allowed to preach. To accommodate the classes which were normally taught there, a building known as the Tin Tabernacle was erected in Court. At the same time the Council launched an appeal which raised £31,000 for a new Chapel. Two years later this had been built. It was 178 feet long, had an interior height of 60 feet and could seat 900.

The exterior of the new Chapel, with its 'squashed Germanic apse' is not considered up to the standard of Bodley and Garner's two finest Neo-Gothic churches, St Augustine's, Pendlebury, and Holy Angels, Hoar Cross. The interior, however, has been called (no less) 'one of the finest creations of nineteenth-century church architecture' (Niall Hamilton). A view from the gallery shows how successfully the architects have created an impression of great length and soaring height. Among many decorations were a remarkable stone reredos, and Stanhope's paintings, which had been taken from the old Chapel and so thoroughly repainted by Stanhope (at Bodley's request, to make their colours harmonise with those of the new Chapel) that they were virtually new. Again Stanhope proved a slow worker. He took all 12 to his studio in Florence and failed to return some of them in time for the Chapel's consecration. Eventually, however, all were hung, and they are now flanked by Marlborough's roll of distinguished old boys. In the years ahead, while chapel remained compulsory, boys whose attention strayed from service or sermon devised their own names for them. 'Abraham Entertaining the Angels' became 'Your Beard is in my Soup', and 'The Sacrifice of Isaac', became 'The Appendix Operation'.

On 29 September 1886, the Feast of St Michael and All Angels, the Chapel was consecrated. Henry Palmer, son of the schoolboy diarist of the 1850s, described the ceremony to his mother.

> After breakfast the choir assembled in the Adderly [sic] library and marched out of C house porch, then came the two clergymen carrying the pastoral staves and the Bishops behind them, then all the clergymen there were about 70 I believe, and in their surplices and last of all the masters and prefects. When the procession came to the gates of the railings round the Chappel [sic] they began to sing, then they marched round the chappel singing all the time; when the Bishops came round to the Doors of the Chappel he knocked with his staff and then the doors were opened and they all marched in and there followed a three hour service and after that a communion service. . . . They had a tremendous luncheon in hall but we had to dine in the Bradean [sic].

It seemed perfectly proper to this great procession of clergy and laymen that the hymn they sang as they circled the new Chapel began 'How dreadful is this place'.

Seven years later (1893) across Court from the Chapel, north of the Bradleian, Bodley and Garner also built the eight classrooms known as North Block, and (1897–9) the Memorial Reading Room with three more classrooms beneath. But it was G. E. Street's son, A. E. Street, who was at last allowed to build the present Museum Block on the site of the old Lower School to provide a museum and further classrooms.

The Museum provided a home for the Natural History Society. Founded in 1864, this had been the first public school society of its kind. When the Marquis of Ailesbury heard of it he was alarmed at what its members would do in the forest and rode to Marlborough where he offered to tolerate a certain amount of poaching if the Master would suppress the society. Bradley refused. But if Bradley chiefly saw the

society as an *alternative* to poaching, the Revd Thomas Preston, its founder, had more ambitious ideas. He wanted it, in the nineteenth-century tradition of amateur science, to have as its main purpose 'the accumulation and publication of scientific knowledge'. 'The boys were expected to devote themselves zealously to scientific observations, and if they did not show enthusiasm, he [Preston] preferred that they should leave the society.'

At first it flourished. There were regular meetings to which members would bring curious exhibits, and lectures on such subjects as 'The Habits of the Honey-bee'. About 45 boys would attend. Two years later the society divided itself into five sections, to study geology, entomology, botany, ornithology and archeology respectively. During these years Farrar, not yet Marlborough's Master, visited the Natural History Society with the idea of starting something similar at Harrow.

But as well as meetings and lectures the society had field-days for which members would be excused school, and many boys joined who

Museum Block and North Block classrooms in the 1890s. Note the 'lime trees' double row which features in one of the school songs. Compare this view with the picture on page 82.

91

were chiefly interested in this privilege. As a result field-days became bucolic romps in the bracken and were suspended; perhaps for this reason the society declined until in 1876 it had only 17 members.

Henry Richardson (see page 110), the master who became its president in 1880, was responsible for its revival. By 1888 it had 163 members and next year 238. Its lectures were now given in the Bradleian, and there, on 23 February 1888, 223 members and guests heard a visitor, J. G. Wood, lecture on ants. Shortly afterwards Preston's ideal boy joined the society. He was William Keble Martin. For his last three terms at the school, Martin was a member of its committee. Seventy years later (1965) the Revd Keble Martin's *The Concise British Flora in Colour* was published. Its hundred plates showed 1,486 British wild plants, discovered all over the country during the years that Keble Martin was a Devonshire parson and meticulously drawn by him in colour. It remains the best of all guides to British wild flowers. It also made publishing history by being the first 'packaged' book – a book sold by the producer to a number of publishers. On hearing the news that it had been accepted, Keble Martin, then aged 87 and a widower, threw his arms round the neck of his housekeeper and asked her to marry him. She refused. But when they heard that the Duke of Edinburgh would write a foreword she changed her mind.

Others besides Keble Martin to survive life at Marlborough as it grew increasingly hearty included E. F. Benson, who became a well-known novelist. His *David Blaize* was based on Marlborough, and he also published anonymously, the year after he left, *Sketches from Marlborough* (1888). It is a delightful and still funny picture of Marlborough in his time (and includes an account of a Natural History Society field-day).

Throughout Bell's time Marlborough remained a well-regarded public school, both by the general public and by parents. One of these, Dr J. B. Maurice, created a record which will surely never be beaten by sending ten sons to the school. When Bell retired Maurice and his sons presented him with a silver cup. Dr Walter Maurice, one of the ten, would tell a story of his time. One summer day the Revd Charles Thorpe, known to the boys as 'Scaley Thorpe', accidentally began to read the prayer for rain, and, once started, did not like to stop. That afternoon there was a cloudburst, two inches of rain fell in an hour, and several boys, including one of the Maurices, who were watching cricket on the Eleven, were thrown from their bench narrowly escaping death, when lightning struck near by. The incident became known as Thorpe's Storm, but Thorpe was not amused and no one dared mention it in his presence.

The school continued, as from the start, to produce many soldiers and sailors. Among the first 199 boys, 48 went into the services, outnumbering the 45 who took holy orders. Among the first 200 boys to enter the school 16 years later the proportions were similar: 29 chose military careers against 28 who took holy orders. Among the first 200 to arrive in Bell's time, however, 34 went into the services and only 16 took holy orders.

About 50 Marlburians fought in the Crimean and Russian War, of whom five died if the Revd George Proctor is included, a master who became a chaplain at Scutari Hospital. A more remarkable number – about 70 – were soldiers in India at the time of the Mutiny. At the siege of Cawnpore, Henry Delafosse was one of only four survivors. At the relief of Lucknow, Nowell Salmon, as a member of the Naval Brigade, was awarded the VC for 'conspicuous gallantry in climbing a tree... to reply to the fire of the enemy'. Had he learned tree-climbing in Savernake Forest? At the siege of Delhi, Edward Thackeray of the Royal Engineers won the VC for 'intrepidity and characteristic daring in extinguishing a fire in the Delhi magazine under close and heavy fire at the imminent risk of his life from the explosion of combustible stores in the shed in which the fire occurred'.

Most outstanding of Marlborough's nineteenth-century soldiers, however, was the same future Field Marshal, M. Evelyn Wood, who remembered being unjustly flogged at the time of the school's rebellion. In the Crimea he fought at Inkerman and Sebastapol before being wounded and sent to Scutari. Here one nurse beat him but the other, Susan Cator, 'always put in 36 hours instead of 24, in order that I might be saved from the presence of the woman I feared'. Forty years later, Wood wrote to the Under-Secretary of State, asking that the Queen should award the Red Cross Badge to Susan Cator, who was now 83 and living in an almshouse, where Wood was sending her 'a small annual sum for pocket money'. For his service in the Crimea Wood was twice mentioned in dispatches, received the Crimea Medal with two clasps, became a Knight of the Legion of Honour and a member of the 5th class of the Medjidie, and was awarded the Turkish Medal. 'Not a bad beginning for a youth of 17,' the *Dictionary of National Biography* observed.

In India during the Indian Mutiny, now in the 17th Lancers, Wood won the VC at Sindhara for routing 80 rebels with only ten men. It was in Africa, however, that he showed his special gift for recruiting local support. In the Ashanti War (1873) he organised the natives into 'Wood's Regiment'; in South Africa he formed a group of Zulus into 'Wood's Irregulars'.

In England in 1888 he spoke at Marlborough's Prize Day, telling the

First photograph of the Rifle
Volunteer Corps, 1861.

A. H. Glennie (seated),
founder of the RVC.

boys that at the school he had acquired little Latin and less Greek, but
learned a more important lesson. When, one day, he persistently assured
a master, the Revd Jacky Biden, that his answers to four arithmetic
problems were not cribbed, Biden said to him, 'I thought you were a
brave little boy, and only cowards tell lies'. 'Now if "Jacky" had ordered
me to "stand round",' Wood said, 'I might have continued to tell lies
till today. I tell you, boys, whether you believe me or not, I have never
told a lie since.'

Marlborough's Corps had been founded soon after the Indian Mutiny,
in 1860. Underlying its founding, however, was a quarrel between
Britain and France. There had recently been a plot to murder Napoleon
III, supposed to have been planned in England. When certain French
officers threatened an invasion, the British government under Palmerston
called for a volunteer force, which soon numbered 150,000, and included
Marlborough's Corps, as well as the Corps of Rossall (the first, it
claims), Eton, Winchester and Shrewsbury.

Bradley encouraged the Corps – he was a keen marksman and would
shoot at the butts beyond the Common – but its founders were boys.
Masters who might have organised it – Bull and Tomkinson, for
example – were busy raising the town's volunteers. It was Alfred
Glennie, son of one of Marlborough's founders, who had the idea. In
the holidays he had drilled with the Artists' Rifles, to which his brothers
belonged. He was supported by Charles Butterworth, William North

and Robert Kitson. Glennie became a country parson, Butterworth an artist, Kitson a west-country banker and only North a solider, in the Royal Engineers.

The early Corps consisted of two companies of 36 and 35 boys respectively. Its uniform was a grey flannel jacket and trousers, to which braid was attached for military use, a leather belt round the jacket's waist and a tin-drum hat with chin-strap. Like some Home Guard units in 1940, it had no rifles and was only able to drill with weapons when the Master acquired some old police carbines. One of the officers' swords was supplied by the matron of B House, whose late husband had worn it when serving in the Honourable Artillery Company in the 1820s. To complete the unit there was a veteran of Waterloo to act as marker at the butts, and another veteran, turned arm-chair tactician, Sergeant Davies, to instruct in drill.

Sergeant Davies, the first Drill Instructor.

The unit was understandably accident prone. A bullet once passed through the tall hat which the marker always wore; when first inspected, a boy accidentally fired a ramrod from his gun which narrowly missed the visiting general. It was by no means always well supported, and *The Marlburian* carried regular appeals for volunteers. *The Marlburian* also published in 1876 an unsigned article on the theme that war, like duelling, would soon become part of our barbaric past.

Furthermore, the Corps was seen by certain masters as a threat, since it might recruit potential athletes; and was despised by some boys because it only recruited those who were useless at games. In 1870, however, it received official support when Bull became the first master to take command. Like Bradley, Bull was a keen marksman. According to John Harrison, 'He was constantly practising on a miniature target fixed to his door. So it sometimes happened that when you opened the door, you were told to stand quite still. "Now I've got your eye!" and you heard the click of the rifle as the hammer fell.' Bull's keenness was rewarded. In 1874 Marlborough won the Ashburton Shield at Bisley.

At first the Corps' most adventurous exercises took place in some nearby piece of open country like Bowood Park. There it would be taken in a train of brakes or wagonettes to practise battalion drill with other local volunteer groups, learning to form échelons or squares, as if still preparing for the Battle of Waterloo. In 1885, however, it took part for the first time in a field-day with other schools. This was also the year its signal section was formed, communicating by lamp and field telephone. A band of a sort probably existed from the first – a photograph of a bugler survives from 1861. In 1887 the *Marlborough Times* reported,

> The inhabitants of Marlborough were treated to a pretty sight early this ... morning, when the Marlborough College Cadet Corps marched to catch the first train for a field-day at Aldershot. Headed by buglers and drums and fifes playing alternately, the Corps were enabled by the great width of the High Street to march in column of Companies, looking remarkably well, though the musical arrangements caused the organs of hearing to detract from the impression made upon the vision.

Meanwhile Marlburians had continued to serve in the country's lesser wars. Before the end of the century, 50 had died in campaigns ranging from China to Somaliland, and five naval officers had been lost at sea. One of these soldiers of the empire, Reginald Hart, won the VC in Afghanistan in 1879 for saving a private under fire.

The school contributed to the Boer War on an equally substantial

First adult Commanding Officer of the RVC, C. M. Bull.

scale. By February 1900, 233 Marlburians were serving in South Africa. Gilbert Fergusson, who formed part of the Ladysmith garrison, wrote to tell his parents of a night operation with a surprising ending.

> Monday night was very dark and wet. Two companies ... under Gough paraded at 1.30 a.m. and sallied forth to take a farm which is about 1½ miles out to our front. We often see men round this place ... and a large number were supposed to sleep there, especially on wet nights.... We took about two hours to get to our positions.... Gough with half A company surrounded the dwelling-house – Harrington with one section watched a railway gate and I with the fourth section watched a path to the hill, a possible retreat of our supposed victims – About 3.30 a.m. I saw a light struck in the house, and we all thought the fun was to begin – 3.45 a.m. the signal to retire reached me, and off we scampered to get back to our quarters before daylight ... the only spoil we carried off were a few cabbages.

Fergusson was killed in a similar sally five days later.

Another who died, Raymond de Montmorency, was one of many Marlborough nonconformists. A contemporary remembered him 'tearing out of the house down to the Bath Road with his tie and collar in one hand, and his coat and waistcoat in the other'. 'It was a common thing', the master, F. E. Thompson, remembered, 'to see him walking down the Bath Road engaged in familiar conversation with a tramp, most happy when he could pick up a French or German wanderer, and enter into his history.' By the time of the Boer War Montmorency was an experienced soldier. At the Battle of Omdurman (1898) he had charged with the 21st Lancers – the charge so vividly described by Churchill. Afterwards Montmorency returned to rescue a wounded man from a large body of dervishes and was awarded the VC.

The Boer War gave Montmorency the chance to employ his unconventionality with official approval. He raised a body known as Montmorency's Scouts, and became, in the words of a journalist, 'the eyes and ears' of his general. When he and a party of his scouts reached a hill top at the same time as a party of Boers, each side 'poured in a pointblank volley at a distance of fifteen paces', and Montmorency died.

One who survived was John Kirk. To his housemaster, Henry Richardson, Kirk wrote from Bloemfontein in March 1900,

> Thank you so much for your kind letter, also for the Marlburian you sent me. I have been able to show it to several O.M.s here,

who were much pleased.... But I must hasten to correct the wicked report of the hospital authorities in calling me severely wounded. I was wounded in the head ... but it was only a scalp wound.... While advancing across the open plain, under a pretty hot fire both from the left and front ... a Mauser shot at a venture, produced the most glorious star I have ever seen in my life. As a matter of fact it chipped my left ear and pierced the scalp behind, then ran round under the scalp for about 4 inches (!) emerging again just beyond the spine and passing out through my helmet ...

I soon realised what had happened and knew it was nothing and tied myself up with the bandages we all carry in a special pocket.... I soon reached the firing line and there we all remained for the rest of the day.

... I felt remarkably callous and indifferent, I think it must have been the bloodletting. I felt as if I had had my shy and won and was out of the running for another somehow, so I simply blazed away for all I was worth and it felt really good to send bullets into those chaps, though I ought not to say such things in cold blood.

When I returned very late, having ... been to a hospital to be bandaged, I found everyone very pensive.... I only learned afterwards that the officers were quite under the impression that I was killed and thought I was a ghost ...

I must get this letter off now so my very best wishes to you and the old House.

The school, of course, celebrated the relief of Mafeking. At Marlborough there was a curious consequence: dormitory chamber-pots in future were supplied with no handles. Ingenious boys had found that when a rope was strung across Court and a chamber-pot started at each end they would meet in the middle with a highly satisfactory explosion.

In 1887 there had been another national celebration, for Queen Victoria's fiftieth jubilee. A whole ox was roasted in the High Street, where 3,000 citizens were fed, and the Rifle Corps fired a *feu de joie*. In the evening one boy remembered being taken in a party up to the great bonfire on Martinsell, and another to 'a hill called four-mile clump from which we could see over 70 beacons and rockets going up in all directions'.

Six years later the school celebrated its own fiftieth anniversary (1893). The event was almost as much a town as a College occasion. Most of the houses put out flags and, according to the College's jubilee book, many of the premises in the High Street were 'tastefully illuminated'. Several hundred Old Marlburians arrived and to accommodate them 'many of the well-to-do inhabitants generously opened their houses'.

The celebration began with a cricket match between the school eleven and an eleven of past captains of cricket. Unfortunately 'just when interest was at its highest' there was a torrential thunderstorm, but the match was finished next day and the school won by 1 run. The storm had passed by 4.30 when the Master and Mrs Bell welcomed the visitors to tea in the Lodge garden, where the college string orchestra played in a tent.

That evening came the great jubilee supper, attended by 250 Old Marlburians and 40 past or present staff. The OMs included 28 who had come to the school before 1847, among them the Revd Clement Cobb, first Senior Prefect; the Revd Henry Palmer, diarist of the 1850s; and Admiral Sir Nowell Salmon, the tree-climbing VC. From later years came the Revd Thomas Papillon and Courtenay Ilbert, the two Balliol scholars, and A. G. Bradley, son of the great Bradley, who that year published Marlborough's first history. Also present were Farrar and Bradley himself, now Archdeacon and Dean of Westminster respectively. The following evening there was a concert in Upper School, at which

Common Room in 1887 displaying a fine array of headgear. Seated are Bell (third from the right), Bull (second from the right), Richardson (far left) and, standing, centre next to Bell, Bursar Thomas.

the Old Marlburian, Henry Irving, son of the actor, recited 'The Hand of Glory' (238 lines) from the *Ingoldsby Legends* and was so 'heartily cheered' that he gave an encore.

A week later there was a boys' supper at which Wilkinson, the college steward, 'surpassed himself'. After 'The Queen' had been toasted, Harold Clayton, Senior Prefect, climbed on to the table to propose 'The School'. Many other toasts and loudly applauded speeches followed, and John Bain, a master, proposed 'The Ladies' in lines which included:

> Who make us dance instead of reading Virgil?
> Who tear us from the noble odes of Horace?
> Who give us tea on afternoons? The Ladies.
> Who come to lectures with the Sixth? The Ladies.

It was no doubt the wives and daughters of staff who took part in Marlborough's first experiment in co-education.

Finally, a week later again, came Prize Giving. This allowed the Master to say goodbye to Charles Bull, the only survivor of the young men Cotton had brought to Marlborough in the 1850s, by this time a Marlborough institution.

Bull, Sellick, Dr Fergus and Bursar Thomas − it was these four who, for 50 years, had given the school continuity as Master after Master came and went. The greatest was Thomas. When he died in 1897, aged only 62, he had been Bursar for 37 years, but the modern associations of the word entirely fail to suggest what he had been doing. To start with, he had organised the huge amount of building which had gone on continually during his time, liaising between Council, Master and architects. Then he had supervised the enrolment of boys, and undertaken all the correspondence and meetings with parents which are now undertaken by the Registrar. He was also college accountant; when on his birthday in 1868 it was announced that the College's debt had been liquidated, a party of boys called on him spontaneously to congratulate him. And he arranged the hiring, housing and paying of staff, and managed the college estates and its catering. He was also from his arrival until his death a form master. In total he did the jobs which at least five people would do today, not to mention their secretaries. As Reginald Bosworth Smith wrote:

> Did a tree need to be lopped, a path gravelled, a cricket-ground levelled, a pavilion built? 'Go to the Bursar'. Is a debt of £40,000 to be gradually paid off and converted into a surplus? Is the old chapel to be pulled down and a new and worthier one ... to be erected in its place? 'Let the Bursar see to it.' How is it possible

that ... at the Jubilee of the College, many hundreds of Old Marlburians can be discovered, invited, classified, lodged, and entertained? 'Ask the Bursar, and it will be done.'

Thomas would even be consulted by the headmasters of other schools. In 1867 he wrote to Benson to congratulate him on appointing Wellington's first Bursar. In March 1872 Benson wrote to Thomas, 'I have heard that you have at Marlbro' some statute, proclamation, or order in Council which forbids [men] to marry.... Here the marrying tendency is so rife that *college* will presently be depopulated and its boys reign alone. I am thinking of issuing some edict and if you ... will tell me how you put such a delicate point I shall be most grateful.'

As for Thomas's outside activities, he was at one time or another a county councillor, on the board of both Marlborough's railways and chairman of the East Wilts Liberal Association.

Part II

Though much that was worthy went on at the school in Bell's time, and it expanded in ways which laid a foundation for its growth in the next century, his long reign was in other ways a period of regression. Douglas Savory (1891–4) recollected, for example, that bullying, which had been reduced under Bradley and Farrar, again became pervasive; and that food was again inadequate. As a little boy he remembered 'waiting outside the dining-hall on a half-holiday and praying that the doors might soon be opened, because I was so exceedingly hungry that I could not settle down to anything in the way of reading or serious study.' The school's academic standards also fell, in particular those of the Modern Side. 'A classical master who found a boy in his form was not making progress would recommend in his report that he should be transferred to the modern side. The modern side therefore became more or less of a dumping-ground for the less able boys.'

The most serious charge against Bell, however, is that it was in his time that athleticism became the school's dominating obsession. Though the same happened at virtually every public school, at Marlborough it became especially dominant. During the first half of the twentieth century Master after Master considered it one of his principal duties to modify this obsession, and one after another only partially succeeded.

The history of games at the school was no tale of steady success. Cotton soon began to arrange cricket matches with other schools, the first of these in 1855, appropriately against Rugby. Rugby won conclusively as it did again in the following two years. Though A. G.

Bradley offered excuses (in 1856 Marlborough's captain was hit by a ball in the eye, and another star player spiked in the head by an opponent's boot), it was clear that the school's cricket was below the standard of other major public schools and the Rugby match was dropped for two years. Marlborough's inadequacy was confirmed by defeats in all three of the early Cheltenham matches. Only in 1859 did it at last win an inter-school match, defeating Cheltenham by 32 runs.

Marlborough now began to play against other schools, but it was the Cheltenham and Rugby matches which became its great cricket occasions. By 1892 Rugby had won 17 times against Marlborough's 11, but Marlborough had defeated Cheltenham in 14 matches and lost in only 13. In the years before 1893 Marlborough produced 20 Oxford or Cambridge cricket blues, a number of whom played for their counties

The first cricket pavilion which was replaced in 1874 (see facing page). The oak tree still stands.

and England. A primitive cricket pavilion of 1856 had been replaced in 1874 by a 'servicable and picturesque' building, while the Eleven had been much enlarged when, at the suggestion of the college steward, a bank to its north was carted away and used to fill the moat round the Mound.

Though Rugby football had been introduced to Marlborough by one of Cotton's recruits, Bere, and a few years later (1860) the football and cricket clubs had separated. Marlborough, like other schools, continued to have its own rules. The difficulties this caused became clear in 1864 when it played its first inter-school match, against Clifton. For this game it was agreed that 'hacking over' (a vicious form of tackling allowed at Clifton) would be forbidden, but when the Marlborough twenty pressed hard, the Clifton players began to encourage each other with cries of

An early picture of the present pavilion constructed in 1874.

'Hack him over'. The match now showed signs of becoming a free fight, and Boyle, Marlborough's captain, asked the Master, Bradley, whether it should be stopped, but Bradley, in the true spirit of his time, told him, 'Win the game first, and then talk about stopping if you like'.

Bradley, the historian, described what followed.

> A few minutes afterwards he [Boyle] got hold of the ball and started for a run. Twice he was brought to the ground by an insidious hack, and twice he struggled to his feet, still clutching the ball in his curious grasp. A moment more, and he had by a brilliant drop, executed just in the nick of time, sent the ball flying plump and fair between the Clifton goal-posts just as for the third time he was rolled over on the grass; and at the sight there burst forth such a cheer from Marlburian throats as has never before nor since been heard on the football field.

A book of rules small enough to be kept in the trouser pocket in case of disputes. Rule 9 reads, 'Though it is lawful to hold any player with the ball, attempts to throttle or strangle...'!

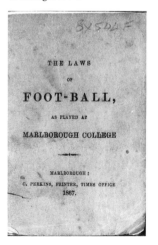

Satisfactory as the victory had been, it was 23 years before another inter-school football match was risked, this an unsuccessful one against Wellington in 1887. Matches against Clifton were resumed in 1891.

At Marlborough football was played by the so-called twenty, forty and sixty (selected by the captain of football) on a ground below the Eleven, and by those not selected on a ground near the sanatorium. There was no space, however, for hockey, and when Richardson introduced this in 1874 it had to be played on the town's common, with the permission of the mayor and corporation. Despite the icy winds which blew up there, five hockey grounds were regularly used.

Some members of the football XX of 1868. Note the long trousers and velvet caps. The team was changed to fifteen in 1878.

If inter-school matches were the year's great sporting events, inter-house games were an equally important feature of school life and involved many more boys. For each game, besides a challenge cup, there were various other awards. Bull, for example, gave the Bull Cap for drop-kicking at football, and Bright the Bright Belt for place-kicking. Housemasters encouraged house rivalry and the house spirit soon came to form part of a comprehensive philosophy of games. In 1867 'Trebla', probably a master, began to explain this in articles in *The Marlburian*. Some of the qualities which he claimed that games promoted were obvious: courage, endurance, the team spirit, hero-worship, patriotism (since love of one's house would lead to love of one's school and love of one's country). Others required more ingenious justification, for example self-denial, since games players could learn to forgo rich foods. In sum, games could change for the better every aspect of a boy's behaviour. 'A truly chivalrous football-player was never yet guilty of lying or deceit, or meanness, whether of word or action.'

Football was Trebla's special enthusiasm. About the football player he wrote, 'Football is his first work. Into that he has to put as much of human patience, common sense, forethought, experimental philosophy, self-control, habits of order and obedience, careless courage, careful patriotism, unity of purpose and harmony of aim as can well be put into a space of six inches in diameter and eighteen inches in circumference.'

Boys responded only too enthusiastically. A boy's poem in *The Marlburian* included the lines,

> ... one athletic rage,
> Has seized Marlburians of every age,
> Now, filled with frenzy, cricket all will play,
> Now, all-absorbing football rules the day,
> Where'er you go, the topic is the same,
> And all our talk at tables is 'the game' ...

By 1893 A. G. Bradley felt justified in devoting 88 pages of his history of the school – more than a quarter of the book – to games.

The effect that all this could have on studious or sensitive boys can be imagined. Savory remembered having a Latin dictionary hurled at his head for winning a prize for a holiday task. When his father wrote to Bell listing 'some well-founded complaints', he got back a postcard reading 'Marlborough is what Marlborough is'. Some found the best escape was to make themselves into clowns. 'No one had anything against E. F. Benson', Horace Mordaunt Rogers wrote, 'beyond that he and E. H. Miles brought considerable ridicule on themselves by wheeling hoops on sweats [runs].' In Bell's last year the school's best-known writer, Siegfried Sassoon, arrived. He was a frail boy who spent much time in the sanatorium, or at home because he had strained his heart 'doing my best to find out how to play "Rugger"'. When his housemaster, Marius Herbert Gould, heard that he was taking organ lessons he said to him, 'So you play the organ, do you, you wretched fellow, you play the organ. I know why you play the organ. You play the organ to get out of playing games, you wretched brute.'

The effect on the future lives of some Marlburians reached a *reductio ad absurdum* with the Revd Sidney Swann (1876–80) whose *Who's Who* entry in the 1930s included,

In Japan won most things started for on land and sea; rowing, hurdling, cycling, running, pole-jumping, weight and hammer;

first to cycle round Syria; rode Land's End to John O'Groats; Carlisle to London in a day; rowed home-made boat from Crosby Vicarage down the rapids of the Eden to the sea, and cut the record from England to France, 1911, rowing the Channel in 3 hours 50 minutes, faster than anyone had ever gone between England and France by muscular power; ... In 1917, when 55 years old, cycled, walked, ran, paddled, rode and swam six consecutive half-miles in 26 minutes 20 seconds.

In 1937, when Swann chased his wife round his Lindfield vicarage with a cook's knife, he had to be taken in a strait-jacket to a lunatic asylum.

Yet the games cult had had opponents at Marlborough almost from the start. Cotton himself became aware of the danger of what he had set loose. In a late sermon he said, 'The applause here bestowed upon success in games is apt to blind a person to his own ignorance, to make him indifferent to the faults of his character, to prevent him from realising that he will be judged very differently when he passes from boyhood to manhood.'

And in the same year that Trebla began to publish, another correspondent to *The Marlburian* deplored hero-worship when it took the form of admiration for brute force. In December 1875 an editorial regretted that so many boys spent the whole of their time at the school thinking about games, and never about politics, history, literature or social questions.

Nor was Farrar an unqualified supporter of athleticism. In a sermon he told the school, 'Do not think I disparage the physical vigour at which I daily look with interest; but it is impossible to repress a sigh when one thinks that the same vigour infused also into intellectual studies, which are far higher and nobler, would carry all successes and prosperity in life irresistibly before you.'

And to be fair to Bell, he recognised and regretted the school's games cult. In his Prize Day speech of 1898 he said, 'We have a very full equipment of challenge cups and shields and it does not seem desirable to add to their number. We offer quite enough stimulus to athletics. I have often wished to see a challenge prize of a similar kind to one awarded in another school to the house which had most distinguished itself in the studies of the school.' A year after he retired, Bell presented exactly such an academic challenge cup to Marlborough: the Bell Trophy.

Against Bell's failure to moderate athleticism must be balanced much good that he did for the school. After its 1893 Jubilee it could well be said to have come of age, and it was Bell, with his long, silver-grey beard, who presided over this achievement.

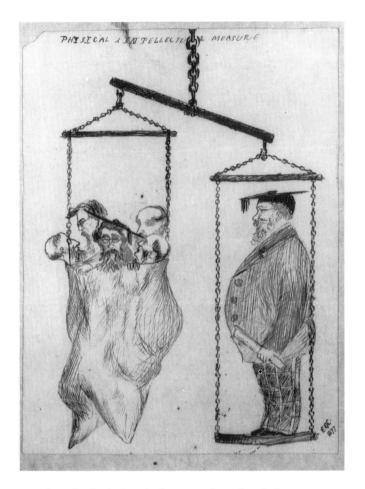

A boy's cartoon 'weighing' intellectuals, including Bell, Bambridge (music), Rodwell (science), Gilmore (maths) against a single physical character, Harding.

In 1890 when he had already been at the school almost 20 years, Bell was interviewed by a visiting correspondent of the *Pall Mall Gazette*. His answers give an interesting idea of his own view of the school.

A great point [he said] is that the masters have a common-room, where they meet daily and hourly, and where the novice meets with kindliest help and advice. You talk about the fierce light that beats on Eton – the light of the London clubs. I think we have a healthier light than that in our common-room. Here everything is discussed, this is the focus of the life of the place. Asked about discipline he said, 'I so much believe in discipline that I have no foreign masters at all. All our French and German is taught, and thoroughly, although not colloquially, by Englishmen.'

'And how, Mr Bell, do you manage to keep in touch with your

staff?' Mr Bell got up from his seat and fetched down a book: 'There,' said he, 'that ... is what we call the Red Book. It always lies, open to all masters, in the common-room. Once a term or so I go right round the forms "reviewing" the work done. In that book I enter quite frankly what I think of each man's work. I showed it once to a well-known headmaster. He said "Capital: but if I introduced it at my school there would be a *coup d'état*".'

Asked if boys were *made* to work, Bell replied, 'Emphatically they are. If a boy does not work his life is made miserable to him. Impositions and judicious canings effectually destroy his pleasure in idleness.'

'And now to conclude a most interesting chat, Mr Bell, ... What kind of article do you turn out of Marlborough School?' The headmaster laughed as he handed me a great book, wherein was entered the name of each boy who had passed through Marlborough since its foundation nearly fifty years ago. 'There, that is the kind of "article" we turn out from here. We have supplied the Church with about 800 clergymen, some 800 or 900 have entered the army, 500 or so have become lawyers, 300 or 400 have gone into business. Wherever you go you will meet with "the articles" we have turned out at Marlborough.'

Harold Nicolson once wrote that when he was a boy headmasters went on being headmasters until they became bishops or certifiably insane. Though Bell had been Master for 27 years by 1903 he was not offered a bishopric. And he was still perfectly sane when, in April that year, he told the Council with characteristic economy that as he was now 71 years old he wanted his job to be given to someone younger.

8

ONE LAY APPLE

1903 – 1911

WHEN FRANK FLETCHER was chosen in 1903 to succeed Canon Bell, there was general surprise. Fletcher came from Lancashire, had been educated at Rossall and Balliol and had then spent nine years as a master at Rugby. He had already applied three times for headmasterships, the last time at Bedford, a mainly day-school, because he had been persuaded by the Revd Herbert James (the one-time Marlborough assistant master who was to become head of Rossall, Cheltenham and Rugby) that none of the great boarding-schools would appoint a layman as their head during his lifetime. When Marlborough Council did just this *The Times* observed that there was now 'one lay apple in the clerical dumpling'.

Frank Fletcher

Other reasons for surprise were that Fletcher had been chosen in preference to Sir Arthur Hort, the retiring Master's son-in-law; and to Frederick Westcott, headmaster of Sherborne, godson of the Bishop of Salisbury, (President of the Council). Bishop John Wordsworth continued to be hostile. After some delay he handed Fletcher 'a legal-looking document for which I had to pay a fee', giving Fletcher permission to preach in the school Chapel provided he did not do so in a surplice, at a communion service or from the pulpit. Learning what had happened, the Archbishop of Canterbury said, 'Our brother of Salisbury has given the new Master of Marlborough leave to preach in chapel provided he does it from a place where no one can hear him.'

In Fletcher's favour, he was a classicist, and on the Council were Old Marlburians like Butcher, Ilbert and Papillon who looked back to Bradley's teaching of the classics as the central feature of a golden age for the school. Fletcher was also, unlike three of his rivals, married. Against him was his obvious youth; he was 33. Earlier that year, when he had met two Marlborough boys on a train and mentioned that he was at Rugby, one had asked him, 'Are you in the eleven?' Parents who came to his Marlborough study would give a start of astonishment when they saw him, or would ask him whether the Master was at home. Ultimately it was his own qualities which got him the job. At an earlier interview for a headmastership he had been asked what he would do if his predecessor had promised a house to a master he himself thought unsuitable. Fletcher replied, as Solomon might have, 'Tell the man that I was bound to offer him the house, but should be unable to advise parents to send their boys to it.'

The boys of Marlborough did not warm to Fletcher. An early visitor to the Master's Lodge wrote, 'They hate Frank but they love his wife.' In his autobiography, *After Many Days* (1937), Fletcher gave his young wife, aged only 24, much of the credit for breaking down this hostility. She made 'the Lodge a place to which intelligent boys liked to come and where they felt that they were welcome. Thanks to her it gradually became what a headmaster's house should be, an intellectual and humanizing centre for the school.'

Fletcher also gave credit to Henry Richardson, by now Marlborough's senior housemaster. 'In countless small ways ... he took pains to bring me into touch with the school, to call my attention to individual boys, to let me know what people were thinking or saying, especially if it was pleasant.' When Fletcher in a sermon had quoted from *Romola*, he received the same day a note from Richardson, 'Dear Master, I asked my form just now whether any of them had read *Romola*. One boy said, "I began it this afternoon".'

Richardson was indeed an outstanding master. He had come to the school in Bradley's last year (1870), had been master of the Lower School, then housemaster of B 2 and of Littlefield. Frederick Poynton (1881–6, later 12 years on the Council) described him as a man who 'always seemed to be in the world and not entirely in the school'. As a new boy, playing hockey for the first time, Poynton had known 'nothing about the game but joined in with zest. Suddenly there was a roar, the game stopped and the Captain of our side addressed me loudly and explosively. What I had done I have no idea, but I imagine I had been busy hitting the legs of my own side instead of those of the opposition. What I do remember was the quiet voice of Mr Richardson, who was watching, say "Don't speak to him like that he is doing his best." Those were the words of a real schoolmaster.'

For many years Richardson's little dog, Bandy, a Dandie Dinmont,

Henry Richardson with
'Bandy' in a Common Room
Group.

was also a school character, a keen spectator of every sort of sporting
event and participator, wanted or unwanted, in Corps outings,
ceremonial processions or group photographs. The only body to which
he seems to have considered it not necessary to belong was the Natural
History Society.

If the boys of Marlborough did not at first approve of Fletcher he did
not approve of the school. At the core of its problems he picked out its
centralised, or so-called 'hostel' system. Though there were now four
out-college houses, 400 of the 625 boys still lived in the old houses
around Court. This was the arrangement which Benson of Wellington
had thought so dangerous and Bradley such an advantage. Fletcher
agreed with Benson.

'A community of this kind', he wrote, 'responds more quickly to . . .

infection from within. ... If the moral tone in any section is low, the evil spreads more easily and more widely than in a system of more water-tight compartments.' When, during his second year, 'various elements of mischief and discontent that had been developing underground came to the surface ... severity was necessary; a bad patch in college had to be cleared; and a few boys ... had to be dismissed or withdrawn.' There followed what Fletcher called 'a row'. At the end of the annual school concert 'an exhibition of bad feeling against me ... was only arrested by the loyalty of the captain of cricket ... with a call of "Three cheers for the Master".'

Fletcher considered that Marlborough's hostel system contributed to the school's games cult. In a community of Marlborough's sort, he wrote, there was the 'danger of a mediocre standard of industry and culture and a sort of hearty, self-satisfied Philistinism'. Marlborough's Philistinism was typified by the observation of a small boy in an essay that it was his ambition to be in the Eleven and also in the Sixth; 'thus I should combine athletics with luxury'.

As Fletcher explained things, boys naturally admired brawn rather than brain, and masters, who were most of them boys at heart, encouraged the same attitude. One result was that it was simplest for housemasters to choose as 'boy-leaders' athletes, who already had 'position and influence' rather than scholarly boys who might need 'more training and more support'. The various captains of school and house teams thus took over the running of the school. In his attempts to change this, Fletcher admitted that he was much helped by one of his Senior Prefects. The reforms this boy made, Fletcher wrote, 'were the outcome of a summer holiday spent with us in Cornwall, during which I outlined to him my conception of what prefect government should mean, and suggested means of organising it. In the course of his year of office he carried out my suggestions, not all at once, but gradually, and never quoting my authority for them.'

This prefect was Geoffrey Fisher, the future Archbishop of Canterbury. According to his biographer, it was Fisher himself who had felt it to be 'unhealthy' that 'the really big people in the school were the athletes, not the school prefects chosen from the sixth'. And it was Fisher who, 'when he became Senior Prefect ... started to reverse the order and make the prefects the prevailing power. This included starting a Prefects' Roll, with a ceremony in which new ones signed, and were admitted into office, to enhance their sense of responsibility. Many, many years later, visiting Marlborough, he found the same book and the same ceremony still in use.'

Alongside curbing the influence of athletic heroes, Fletcher put much emphasis on improving the school's academic standards. At first he continued to conduct Marlborough's termly assessment, the 'Review', regularly reporting the results, class by class, in the Master's Red Book. The entries would include comments like 'The spelling of the word "prejudice" was a great stumbling-block to many', and would end with the names of boys whom he had ploughed. In 1906, however, he substituted visits without notice to various classes. Other entries in the Red Book included, 'I have posted a notice that "The buying of Sunday Papers is forbidden"'; and, 'It is most undesirable ... that corporal punishment should be inflicted on Sundays.'

Almost as well liked as Richardson among early twentieth-century masters was John 'Pat' O'Regan. 'Sometimes he read us a little poetry,' Siegfried Sassoon wrote, 'and when we had an odd twenty minutes to fill he would, if the spirit moved him tell us to write some ourselves, and offer a prize of half a crown. Thank you, Mr O'Regan, for those half-crowns (I nearly always won them). You were the only person at Marlborough who ever asked me to write poetry. The first time I won the prize you had my verses framed and hung them in the form-room.'

> School Life
> My life at School is fraught with care,
> Replete with many a sorrow.
> When evening's shadows fall, I dare
> Not think about tomorrow.
>
> The extra lesson doth correct,
> My wandering attention,
> And other things which I expect
> It might give paine to mention
>
> But extra lessons cannot kill,
> And blows don't fall so hard,
> That they will end the life of this,
> Ambitious little Bard.

O'Regan, an exceptionally small man who never lost his native accent and would always refer to Ireland as 'my poor country', was, in Fletcher's opinion, 'essentially out of the ordinary', and it was 'good for boys' to have masters of this sort. Among other eccentricities, he joined the Corps as a private, though he was incapable of marching in step or keeping his puttees effectively tied. 'How many years have you been at Marlborough?' an inspecting general is said to have asked him. 'Twenty years, sir,' the small soldier replied.

At first O'Regan's relationship with Fletcher was not good. They had been contemporaries at Balliol, where O'Regan had also been a hockey blue. 'His sentimental Irish conscience', Fletcher wrote, 'made him alternately reproach himself for being jealous of an old friend and hold aloof from me lest he should seem to be presuming on the previous intimacy.' But they were on better terms by the time O'Regan made his most important contribution to the school: the transformation of history teaching into a separate discipline, this leading in 1918 to the establishment of a history Sixth. For O'Regan it was the discovery of his vocation. 'I have at last got a proper job – History teaching – which will expand my mind instead of stifling it.'

To his history classes O'Regan would bring all manner of visual aids, from bows and arrows to original historical documents. Once it was a suit of chain mail. When no boy was small enough to fit into this he put it on himself. 'Unfortunately it was impossible to get it off again,' John Goldschmidt remembered, 'and I had to go to his house and fetch an overcoat so that he could return there inconspicuously and summon the local blacksmith.'

There was an innocence about O'Regan which made some boys unjustly consider him humourless. A history exam he set his class included the question, 'Explain A.M.Z. – The Triple Terror – Kethandothi – The Shedistic Question – The Vocanic Decrees.' The class struggled earnestly with this and four similar problems for an hour before suspecting that something was wrong.

Alan Lascelles, later Private Secretary to King George VI, remembered O'Regan as 'one of the few teachers at Marlborough who succeeded in teaching me anything'. Lascelles wrote a parody of Scott's *Locksley Hall* which was rejected by *The Marlburian* because it included the disrespectful lines,

> Many a time from yonder ivy casement in the west
> Have I watched the great O'Regan sloping slowly to his rest.

In 1912 his marriage forced O'Regan to give up his house and move to the Roman villa, Killycoonagh, which he had built on the hillside above Marlborough's High Street. Beverley Nichols, one of his pupils, fictionalised this in his novel, *Prelude*.

> It was a perfectly charming place; goats roamed in and out of the little marble hall, known as the Atrium, a tame raven made dirge-like noises from the flat roof, and wherever one stepped there was always a chance of stepping on a pig. And Mrs O'Rane ... how charming she was! Rushing in and out of the villa, followed by her small son ... she was the soul of the place ...

114

Admirable teacher as O'Regan was, he was also an expounder of the philosophy of the time which wrapped up the house-spirit, patriotism, chivalry, games and war in one big bundle. When his house won the hockey final his victory speech to the boys included, 'The Eleven came on the ground full of fight and in deadly earnest, scored almost immediately, and *in consequence* utterly demoralised the enemy, through whom they went like a charge of cavalry.' 'You must worship the house as a keen man worships his regiment.'

A housemaster who more emphatically encouraged the house-spirit as embodied in athletic prowess was Temple Charles Gabriel Sandford. Ulric Nisbet described life in Sandford's house (after it had moved to Field House in 1911). 'The Spartan discipline he inflicted upon himself was reflected in our own customs and doings. There were two pairs of hanging rings in our long dormitory, and upon these each Saturday night new boys, and sometimes not so new, were made to carry out an excruciating exercise called "pull-through". Failure was punishable with three strokes – in pyjamas.' When Sandford died during the Second World War, his *Marlburian* obituary recorded that he had contributed to the college 'a career of athletic service ... unequalled in the school's history'. The ring ritual survived into the 1930s.

Among boys at Marlborough in Edwardian times was George Turner, the future Master. There was still a medieval flavour to the medical treatments provided, Turner remembered. After measles and pneumonia, part of the cure prescribed by Edward Penny, the school doctor, was 'the application of leeches, an itchy business; and when I was very kindly asked to the Lodge as a convalescent, the master's prescription was a glass of champagne every morning. Thus I gained not only my first acquaintance with that encouraging drink but also the start of a life-long friendship with Sir Frank and Lady Fletcher.' (Fletcher was knighted in 1937.)

Turner was one of the four boys who published a curiosity: *The Marlborough Struwwelpeter* (1908). All four won Oxford or Cambridge scholarships and the author/illustrator, Arthur de C. Williams, became a distinguished Indian civil servant. The book was a full-colour parody, with sinful Marlburians substituted for the originals, and must have seemed hilarious to those who could identify them; some in addition are perennial school types: Johnny head-in-tome, who fell into the swimming-pool, and Tomkins, who experimented with tobacco and set himself on fire by hiding his pipe in his pocket. All are historically interesting for their clothes.

Uniform had developed slowly at Marlborough. Though Wilkinson introduced white ties for Sixth Form boys on Sundays, Cotton's circular letters asking parents not to dress their boys in rough or parti-coloured

'Story of Tomkins the Smoker' in the *Marlborough Struwwelpeter.*

Editors of *The Marlburian* in 1909, including the author of the *Marlborough Struwwelpeter*, A. de C. Williams (seated, right) and J. Bell (seated, left) to whom the book is dedicated. Also in the picture is G. C. Turner (standing, left) who later became Master.

clothes showed that these were still normal. Top hats for the Sixth on Sundays, which he also suggested, had disappeared by 1860. Bradley, however, made a determined effort to introduce uniform hats, getting an Oxford tailor to send samples, and one of these eventually developed into the black peaked-cap which Marlborough's Struwwelpeter wears – the sort worn by the boys of every nineteenth-century school story. Round his neck he has a stiff white collar and black tie, and below these a black jacket with five buttons, grey striped trousers and black boots. Under his arm he carries that Marlburian peculiarity a kish (the 'i' as in 'rice'): a cushion, black on one side, coloured on the other which could be sat upon, or folded, coloured side inwards, to enclose books. Tomkins,

116

the smoker, on the other hand, wears a straw boater, doubtless normal in summer; and Cruel Dix, a prototype athlete, who threatens to strike his house prefect with a walking-stick but is laid out by one of his own Rugby forwards, is dressed for sport in bright blue blazer and shorts and a bright blue cap with white tassel.

Fletcher's last year as Master was also the last year at the school of William Bambridge, the organist and Director of Music for the previous 47 years, outlasting even those four long-lasting figures of the previous century, Bull, Sellick, Fergus and Thomas. He did not bring music to Marlborough. The school's first organist, James Whitehead Smith, had been appointed in 1848 and the Music Society was formed the same year. Both the boys whose diaries survive from 1850–2, Somerset and Nunns, took regular music lessons. The Society's Christmas concert, the first given in 1849, soon became an annual event, and an occasion when Old Marlburians would visit the school. By 1893 A. G. Bradley was able to report that when 'Auld Lang Syne' was sung 'the grey-haired veteran and the piping treble' could be seen 'gripped in one another's clutches amid the dust and uproar'.

Also in 1848, when the first Chapel had been built, a school choir was formed, one of the first at any public school. Its singing was admired, even by a boy like Edward Lockwood, whose thoughts were usually on poaching. 'We were all driven, much against our will, fifteen times a week to chapel, where the services were rendered far less irksome than they would otherwise have been, by the singing; for sufficient voices were found among the boys at school to form a choir, which, had I not known the boys, and watched their distorted faces whilst they sang, I might have imagined came down direct from heaven.'

Cotton had compiled the school's first hymn-book. It was Bradley, however, who had appointed Bambridge in 1864, then only 21, but already known to be an exceptional pianist. Besides the piano, he played the organ, the cello in the school orchestra and the euphonium in the brass band. He wrote many of Marlborough's hymn tunes. He endeared himself to the boys by also being, in the words of his obituary, a 'long-legged, elusive half-back', an 'astonishing dribbler' and a 'tall, gaunt, nimble-fingered bowler of googlies long before the googly had a name'.

'No one except Dean Stanley knew less of music than Farrar,' John Rogers wrote, but at Marlborough Farrar encouraged it, in 1872 presenting two prizes for solo singing. The same year the first inter-house competition was held. Each house which could produce ten singers sang the same two part-songs. But hearing five houses practising these day after day became a public nuisance and, according to A. G. Bradley, when one of the songs was 'Where are the Boys of the Old Brigade?'

Cover of the *Marlborough Struwwelpeter* depicting a typically dressed boy of the period in black jacket and black cap with his 'kish' under his arm.

A scene evocative of the period (*c.* 1908). Bambridge holding court with his band in the garden at 'Wiamate' his house in Pewsey Road. He came from New Zealand; hence the house name.

a reward was offered for their discovery, so that the search could be called off. Presently competitive instrumental performances were substituted.

Also in 1872 the brass band was formed, to supplement the drum and fife band of the Corps. Horace Mordaunt Rogers remembered hearing the news of this and rushing to find Bambridge. 'I did so want to play the cornet. I envied those men who played outside public houses with a harpist or on board a steamer or on *The Skylark* skippered by the famous Captain Collins at Brighton.

'Bam looked at me a moment and then with a whimsical smile said: "I think with your mouth I should recommend the saxhorn." I thought this was somewhat of an outsize criticism but the saxhorn it was and I grew to love old Bam.'

Two years later (1874) 'Penny Readings' began. At first these were staged in the Bradleian and were entirely musical, apart from a reading by the Senior Prefect. The choir would sing, the brass band play and there would be solos on the piano and other instruments. But by the end of E. F. Benson's time (1887) a dramatic event had been introduced.

The next item was the removal of the piano by two strenuous college servants. A protracted struggle took place, but the piano was eventually out-manœuvred. Immense applause among the audience. Then a song was sung by the choir, but as it was soft, and was not out of tune, the School did not encore it. . . . This was succeeded by several minor events: the most important being a cornet solo, which was very loud and clear, and consequently most popular. Then came the event of the evening, the Penny Reading itself. N.B. 'What is not needful is dear at a penny.' Hint for the committee given gratis. It was of a funereal type, but was accompanied with a great deal of by-play, which is always charming. After that came the three humorous chafers. They always do have chafers at a Penny Reading.

In Benson's time seats cost 3*d*., 6*d*. or a shilling each, and there was usually one Penny Reading a term. By 1909 there had been a hundred, and they were so popular that they had been moved to Upper School.

The newly built Field House (1911) and bridge. According to one of the inmates of the house, there was a strict rule that the bridge must be used 'because the horses and carts on the road were so dangerous'.

Benson called his Penny Reading conductor Whiston but this was undoubtedly Bambridge. When the orchestra played the Toy Symphony, 'Whiston was also wonderful. He beat time to all the performers with one hand, and held a tin trumpet to his mouth with the other. I rather think he turned over the page with his nose, which is long enough to be useful.'

When Fletcher had been at Marlborough only six years he was encouraged to apply for the headmastership of Rugby, but declined, considering this unfair to Marlborough. Two years later when the Archbishop of Canterbury wrote to press him to accept the headmastership of Charterhouse he felt he could not refuse. By then he considered that his work at Marlborough was as complete as he could make it. The culmination of his efforts had been the opening of Field House, across the Bath Road from the Porter's Lodge. Because this was an in-college house it had to stand close to the road and be connected to the main college buildings by the now little-used footbridge. It would accommodate a hundred boys, and into it moved B3 and C2 houses.

'At Charterhouse', Fletcher wrote, 'the difficulties to be faced were far greater than those we had found at Marlborough; but ... the task was made easier by the fact that we came to a school dissatisfied with itself and conscious of the need for improvement.' This, he implied, had not been the case at Marlborough.

Frank Fletcher in his later years as Headmaster of Charterhouse. The pupil at the extreme right is a future Marlborough Master, Tommy Garnett. *Reproduced by kind permission of the Headmaster and Governing Body of Charterhouse.*

9

THE BOODLE AND THE BOOT

1911–1926

Part I

WHEN FLETCHER RESIGNED in 1911 the Council as usual advertised for a new Master, and invited the six short-listed candidates to attend for interview. On the appointed morning five came, but the Council remained dissatisfied and sent for the sixth, the Revd John Basil Wynne Willson. Several members then explained that they had other engagements that afternoon, so a vote was taken and Wynne Willson arrived just in time to be congratulated on his appointment.

The Council may have chosen the new Master because, for the past six years, he had been headmaster of Haileybury, a school which had a 'hostel' system like Marlborough's, and which charged the sons of clergymen lower fees (as Marlborough had done until 1870 and continued to do in the form of Foundation Scholarships then a reintroduced but smaller general reduction). He was a likeable man, who soon became known to the boys as 'The Boodle', but he was not a forceful one. Robert Bennett's story of the end of term hymn, 'Lord Dismiss us with Thy Blessing', catches the flavour of his regime. It was the custom to sing this hymn with irreverent enthusiasm, so a new tune was ordered. 'We were all horrified.... The first verse was sung only by choir and organ while the whole 700 took no part. As the second verse began one bad lad started singing the old tune and by the end of the verse it was sheer pandemonium. For the third verse the organ swung

Basil St John Wynne Willson (hands clasped) in the Lodge garden with his Chaplain, J. M. Lupton, and two Housemasters, A. H. Wall and M. H. Gould.

back to the old tune. Next day another notice appeared stating that as the school seemed so attached to the old tune it would be used as usual.' It is difficult to imagine earlier Marlborough Masters accepting such a defeat.

Wynne Willson was a firm believer in the benefits of a public school education. 'But for our public schools', he told the *Church Family Newspaper*, 'you would never get the successful administrators of Empire which England produces in such numbers. The elder boys in our public schools, having to exercise a certain rule over their juniors, gain an experience which is distinctly good for them.' This was an argument in support of the prefect system which neither Arnold nor Cotton had used.

Asked if boys were badly fed he replied, 'Don't listen to such complaints. Boys are born grumblers.' Asked if there were boys for whom public school life was not the best, he would only admit that 'The morbidly sensitive boy or the eccentric genius may perhaps find the atmosphere uncongenial.'

Uncongenial it certainly was, according to Bennett, who came to the school a year after Wynne Willson and found little evidence that Fletcher's restoration of the prestige of scholarship over athleticism had survived. 'Everyone was passionately fond of games.... There were of course other activities such as music, natural history and a debating society, but generally speaking ... we were the reverse of highbrow.'

His contemporary, Nisbet, remembered that 'besides getting to know the bloods by sight, name and initials, I began to worship from afar the greatest of them. On one unforgettable evening my hero came to take prep and prayers at the House. Being a new bug, I was kept ... in the background. It was just as well; had he spoken to me, I would have passed out!'

Bennett and Nisbet began their time at Marlborough in small out-college houses – the Priory and Upcot respectively. Even here life was basic. At the Priory, in Marlborough's High Street, there were outdoor earth-closets. Both of them moved to one of the in-college houses where conditions were equally rugged, and while they were juniors had as their day-room the old Upper School. It was popularly supposed, Nisbet wrote,

> to be the largest structure of its kind without interior supports in England, and to have been guaranteed for only 6 months. This did not prevent my sharing its doubtful amenities seventy years later with some two hundred and fifty companions.
>
> ... in this barrack-room of ours, three-quarters filled with rows of knife-eaten, time-darkened desks [there were] at one end, brewing lockers and the captains' tables; at the other, a raised throne; above the throne and continuing around the walls long, dusky panels commemorating prize-winners. To complete the scene, add two fire-places – one shared by eighty-five per cent of

Upper School as it was in the days of Betjeman and MacNeice. The basket (left) is the kind which was used for 'basketing' (see page 135). The Big Fire is on the right.

the occupants, the other exclusively reserved for the four captains and their friends.

When I was a member of the Upper School the rules of the place were as singular as the place itself. No one who did not belong to it was ever permitted to enter it; and everyone in it was waiting to be promoted out of it. By day it echoed with whistling and song; during the minutes preceding evening prep, it resounded with a din that shook the college.

There was a reason for this uproar – a final letting off of steam before the re-entry of the captains. At a few minutes past seven they retired to the draughty shelter of Brad. arches. At seven fifteen they returned.

These 'captains' (prefects) were allowed to beat but only to give three strokes, and only with a master's permission. Punishment took place after the masters had retired. Then, 'A large circle formed round the victim and executioners and each blow was loudly counted, sometimes with much hilarity.'

Upper School was lit by gas and one of the boys' diversions was filling a large biscuit-tin with gas, making a hole in each end, balancing the tin on two books and lighting the top hole. After a time, when the gas and air mixture was right, there was a highly satisfactory explosion. Bennett remembered a short-sighted master arriving at the critical moment and peering 'closely at the contraption in spite of the pleading of the owner. Then it went off. No rule had been broken but of course it was forbidden for the future.'

A master who came (and left) in these years was Geoffrey Fisher, the Senior Prefect who had helped Fletcher. Nisbet described the future archbishop as 'young and fiery. Finding his eye too penetrating at the top of the class, I sank by means of *viva-voce* questions, to the bottom. Here I was joined by my friend Willie Booth, with whom I spent an exciting term, penning on our brand-new desks the story, from Hilaire Belloc's *Nonsense Rhymes*, of a lad named Jim, who left his nurse at the Zoo and was eaten bit by bit by a lion.'

Bennett was in Upper School when Fisher stopped a riot there.

The end of the term was only 2 days away and everyone was very excited. Suddenly they seemed to go mad. They smashed all their incandescent mantles, strewed paper all over the floor.... Two hundred desk lids crashing down Bang Bang – Bang Bang Bang makes a tremendous noise.... As soon as Fisher came in everyone accepted that 'Authority' had come in. He just ordered everyone to clear up the mess and the matter ended there.

Not according to Fisher. He told his biographer:

> But I didn't think that was quite enough. I therefore ordered that
> all the senior boys should come in on the following Saturday
> afternoon. I then had the problem of settling what to do with them
> for two hours. I went to my friend, the chief mathematical master,
> and said, 'How can I keep these people occupied ... for two
> hours?' He replied: 'Set them on to multiply one by two and the
> result by three, and the result by four ... and so on indefinitely,
> and I will give you a check so that you can see what is the right
> answer when you get up to ten, and what is the right answer when
> you get up to twenty, and nobody will get beyond that.' It was
> magnificent because there they were, doing this menial task of
> multiplying, and I would walk round quietly, and just from the
> check scratch a notebook and say 'Wrong. Begin again from the
> beginning.'

At Marlborough Fisher soon took holy orders, then left to become
headmaster of Repton, Bishop of Chester, Bishop of London and finally
in 1945 Archbishop of Canterbury.

'We endured it as being inevitable', Bennett wrote, summing up his
feelings about Marlborough immediately before the First World War,
'deriving what fun we could manage, even if sometimes rather childish.'

The official version of these years can be found in Wynne Willson's
Prize Day speeches. In 1912 he said, 'As to the history of the school in
the past year, it has been a smooth course.... The health of the school
has been good and it has been a year of peace.' The same tone of self-
satisfaction permeates the speeches of 1913 and 1914. Each year he named
prize and scholarship winners from a list which continued to be
impressive. Each year he referred to victory or hard-fought defeat in the
Cheltenham match. The only hint of the disaster which lay ahead came
in references to the Corps. In 1912 he reported that 'the numbers this
year have reached 550' (Applause). In 1913 he said, 'Next I refer to what
does not quite come under the head of games, but forms a very important
part of school life – the Officers' Training Corps, which now numbers
570, and I believe I am right in saying it is the biggest Officers' Training
Corps in existence.'

Though Marlborough's Corps, since the 1870s, had been a more
important part of the school's life than the corps of most public schools
(those of Cheltenham, Wellington and Eton had also been important) it
had nevertheless throughout the nineteenth century given its members
little effective training. The Boer War, however, with its humiliations
for the British army, together with Germany's increasing military

strength, changed British attitudes, and Marlborough's corps, along with those of other schools benefited. These were years when the Navy League and the National Service League campaigned for conscription to give Britain an army which could compete with the huge conscript armies of Germany and France. In 1906 Lord Roberts, victor of the Boer War, told a Scottish public school, 'I look to you public school boys to set an example. Let it be your ambition to render yourself capable of being leaders of others who have not your advantages, should you ever be called upon to fight for your country.'

In 1904 there had been a Royal Commission on the Militia and Volunteers, which took evidence from public schools. Four years later came Haldane's army reforms, and in the same year, the Corps ceased to be the Rifle Volunteer Corps and became an Officers' Training Corps. Its purpose now was 'to give students elementary military training, with a view to their eventually applying for commissions in the Special Reserve of Officers or the Territorial Force'. Boys who gained a certificate in the OTC would be exempt from certain examinations. Another 94 recruits joined the Corps in the year it became the OTC.

Charles Sorley, Marlborough's war poet who was to be tragically killed in 1915, was one boy who obtained a certificate. In December 1911 he wrote to his parents describing the examination at Devizes Barracks, which was divided into three parts: Company Drill, Tactical and Musketry.

> For each part the full is 100, and to pass one must get at least 50 in each subject and at least 180 in the whole.... My lot was

The OTC in 1913. Numbers increased steadily as war loomed.

126

Charles Sorley (seated with bare feet) at Corps Camp.

Musketry first, of which I was glad as lack of time has forced me to take it practically unseen. There was a horrible dark little rabbit-hutch, concealing a gawky subaltern with a rifle. We went there one after another alone, and an air of sanctity hung over the whole proceeding. I entered with fear and trembling. Twenty questions I was asked, and I looked sheepish and I said 'Don't know' to each one. Then he said, 'Is there anything you do know?' and I gave him the two pieces of knowledge I had come armed with – the weight of a rifle and episodes in the life of a bullet from the time it leaves the breech till it hits its man. Then I saluted really smartly, and the gentleman gave me 60 out of a hundred. Company drill came next which merely consisted in drilling a Company ... of most alarmingly smart regulars. For this I got 70 (every one got 70) ... Tactical was equally a farce. I was told to send out an advance-guard, lost my head, sent out a flank-guard, scored 70 per cent ...

We left the barracks about 2.30: only three people had been ploughed – they must have been bad. It was a very fine afternoon and a good drive home. I only wish they had not been so kind in marking me so that I might have tried again in the summer.

Corps Brews at the Town Hall were a traditional conclusion to the field-days of these times. 'I think our Corps Brews are the most perfect

127

The Marlborough Corps marching on Bath Road, 1912.

type of a Mutual Admiration Evening,' Sorley wrote to his parents.

We go away thinking each of us personally is the smartest member of the smartest corps in the world. But this time a very fortunate incident occurred on the way home. The band were so puffed up by the nice things that had been said about them, that they were making a great deal more noise than was right at 10 p.m. The result was that the first horse we met bolted. We were marching on the left of the road and the horse was on the right, and you know how broad the High Street is. There was no danger; even the horse was not very frightened. But College Corps were! In a second we were all on the pavement, making for the wall; and we had been marching at attention under military discipline. I have never seen anything so disgraceful; but it just reminded us that we weren't all Wellingtons yet. I think this should be arranged to happen after every Corps Brew.

Marlborough's Corps continued, however, to flourish. At the Prize Day of June 1914 the Master said, 'One of the most energetic parts of our school life is the Officers' Training Corps.... I never feel so proud of the school, I think, as when I see it going to a field-day, swinging by on its way down the High Street.'

Words like these now seem to hang ominously over those last months of peace. When, at Lords, on a July afternoon of 1914, Nisbet said

128

goodbye to his cricketing hero, 'nothing in the talk around us even remotely suggested that we would never meet again'. A few days later members of the Corps were attending the annual camp on Salisbury Plain, and though 'the usual ingredients of Corps life were there in plenty' and 'there were sing songs, blanket tossing ... the cloud of War that overhung us was a ... factor which could never be entirely disregarded'. 'On Monday', *The Marlburian* continued, 'it was expected that General Sir H. Smith-Dorien would address the Brigade but the crisis rendered his visit impossible ... war was on this day so much in the air that it was impossible to think of anything else.' The Marlborough contingent returned to the college at 12.30 on 4 August. A few hours later war was declared.

When the school reassembled in September Bennett discovered that 'all the young masters not in Holy Orders had disappeared and their places were filled by a lot of dugouts. Some I fear found the going a bit hard.' The term's first issue of *The Marlburian* (8 October) carried a single notice on its front page:

> The Editor would be pleased if all Marlburians who are serving in any capacity in any of His Majesty's forces ... would communicate particulars as to commissions, enlistment, etc., and all subsequent doings, for insertion in 'The Marlburian' and also for a list, which will be posted in the College, on which an account of each O.M. serving will be recorded up to date.'

Inside it reported that 50 boys who would otherwise have returned that term had instead 'received the summons'. Nine days later the Battle of Mons had been fought and it printed the first, black-edged casualty list — 9 dead, 6 missing, 18 wounded, 6 prisoners of war. One of those killed was Harold Roseveare. Only the previous term he had been the school's Senior Prefect and Cadet Captain of the Corps. The same issue published an extract from one of his letters.

> At present I am crouching under a wigwam made of sticks and a waterproof sheet, and as it is pouring with rain, I am suffering from a constant stream of muddy drops. On the whole I haven't done much except march, march, march.... For some days we marched at top speed *from* the Germans; then we turned and did a little marching *after* them for a change. Have marched some 200 miles or more since I came out.

Three days later he was shot in the chest, leading an attack on a German machine-gun at Vailly and died next day.

Many Marlburians had joined the Public School and University Brigade, billeted at Epsom. Here 'some of the more ambitious of us are seeking commissions, but most of us are content to shoulder the rifle – which by the way we have not yet got.' This Old Marlburian named 21 others who were either privates in the brigade or in an officers' training-camp on the downs, which was 'generally regarded here as rather of the "picnic" order'. Many of them were 'having trouble with their feet – or as "The Epsom Herald" has it, their "pedal extremities".'

At the school 'large and important additions' had been made to Corps activities. There were uniform parades on two afternoons a week and another in mufti on Tuesday mornings. On Saturdays there were sometimes night operations. Though the Corps had lost 115 members that term, 76 new recruits had joined and the roll was 529. Meanwhile half its rifles had been commandeered by the government.

Soon *The Marlburian* began to carry descriptions of the heroic deaths of Old Marlburians in France. A few must stand for the great number which appeared in issue after issue over the next four years. About Edward Bradbury (1894–98) killed at Néry on 1 Sept 1914, a fellow officer wrote:

> The battery he was in was surprised by a German battery in a mist early one morning, and poor old 'Brad' was killed. 'Brad' served a gun himself, and during that time knocked out one German gun completely.
>
> He first had a hip and one leg shot away, and still managed to fire off a round or two more, until the other leg was taken off just above the knee.
>
> The doctor who told me about it afterwards said that all he asked was for heaps of Morphia, so that the men should not hear him screaming, and that he might be taken quickly to the rear. The whole story is that 'Brad' died as one felt he would.

On 30 July 1915 Sidney Woodroffe died at Hooge in the Ypres salient. His brother, Leslie, was severely wounded in the same action, and another brother, Kenneth, had already been killed. Sidney was posthumously awared the VC, the citation reading,

> The enemy having broken through the centre of our front trenches, consequent on the use of burning liquids, this officer's position was heavily attacked with bombs from the flank and subsequently from the rear, but he managed to defend his post until all his bombs were exhausted and then skilfully withdrew his remaining men. This

very gallant officer immediately led his party forward in a counter-attack under intense rifle and machine-gun fire, and was killed whilst in the act of cutting the wire obstacles in the open.

The Marlburian published Charles Sorley's poem on Woodroffe's death.

There is no fitter end than this;
　　No need is now to yearn or sigh.
We know the glory that is his,
　　A glory that can never die.
Surely we knew it long before,
　　Knew all along that he was made
For a swift radiant morning, for
　　A sacrificing, swift night-shade.

Immediately below came a poem by another poet on Sorley's own death, shot in the head by a sniper at Hulloch on 13 October 1915.

Sorley had been no conformist at school, and though a prefect, had deplored the effect that seniority was having on him. 'When one reaches

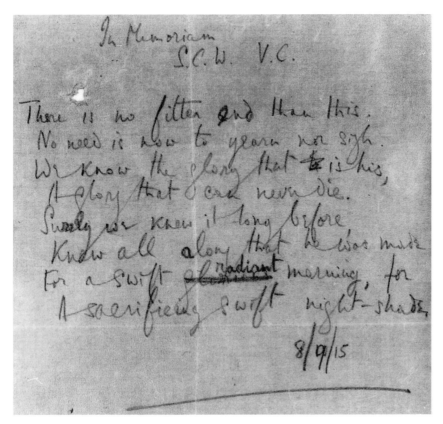

Sorley's manuscript epitaph, written in the trenches on a flimsy piece of paper, on hearing the news of the death of his old school friend, S. C. Woodroffe, posthumously awarded the VC.

the top of a public school, one has such unbounded opportunities of getting unbearably conceited that I don't see how one survives the damage that must come when the tin god is swept off his little kingdom and becomes an unimportant mortal again.'

Arthur Pelly, a close friend, remembered standing with Sorley at a C House upper window looking down on Court when Sorley composed 'for my entertainment', the first lines of his poem.

> O come and see, it's such a sight,
> So many boys, all doing right . . .

He also remembered 'Sorley refusing to be confirmed and then later agreeing . . . on his own terms. The Master took confirmation classes in Chapel. Boys always entered by the west door, and we were not supposed to use the south door at the other end. On one occasion . . . when we were all assembled in our places like good little boys in plenty of time, with the Master in his seat, the south door suddenly opened and in walked Sorley. He strolled the full length of Chapel and reached his seat in the nick of time with the Master glaring at him. Sorley looked up, took his watch out, looked at it and held it out to prove that he was not late, and smiled at the Master who could not conceal his annoyance and fury.' On another occasion Wynne Willson gave Sorley 'lines' but 'Sorley found in some old book of College rules that prefects could ask to be beaten. The Master refused to beat him: Sorely refused to do the "lines"; so that deadlock ensued.'

After winning a scholarship to University College, Oxford, Sorley spent the first six months of 1914 in Germany, and as a result saw the mistakenness of what was happening earlier than, for example, Graves or Sassoon. In October 1914 he wrote 'I regard the war as between sisters . . . the efficient and intolerant, against the casual and sympathetic. Each side has a virtue for which it is fighting, and each that virtue's supplementary vice. And I hope that whatever the material result of the conflict, it will purge these two virtues of their vices, and efficiency and tolerance will no longer be incompatible.'

In July 1916 the first Battle of the Somme was fought, the most disastrous engagement ever for a British army, as well as for the British middle classes. On the first day alone there were 60,000 British casualties most of them the volunteers of Kitchener's New Army, as line after line advanced across no man's land with crazy bravery, to be mown down like corn by German machine-guns. It took the British four days to admit that it would be safer to advance in short rushes. Leading them, easily identifiable because they carried revolvers or swords, not rifles, were the sort of young men whom Marlborough produced. The first issue of *The*

Marlburian to begin to reveal the consequences (31 July 1916) listed 17 Old Marlburians who had died. The next (17 October) added 60 more. Again it printed tale after tale of heroic death. 'He will be sorely missed in the regiment', 'His men would have followed him anywhere', 'He died as he would have wished to die' ... there is an awful similarity about these notices which unites them into a single memorial to a generation and its beliefs.

Though in some ways life at the school continued as normal, for most boys it was overshadowed by such events. 'It was uncanny', one of them, George Lowndes, remembered, 'to look across Chapel to the back row opposite and realise that within six months half of the boys there would be dead.' 'Every week', Bennett wrote, 'someone heard that a brother or a friend had been killed or wounded, and immediately we left MC death, or if we were lucky wounds, would be our inevitable lot.' When Bennett left three and a half years later, he was in the army just five weeks before being seriously wounded. In all 742 Marlburians died.

Prospects of this sort made some boys reckless. When an Old Marlburian landed his plane, a BE2C, on the Common, one of them took a joy-ride with him. Another, in the forest, accidentally shot his friend in the leg with a 'saloon pistol'. Masters were affected differently, as they heard of the deaths in their early twenties of boy after boy to whom they had devoted their care and affection. There is little doubt that cumulative dismay caused Wynne Willson to leave Marlborough in 1916, after only five years. He became Dean of Bristol, then Bishop of Bath and Wells (Bath and Wills, to wits, since he had married a daughter of the well-known Bristol tobacco family).

Making ice-cream for Prize Day 1913.

Part II

To replace Wynne Willson the Council first invited an Old Marlburian, Cyril Alington, future Provost of Eton, but when he refused the job, chose instead Cyril Norwood, headmaster of Bristol Grammar School. Norwood was a formidable figure, later the author of *The English Tradition of Education* (1929) and editor of the so-called 'Norwood Report' on curriculum and examinations (1943). He has been described as 'perhaps the last in the tradition of great Victorian headmasters'.

He took office early in 1917, when almost two years of war were still to come, and hundreds of Old Marlburians were still fighting. Sassoon was as gallant as any of them – he fought at the Somme and described the experience in *Memoirs of an Infantry Officer*. But his poem 'The General', suggested the growing disillusionment that he and others were feeling:

> He's a cheery old card, grunted Harry to Jack
> As they slogged up to Arras with rifle and pack ...
> But he did for them both with his plan of attack.

Finally he wrote letters of protest to the press and failed to report for duty, offences from the consequences of which Robert Graves saved him. When he returned from a hospital for the shell-shocked he fought again in the trenches, but it was about Armistice Day, 11 November 1918, that he wrote his best-remembered poem, 'Everyone Sang'.

The boys of the school celebrated less decorously.

Cyril Norwood.

After breakfast [Arthur Bird wrote] we all streamed down the town (against rules) to hear the mayor, Hughes, one of our masters, announce the news. There was a lone Scottish piper marching up and down playing his doleful tunes and that was all. When we got back to the school, the boys in Upper School began to throw anything, books, kishes, ink-bottles, coal through the large windows and out-college boys who were in for lunch threw them all back again; the waste-paper baskets were burnt and I personally burnt all the notices. There was an unholy mess. A list was put up so that boys who had taken part in the destruction could put their names down and have ten shillings added to the bill or pay the ten bob themselves, quite a lot squeezed their pocket-money and paid.

It is possible to paint two pictures of Marlborough in Norwood's post-war years, apparently irreconcilable, but both in part true. Much of the first is based on the dislike which poets and intellectuals like John

134

Betjeman, Anthony Blunt and Louis MacNeice felt for the school. They found it still an uncivilised, games-obsessed place, where bullying and beating were regular and the curriculum little changed since the last century. As in Wynne Willson's time, they picked out Upper School to represent Marlborough's ruggedness. MacNeice described it as 'just a great tract of empty air, cold as the air outside but smelling of stables, enclosed by four thin walls and a distant roof'.

The group who monopolised the biggest of the two fires which alone provided any heat, was known as Big Fire, like some gang of Indian braves. One of Big Fire's practices was 'basketing'. Betjeman's claim that he was basketed was denied by John Bowle, and the practice was in fact rare. Another contemporary, Maurice Hayward, saw it only once. 'The victim's coat and waistcoat were removed and he was placed in one of the enormous waste-paper baskets with his head and feet protruding. A dollup of treacle was poured on his hair, and the basket hauled up about 10 or 12 feet by a rope slung round a roof beam for all to see. After a short period the unfortunate fellow was let down in time for him to get to his desk before the presiding master arrived.'

Hayward remembered another barbarity. To go to the lavatory during daytime, small boys of A House had to cross Court to reach the school latrines behind the Bradleian. These 'provided a double row of doorless compartments ... [which were] substantially flushed down a common drain about every twenty minutes. [They] also had a constant slow flow [on] which lighter hearted jokers used to float rafts of burning paper to singe other occupants.'

About the school's curriculum John Bowle wrote: 'The only part ... that was taken seriously was classics. If you weren't good at Greek and Latin, you were regarded as expendable.' Betjeman was not good at Greek and Latin, and was so severely criticised for this by Alec Gidney, master of the Lower Sixth, that he was still writing bitterly about him 50 years later. In 1958 he told a *Daily Mail* interviewer, 'I was bullied and crushed by a master, and it is immensely gratifying to me to know that the hide-bound old prig is still alive and occasionally reading my name.' In 1974 his poem, 'Greek Orthodox', contained the lines,

> What did I see when first I went to Greece?
> Shades of the Sixth across the Peloponnese
> Though clear the clean-cut Doric temple shone
> Still droned the voice of Mr Gidney on.

On the other hand, Sorley, who had Gidney as his English master, described him as 'a very inspiring teacher'. And perhaps Gidney was provoked. As an old man, still living at Marlborough, he told Betjeman's biographer, 'at the beginning of one term when the form list was being passed round, he said to me: "Please, sir, I can't remember whether my surname is spelt with one 'n' or two." He was posing as usual, you see. So I said: "Make up your mind and let me know when you've decided".'

Certainly much of Betjeman's school misery was an invention of later years. Blunt considered that he was quite capable of protecting himself. 'He had this marvellous sense of humour, and when the toughs tried to be bloody, he simply laughed in their faces: and, as you know, when John Betjeman laughs it's quite something. They were absolutely routed.' And although the school was again dominated by games-playing toughs, there had been a change. Boys who hated games were now sufficiently numerous (and felt themselves to have enough support in the outside world) to create a self-supporting, even self-satisfied group. Together they devised forms of defiance which ranged from straightforward protest to ironic self-mockery. According to Blunt, Betjeman once bowled a hoop through Court with a green feather behind his ear, coping (like E. F. Benson) with hostility by making himself into a joke; Blunt himself and MacNeice played conspicuously on the rounders pitch with a big rubber beach-ball. These three, together with Bowle and John Hilton, founded an Art Society, of which the master, Clifford Canning, agreed to be president. When the Art Master, Christopher Hughes, claimed that he should hold this position, Blunt persuaded the society to dissolve itself and reform as the Anonymous Society. Of this, significantly for Marlborough, George Turner, the future Master, agreed to be president. Betjeman read a paper on Victorian Art to the Anonymous Society.

It was Matthew Wordsworth, however, son of the Bishop of Salisbury who had forbidden Fletcher the pulpit, who in March 1924 suggested publishing a magazine. *The Heretick* was intended, in Blunt's words, 'to express our disapproval of the Establishment generally, of the more out-of-date and pedantic masters, of all forms of organised sport, of the Officers' Training Corps and of all the other features that we hated in school life, not so much the physical discomforts – they were almost taken for granted – but ... the intellectual discomforts of the school.'

The first issue appeared on 29 March, the cover, designed by Bowle, showing a hearty with a hockey-stick, being teased by aesthetes in the form of fauns playing pipes in the branches of surrounding trees. Betjeman contributed three pieces, including an account of the 'Dinner of the Old Marlburian Centipede Farmers in Unyamwazi, S.A.'. In his diary Bowle wrote, 'Court alive with orange covers on black suits. A strange silence in Hall, everyone reading it.' The hearties did not like what they read, and Bowle was so convinced that they planned to attack him after the end of term concert that he equipped himself with a squaler.

The Master also read the first issue and in his final sermon of the term spoke about its motto, 'Upon Philistia will I triumph'. If this meant 'overcoming the philistine in all of us', he approved, but if it was 'an expression of intellectual snobbery' he did not. Norwood's reaction fairly represents him. To an extent he sympathised with the aesthetes of the school and shared their desire to modify its games culture, but he was too distant and conventional to seem a satisfactory ally. To Maurice Bowra he looked like 'an Edwardian policeman'. Hayward claimed that he was once seen wearing button-boots. (He was known as 'the Boot' because of the number of boys he sacked.) Betjeman would imitate him 'telling God what Marlborough stood for' as he rode uphill on his bicycle. He had, Bowle wrote, 'a terrifying exterior'. On the other hand Bowle admitted that this concealed 'something like genius. He certainly had a very great impact on all of us, including John [Betjeman] ... Underneath his forbidding exterior, Norwood concealed a great sense of humour and great perceptiveness about character.'

Norwood might have tolerated the second issue of *The Heretick* which appeared the following June, but Blunt's article, suggesting that there could be no morality in art, so provoked a parent that he threatened to remove his son unless the magazine was suppressed, which it duly was.

Norwood's undoubted achievements are the basis of the second picture of the school during the early post-war years. The curriculum may have remained old-fasioned, but he made significant reforms, expanding science and rearranging all the teaching so that boys could take School Certificate early and be free from the Fifth Form upwards for more advanced work. The success of these changes soon showed in the increased numbers of Oxford and Cambridge scholarships which it began to win: 30 in 1925 and 24 in 1926. And these helped to increase steadily the school's numbers which rose from 700 in 1918 to 750 in 1921, with a full waiting-list for the next five years.

Though the increased numbers were accommodated without the building of a new house, the school in Norwood's time acquired the most important addition to its buildings since its new Chapel: the Memorial Hall. The idea of a war memorial had first been discussed at a meeting of Old Marlburians in April 1917, when it was agreed that this should take two forms, a Speech Hall, and a fund for the education of the children of Marlburians who had died. Two years later (February 1919) the Council agreed that if the College War Memorial Committee would erect a 'suitable building or buildings' it would give free education to boys nominated by the Marlburian Club. That September the first boy to be chosen entered the school, and next month the committee held a public meeting in London to discuss what it should build. It settled on a Memorial Hall (rather than a cloister), and arranged a competition for its design among Old Marlburian architects, at the same time expressing 'a strong preference for a Hall in the Amphitheatre style'. It also chose the site, which its minutes ominously described as 'the water meadow below the chapel adjoining the Bath Road'.

Towards the end of 1920 the President of the Royal Institute of British Architects chose the design of the Old Marlburian, William Newton (who had served in the Artists' Rifles and won the MC). His plan proposed the Memorial Gardens, much as they can be seen today, backed to the south by a magnificent pillared hall to seat 1,500. Because of the nature of the site this would have to be built on a concrete raft. The total cost was daunting: about £100,000. The Committee believed, however, that the price of building materials would fall, and postponed its first appeal for a year.

Even when it was proved right and the expected cost fell to £75,000, this was more than a succession of appeals could raise and the committee was forced to ask Newton to draw up reduced plans. These meant that the hall would have to seat fewer and there were discussions about whether the average boy should be allowed 14 or 16 inches sitting space. Eventually a hall for 1,150 was agreed and building began. All was expected to be ready by the autumn of 1924, and though various celebrities including Marshal Foch had declined to perform the opening ceremony, the Duke of Connaught had agreed.

On 21 July, two months before the chosen date, the Committee was called to a meeting to hear a statement from Newton. In layman's terms, he told it that the Memorial Hall was sinking. 'The raft had been ... inspected and passed by a very distinguished expert. When the new scheme was adopted with a Hall of altered design the raft should have been inspected again, but the reinforced-concrete expert ... expressed no doubt as to the capacity of the raft holding a different distribution of weight.' Nevertheless, at the end of May when timbers supporting the roof were removed, cracks had appeared in the walls.

Piles had to be sunk at the rear of the raft and horizontal girders inserted below it to prevent further damage. The final extra cost was £2,600, most of which Newton recovered by economies; he also charged no fees for his services. The grand opening, however, had to be postponed and eventually took place eight months late on 23 May 1925. Apart from being of great use to the school, the Memorial Hall was widely admired by architectural critics of the time.

Cyril Norwood with the
Duke of Connaught on the
occasion of the opening of the
Memorial Hall in 1925.

Below the Memorial Hall's auditorium, at the suggestion of Dr
Ivimey, a number of new music rooms were built. Since 1911 three
Directors of Music (George Dyson, Arthur Heberden and Noel
Ponsonby) had attempted with fair success to fill the gap left by
Bambridge, but it was only when John Ivimey came from Cheltenham
in 1919 that the department had a director who stayed long enough to
make a real impression. Hayward remembered that 'Despite his

administrative responsibilities, Dr Ivimey remained a personal teacher for piano and organ playing ... and himself attended to all first year entrants before passing them on to his assistants. This personal touch stood out in contrast to the ministrations of form and set masters ... whose task it was to urge one on to say farewell as soon as possible on promotion to a higher form.' Ivimey gave lessons in his 'cramped quarters above the porter's lodge' into which he 'somehow squeezed his massive form and a grand piano'.

In the Bradleian he gave a course on the great classical composers accompanied by gramophone recordings, and 'enlivened by his own disciplined rendering of extracts on the piano'. He also composed the music 'in a Sullivan style' for *The Headmistress*, a school operetta written by the housemaster, Charles Boughey.

Ivimey was not just a teacher of music.

> As a reward for the extra practices the treble choir had to attend, he gave us an afternoon outing to Avebury in a horse brake. Most of us had to crowd onto the off-side seat to balance the large figure of our conductor on the other. The slow amble of horse travel gave him plenty of time to introduce us to the mystery of the enormous man-made mound of Silbury Hill.... Pompous he may have been but his kindly manner led us to listen to his every word.

£4,000 of the cost of the Memorial Hall was contributed by Herbert Leaf, a member of Council. Leaf had by this time spent three periods as a master at Marlborough, the first under Bell. He was probably the college's greatest benefactor. His contribution to the Memorial Hall was merely what was left from the £30,000 he had given so that electric lighting could be installed throughout the College.

Council had agreed in principle to this civilising innovation in May 1922, Leaf had promised the money next month and by February 1923 the wiring had been completed. That November the Council signed an agreement under which the *college* would supply electricity to Marlborough town. For many years it continued to do so, from a generator which stood behind Newton's new laundry in Pewsey Road. (The latter had replaced Blore's original laundry, as part of the plan for the Memorial Hall.)

Leaf lived 'in some state' at No 1 the Green, where he was the most available Member of Council when a signature was needed. Howard Lansley, a junior accounts clerk (who later became Mayor of Marlborough), remembered going on these errands 'with some trepidation.... But he [Leaf] was not really a frightening person. He was short, fairly plump with a ruddy face with a white trimmed Van

Dyke beard. One was shown into his drawing-room ... and he talked quietly as he was signing.' Leaf also paid for the Rose Garden, in memory of his wife, Rose, and when he died in 1936 his bequest to the college was used to build the Leaf Block of classrooms.

If Norwood had some sympathy for non-athletic boys, he believed in healthy exercise. He initiated 'the experiment of having about twenty minutes of Swedish drill exercises in mid morning in house squads in Court to sharpen our wits' (Hayward). He also believed that the school had responsibilities towards less privileged sections of society. *The Marlburian* of June 1920 carried an appeal from the Master for support for a town Institute. In Marlborough, he wrote, 'there is very little provided at present for the young men and women of the place ... the town has subscribed £500, the college has added £100, and a site and premises has been purchased in Kingsbury Street. Here we hope to provide a canteen, reading-room and small library, rooms for men and women's societies, a billiard room, a hall for recreations, lectures, and concerts and baths for men and women.' He asked members of the school to contribute towards the £2,000 all this would cost. 'For the sake of old associations', he added, 'we do not wish to sever connection with the Tottenham Mission; we shall continue to support it, though less liberally than hitherto.'

Marlborough's Tottenham Mission had been founded 40 years earlier at the start of the 1880s, at a time when the Anglican Church felt that it should give as much attention to shepherding the heathen of England's vast working-class suburbs as it gave to converting Africans, Indians and Eskimos (as one Old Marlburian attempted in Lapland). Various schools had already established English missions, and it was the examples of Winchester in 1876 and Eton soon afterwards which inspired an Old Marlburian, the Revd Henry Walsham How, to suggest that Marlborough should do something similar. The following month (November 1880) both the school's Sixth Form and a meeting of masters approved the plan and in December a meeting in the Bradleian chaired by the Senior Prefect agreed to raise money to pay a stipend of 'say £150' to a mission clergyman.

Early next year (February 1881) the Master announced that £50 had been raised, but 'it remained to find a fit man, if possible an Old Marlburian'. Soon afterwards the Church authorities assigned to Marlborough a district in the parish of Tottenham. Here there was church accommodation for only 4,000, but already a population of 30,000 which was expected to expand to 180,000 as more and more houses were built for workers who would use the new Great Eastern station at Enfield to travel to work in London.

By July the Revd E. Bailey Churchill had been appointed Missioner, but he was, in Bell's words, 'unsuited for the task', with the result that 'the mission was . . . in danger of shipwreck'. In March 1883 he was succeeded by Edward Noel Smith, Old Marlburian, brother of that most loyal Marlburian, Reginald Bosworth Smith, for this reason known as 'Little Bos'. (It was 'Bos' who might have been Master instead of Bell, if only he had been in holy orders.)

Little Bos and the Tottenham Mission are a single subject. For just over 25 years he devoted his life to it, before dying, aged only 48, of appendicitis. 'A great beggar he was,' an obituary said. His begging produced five buildings at Tottenham. First came the church, consecrated in 1887, to which Marlborough contributed £4,400 of the

St Mary's, Tottenham, in the 1930s.

total cost of £10,000. Two years later came the vicarage, and in 1891 Stoneley South, a mission building in the poorest part of the parish. A parish it had become, once it had its own church, and Marlborough's contribution then went towards the stipend of its curate. In 1899 a working man's club was built, and finally, in 1907, the Marlborough Boys' Hall was opened to serve as a Sunday School and the headquarters of the Church Lads' Brigade.

The school contributed men as well as money. Old Marlburians who worked at the mission included Robert Fisher, later a West African missionary, Geoffrey Evans, killed in the First World War, and Arthur Thomas, son of Bursar Thomas. Parties of prefects from Marlborough made regular visits to Tottenham at Christmas. In return Noel Smith visited Marlborough. In 1883 he gave a well-attended meeting 'an interesting address, richly stored with humorous anecdotes of his past year's work'. He now had Sunday congregations of 250 in the morning and 400 in the evening, as well as a choir. 'Among the most marked of the civilising effects of the Mission had been the reformation in manners and mode of dress he had succeeded in introducing among the factory girls.'

To Marlborough came parties of lads from Tottenham, and on 7 July 1912 Sorley had been the escort of one such party. To his parents he wrote:

> Some were completely mummified and dazed, as if being led about in another world, but most were exceptionally lively and interesting – and oh! their intelligence! I took a couple up to the Museum, and they turned out to be disappointed Darwins. The amount I learned from them was simply stupendous.... They had twenty thousand humorous stories about the doings of toads and bugs; there wasn't a shell for which they couldn't give the Latin name. They were simply brim full of information and delighted to find someone to whom they could impart it. Others were earnest devotees of the Mission ... one was 'very fond of pretty poetry' ... And one had a sister in the service of the Duke of Marlborough, whom she fondly believed reigned over this part of the world. And a few – poor fellows – in clothes as old as themselves, would not talk a word, but they ate heartily and, I think, enjoyed themselves.

The First World War had more or less ended Marlborough's connections with the Tottenham Mission even before Norwood's suggestion that the school should contribute instead to a town institute. Two years later he promoted a new idea: that 50 boys from Swindon elementary schools should come to Marlborough in the summer holidays to camp with a number of Marlborough boys. In March he put this to A. E. Bullock, the Swindon headmaster who became the Marlborough – Swindon Camp-Club secretary, and that August the first Swindon boys came and camped with ten Marlburians. One of these was Henry Brooke (the future Home Secretary, who 50 years later became Marlborough's first lay chairman of the Council). 'Will any of us ever regret that we had that experience?' Brooke wrote. 'All my life I shall be grateful for it.'

During the camp there were daily services in the Chapel but, unlike the Tottenham Mission, its chief purpose was social, rather than religious. The idea, Bullock believed, had come from Marlborough masters who had served in the War and who thought that 'many of the troubles of the country can only be solved by better understanding between all classes of the community, and the way to find the other fellow's point of view is to live with him on equal terms, for a while'. The master responsible for the idea was in fact Henry Flecker, brother of the poet, James Elroy Flecker. At camp the boys were divided into so-called houses, ten Swindon boys and two Marlburians in each, and spent most of their time playing competitive cricket and football. From 1924 to 1939 there were camps each year at Marlborough.

And at Swindon a mission-style club was soon established, and expanded so quickly that it had to move from building to building, ending in offices next to the Great Western Railway station. Here typical boys' club activities went on, from ping-pong and billiards to gymnastics and amateur dramatics. Throughout the inter-war years club teams played soccer matches with Marlborough houses. Because Swindon was close, Marlborough boys were able to have much closer contact with the Swindon Club than they ever had with the Tottenham Mission. Three to four hundred club and Marlborough boys would attend the annual December reunion teas.

The Club held its first post-war camp in 1948, and survived for a while. In the 1950s club boys took part in the restoration of Castle Farm (see below). But in the 1960s, together with Swindon's cloth-cap working-class, it gradually withered away.

Perhaps the best aspect of Marlborough under Norwood was its masters. George White, an Irish boy who later became headmaster of St Columbus College, believed that they differed from those of other schools by being 'on easier and more friendly terms with the boys'. He picked out in particular Alec Gidney, Betjeman's old enemy, 'whose humourless personality and reverberating tones made him an exquisite comic object for imitation': and another classicist, George Sargeaunt. When a boy 'was faced with a Greek phrase meaning literally "the

wrapping round the private parts", Sargeaunt with an expressionless face said, "Say *loin-cloth* – that covers the whole thing". As we with difficulty suppressed our laughter he looked at us with no change of expression, but I knew he was getting from the situation an amusement all the more intense for his concealment of it.'

Norwood himself, however, dominated the school. He was, White wrote, 'an impressive and eloquent rock, immensely able and full of moral fervour. Much later I discovered that he was not quite perfect . . . but at the time I simply felt that as long as he was there nothing could go really wrong, and when at the end of 1925 he told us that he was leaving to go to Harrow the ground beneath my feet seemed to be disintegrating.'

Gates and Court in Norwood's time. The old Dining Hall, in the far right-hand corner of Court, was replaced in the 1960s. The trees went at the same time. The occasion depicted is possibly the start of the autumn term.

145

10

BOY, BEAK AND MASTER

1926–1939

T HE NEW MASTER, George Turner, was chosen by the Council
from ten applicants, but not before 'prolonged discussion' and the
defeat of a motion by the Bishop of Winchester proposing an
adjournment for further enquiries. He was the first Master to be
appointed from Common Room.

Many years later, when Turner was visiting Marlborough on leave
from his subsequent position as Principal of Makerere College, Uganda,
he met a parent in Court who suggested to him that in Africa 'they must
need sturdy young Britons to help them build the country. Tilting his
head on one side, Turner remarked distantly, "Well, they do . . . and
they don't".' Just as Turner was to prove an imperialist of a new sort,
so he was to be a new sort of Master.

Not that he had failed to serve courageously throughout the War. It
was generally believed that he had won his MC when he captured single-
handed a group of Germans by telling them, 'Come along with me'. He
had later commanded Marlborough's Corps – and recalled an occasion
when, 'after an eloquent lecture on such homely subjects as the care of
feet on the march . . .' he found a boy's notebook with the title, 'Major
Turner on the Art of Killing'.

Though he was a small man, 'yet there was a dignity and a sort of
nobility about his bearing which none could deny', Kenneth Carey, Old
Marlburian Bishop of Edinburgh, remembered. 'There was, too, a
fastidiousness about his clothes, his manners, and his general way of
living which gave his whole life the sort of proportion which only great
good taste and great manners can supply. His silences were the most

George Charlewood Turner in the Lodge garden.

formidable thing I have ever known. . . .' 'His gaze', another Old Marlburian remembered, 'had a disconcerting way of travelling through one and out the other side.'

His manner was paralleled by his home life at the Lodge. As a bachelor, he lived there with his sister and mother, 'a little old lady in black'. The same Old Marlburian remembered being entertained to tea there as a new boy, the two ladies sitting one at each end of the large dining-table. Presently, 'overcome by the formality . . . the boy next to me suddenly hid his face by turning it into mine, his features convulsed with soundless hysteria. Appalled, I stared past him fixedly at the Master's mother, chewing my piece of cake as solemnly as an owl, until the boy recovered himself.'

His mother alone could dominate Turner. 'George, fetch the sugar,' and the Master would fetch it. Michael O'Regan – son of the history teacher, Pat O'Regan – remembered an occasion at the Lodge when the members of a visiting team from Harrow were behaving in brash, Harrovian style, and Turner's mother suddenly appeared at the head of the stairs. Without saying a word she restored good manners.

Though Turner, like his mother, could impose his authority, other aspects of his character were more important for the school. When a housemaster reported an illicit wine party, Turner observed, 'On occasions such as these I wish I were like some of those splendid old predecessors of mine, all covered with hair and indignation.' He added, 'and such inferior claret'.

Turner was no more enthusiastic about Marlborough's athleticism than Fletcher had been. In his first sermon as Master he said that sometimes his eyes strayed away from the match he was watching 'to the sunset dying away over the Kennet – for that is a sight which will remain to you long after the sound of the cheering has died away'.

> He was never angry, [George White wrote] and all exaggerated displays of emotion were to him distasteful or ludicrous.... He shunned action for action's sake, never feeling impelled to bustle about in order to convince himself and others that he was doing his job.... Once when I was travelling with him on a ship I remarked that it was very pleasant sitting there with nothing that had to be done. He replied, 'Ah yes, but to get the full flavour of idleness there should be a great many things that one ought to be doing. Sometimes when I have a great deal to do I sit down and do nothing for two or three hours.' ... One of the most remarkable things about his professional life, was ... his freedom from conventional ideas. This man, who came to the Mastership of Marlborough with no school experience elsewhere, having been both a boy and assistant master there, carried out in the school changes which amounted to a civilising revolution.

'He believed intensely in allowing boys to develop along their own lines,' Robert Birley wrote. Turner had already shown this by defending Betjeman, Blunt, MacNeice and their aesthete friends. Successors like Bernard Spencer continued their conflict with the school hearties. 'I have a copy of [*The Heretick*] before me now', Turner wrote forty years later, 'and find it more to my taste than much that I have since read in school magazines. It is rather arrogant and a trifle cynical, and it lacks the fine compassion of Charles Sorley's 'A Tale of Two Careers'; but its producers ... were talented boys who felt keenly the lack of interest at Marlborough in the things they cared for most.'

Eventually, one Sunday in 1928 there occurred the notorious swimming-pool affair.

We gave a party that evening to the prefects in the Lodge garden. I noticed that they drifted into two groups and that there was tension in the air. Later enquiry disclosed a sad incident. Some of the prefects had decided that certain boys who seemed to give themselves airs as superior persons needed to be suppressed: so they had caught some of these after chapel and thrown them into the bathing-place, Sunday clothes and all, from the roof of the shed. But other prefects had disapproved and one of them, James Mason

The bathing-place in 1948, much as it was in Turner's day. The flat roof on the left was the scene of the prefects' incident when James Mason threw a fellow prefect into the pool. Bathing in the nude was the regular practice until the advent of girls in 1968.

U Dormitory in C House,
1948, in the days of water-
fagging. Chamber pots
(beneath wash-stands) too!

(later famous on the screen), had pushed in one of the throwers-in,
white tie and all. Hence the grouping in my garden. This affair,
of which we all felt rather ashamed, was a *reductio ad absurdum* of
the war between 'athletes' and 'aesthetes', and I think it helped the
growth of some mutual tolerance and respect. It all seems rather
petty now, but how worrying it was at the time.

Two of Turner's reforms epitomise his civilising influence. Ahead of
all other major boarding-schools he abolished personal fagging. Fags
were still required to perform duties which benefited their house or their
fellow boys. Thus water-fags still carried jugs of hot water from
basements to dormitory basins for general use, and time fags called out
the time every half minute as 7.00 a.m. approached. But fags no longer
polished prefects' Corps boots or pressed their trousers.

Still more symbolically, Turner had that most notorious of the
school's buildings, Upper School, demolished. For his first ten years it
had remained a barbarous place, even though hot-water pipes along one
wall and two stoves along another replaced the old open fires. In the
summer of 1931 it was the setting of a riot. Unlike the spontaneous
outbreak which Fisher quelled 20 years earlier, this was premeditated.
'All in-college was aware the riot was scheduled to take place,' the boy,

Cecil Rogers, wrote, 'except the powers-that-were who were taken by surprise.' But the exact cause, and the consequences, if any, remain obscure.

When Upper School went, most of the site became the grass plot it remains today, though out of one end a new study block was built. This is now part of New Court (girls) House. 'Upper School', meaning the 200 junior boys of in-college houses, was not, however, abolished. These boys were given a new day-room in New Court, the old north and east wings of the Castle Inn's stables. New Court now became New Upper School and remained so for another 30 years. It was an improvement on Blore's icy barn, but confining so many junior boys in one room remained unsatisfactory, and the fact that it was L-shaped made keeping order even more of a problem.

Here and elsewhere, the maintaining of order remained largely the responsibility of the school's prefects. Year after year Turner thanked them in his Prize Day speeches, and on the whole the arrangement worked well. A House was an exception. Here, where juniors still spent their first three terms, new boys were tyrannised by third-term boys. In the 1930s its rituals had become standardised. Two weeks after they arrived they underwent an examination on the school's customs, prominent boys and masters. They would be asked, 'How many masters are there?' (Answer: one Master, the others being housemasters or beaks); or 'What is the Turret and Testicle?' (Answer: the Castle and

New Court in 1938, just after demolition of the old Upper School. The low wall surrounding the lawn marks the line of the walls removed. The building beyond is a study block formed out of the far end of Upper School, now part of New Court House.

151

The new Upper School (drawn in 1948) was used from 1937 to 1969. The L-shaped room was formed out of the ground floor of the old stable block.

Ball Hotel in the High Street). They would have to know the elaborate rules about dress which included the number of jacket buttons boys of various seniorities could leave undone (the more, the more senior), and the colour and style of the trousers which they might wear (dark grey with narrow legs as a junior, brightening to almost white Oxford bags with legs up to 22 inches in diameter as a blood).

They would also be questioned on the school's vocabulary. Though Marlborough's did not include the sort of words with middle-English derivations preserved in Eton's or Winchester's vocabularies, by this time it contained words which had been in use for 80 years ('bolly' for pudding, 'oiler' for waiter). Some were obviously derived from their meanings ('sweat' for a cross-country run; 'fag day' for a day with afternoon school). Others were merely distortions: 'congregagger-pragger' for congregational hymn practice.

Others again referred specifically to A-House practices. An A-House senior could tell a 'new bug' to 'turf ten': distance himself by ten feet; or could punish him with a number of 'basements'. At this time the building's central well extended from basement to roof, and one 'basement' meant running down the stairs from the ground floor to the basement and up again. 'The normal infliction was ten basements', Mark Moore remembered, 'and one's tormentor would stand at the top counting the seconds to make sure there was no slacking.'

152

Near the end of a junior boy's first term came initiation ceremonies, one of them known as 'Running the Gauntlet'.

> Our terror [remembered Robin Swann, son of the great athlete, the Revd Sidney Swann] was heightened by not being told what it entailed. Came the evening. All new boys were herded into a room at one end of the long wide corridor, stripped naked and told we had to run up the corridor one by one between two lines of old hands. I had visions of arriving at the far end lashed to pieces and pouring blood ... visions which were powerfully enhanced, for us still waiting, by the sounds of leather on flesh and shrieks of anguish from those ... already half way up the corridor.... I thought 'Come on: there's sure to be a Nurse around someplace, with iodine. Let's go.' I dashed for the corridor and sprinted. The 2nd and 3rd termers, lined up on both sides, each carried a pair of leather-soled slippers which they were lashing together as noisily as possible, simultaneously letting out shrieks of anguish.... I kept sprinting.... Of a sudden, I realised I was untouched. Another 4 yards and I was safe. All the naked runners were in the room at the end. Cowed. Sweating profusely. Not a scratch between us, but feeling no end of fools.

In the school as a whole, however, bullying became rare in Turner's time, and in other ways life contrasted dramatically with earlier days. Lawrence Waddy, later headmaster of Tonbridge School, remembered that 'Every day for six years I ate all I could get, which was plenty: a cooked breakfast, two helpings of two courses at lunch, tea and "hallers" [large, hard biscuits] at 4, and a high tea at 6.'

In the outside world others were less well fed in these depression years, and in 1932 a group from the school, led by a boy, Michael McAlpine, began to help the local unemployed. At Swindon they acquired and organised 120 allotments, providing a hut for the users; at Marlborough they arranged 'games, lectures, a library, and carpentry and cobbling' for the unemployed. 'I think this effort', the Master said on Prize Day, 'gives some answer to those who denounce our schools as complacent homes of privilege.'

The depression also affected Marlborough parents. 'I know well', Turner said, 'the great sacrifice many parents are making.... Undoubtedly the most satisfactory step would be a considerable reduction in school fees all round: but ... in an unendowed school of nearly 750 boys quite a moderate general reduction ... would absorb the whole of the working balance upon which we depend.... We decided therefore, for this difficult year to aim rather at offering more considerable assistance where it was most needed.' To provide this the Council had established a special fund.

In spite of the slump, the school continued to build, in particular to provide what it most needed: proper science laboratories. In 1932 the Council rejected Newton's first plan for these as 'too expensive and not big enough for possible expansion. I went to him,' Turner continued, 'with the sort of request that is familiar to architects – I asked for more accommodation for less money. I told him that the building in my mind's eye was not so much an academic block ... as an elegant factory.' The result was the science block, hardly elegant by today's standards but a classic of its time, one of the first buildings to use shuttered concrete, and now officially listed.

The realisation of Turner's dream of an 'elegant factory', designed by W. G. Newton, an Old Marlburian, and completed in 1933.

The same year, 1933, the school launched a Centenary Fund appeal, in preparation for the year 1943. 'A centenary occurs but once in a hundred years,' Turner explained, and it should be celebrated by giving the school 'something more than strict necessity demands'. Precisely how the fund would be used was left for a meeting of subscribers to decide in 1943.

The science block was built towards the end of the time during which Ashley Gordon Lowndes taught biology at Marlborough (1921–38), years in which he produced a generation of scientists which few schools can match. Best known were Sir Peter Medawar, winner of the Nobel Prize for Medicine in 1960 (for his work on the immune-response system), Sir Arthur Bell, gynaecologist to the Royal Family, and Francis

154

Camps, professor of forensic medicine, but a dozen others rose to the top in their fields.

Tubby Lowndes was a barrel-shaped man, who would address his pupils in West Country style, 'Now, my zun ...'. John Cloudsley-Thompson, Professor of Biology at Birkbeck College, explorer of the Sahara, remembered him as 'terrifying', but at the same time 'always fair, very kind-hearted and a magnificent teacher ... he never sent people "with a note to their Housemasters" (which meant they would get the cane) ... His worst punishment was to make one come in after lunch, be given two earthworms and told to dissect out their ovaries – you still had a chance if you missed one. It did not take long once you had acquired the knack but, if you made a mistake, you could spend hours in fruitless searching. It taught us a great deal about careful dissecting.... I am well aware of the enormous debt that I owe him for directing my studies so well at their outset.'

At one point Lowndes's teaching overlapped another of Marlborough's enterprises of the 1930s, when a paper by his pupil, Peter Moore, entitled *The Genus Micraster around Marlborough* – of remarkable maturity for a schoolboy – was published by the Marlborough Press. The founder of this private printing press was an Australian Rhodes scholar, Brian Hone, who was appointed to Marlborough in 1933 as an English master. Hone's intention was to give boys who were not particularly good at work or games and who hadn't any special musical or artistic talent, the chance to learn and perhaps excel at a craft. He also wanted to show that he could do something besides play cricket – he had played for Cambridge for three years, captaining the side in the third, and at Marlborough he was responsible for cricket. Turner approved of the idea of a Marlborough press and gave Hone £100 to buy equipment. Hone only discovered later that this was a gift from Turner personally, not from the school.

During the Christmas holidays of 1933–4 Hone worked in Oxford at the Shakespeare Head Press and when he returned established Marlborough's press in some old huts on the present armoury site. Soon after its foundation the press amalgamated with a private press which had been started by two boys of the school, Dick Maurice, a son of one of those ten Maurice brothers of Canon Bell's time, and James Elverson. In Elverson's parents' home the two ran the Green Street Press, which did local jobbing work. Maurice was the earliest Marlburian to set out on a printing career as a result of his printing experience at Marlborough – though in fact he became a well-known Marlborough doctor. Many other boys from the Press, however, became printers or publishers, including L. John Randle, owner/manager of the Whittington Press, which prints high-quality limited editions; and Richard Russell, of the Oxford University Press, who published a history of the Marlborough College Press to celebrate its fiftieth anniversary.

In those 50 years it had produced a number of fine items, now much valued by collectors, one of them, designed and set by Russell himself, *The Marlborough Litany* (1949). This work, printed in black, red and blue, led to a disagreement with Archbishop Fisher, who considered that the word 'Marlborough' should not form part of the title of a part of the Prayer Book and refused to buy a copy. It was the archbishop's loss, wrote Russell; Morocco-bound copies were originally sold for £3.12s. 6d. In 1980 Russell was offered £300 for his own copy.

Among the Press's more enterprising pieces of ephemera were cricket score-cards for school matches, printed in the pavilion loft, brought up to date by a telephone line to the scorebox. Hone was later knighted for his services to education in Australia, where he became headmaster of Cranbrook, Sydney, and later of Melbourne Grammar.

The Press continued to flourish after Hone had left. One inspiring master to take charge was Edward Walters (1942–6). According to Russell, Walters was 'a gentle person, not born to be a school-master', but his style 'is stamped through the work of that golden era'. In 1972 the Press produced *The Marlborough Anthology* which included poems by Sassoon, Sorley, MacNeice and Betjeman. R. A. Butler, the Marlburian whose Act of Parliament of 1944 had more influence on English education than any other this century, wrote the introduction.

When cricket was under Hone's control it ceased to be compulsory. This was part of a general liberalising of games, in the form of a move away from the three 'major games', Rugby, hockey and cricket. All of these had been compulsory for all boys, but now in summer tennis was allowed, and also athletics, as these had been moved from the Lent to the summer term. Since then, fives, rackets, gymnastics, golf and swimming have all been accepted as alternatives to the major games, but games of some sort are still compulsory on at least two afternoons a week.

In 1936 the school lost an institution almost as immemorial as Upper School when Gate-Sergeant Sheppard retired. Percy Sheppard had come to Marlborough to work in the laundry when he was 18. In 1902 he and his first wife had been called to the Steward's office to be told that they had been 'chosen for the Porter's Lodge'. In 1918 Sheppard's first wife died, but in 1923 he married a dormitory maid from Field House. Many years later Mrs Hulbert (as she had then become) remembered life with Sheppard at the Porter's Lodge.

In term time it was hard. Twenty-four times a day Sheppard would

Gate-Sergeant Sheppard's autographed copy of his photograph in *The Marlburian* marking his retirement after 34 years living in the Porter's Lodge.

climb to their bedroom to reach the bell-pull and ring the school bell. Weekly the two of them would clean the whole Chapel. 'Start on Wednesday. I had someone to scrub the chancel stone slabs on Fridays.... When we finished we were both proud of it. All books straight. At different times we changed the colours of the altar frontals and bookmarks. I also saw that all the linen was clean.'

In the holidays, however, the college servants emerged as if from underground, to lead a communal life of their own. 'There were the Servants' Cricket Club. Sheppard was very keen on cricket and was

Captain and Secretary for over 20 years.... Also there were away matches such as Eton, Winchester and Oxford and that gave myself and others a chance to look over the colleges. In the summer holidays we had our annual outing to the sea. This we paid for and I remember our first when [a number of] 32-seater charabancs left the courtyard. Sheppard collected the money and this amounted to £1,000. The end of the Christmas term we were given a dinner in dining-hall and a service in Chapel. We all appreciated being waited on by the masters.'

Mark Moore remembered a less dignified experience for Sheppard. Daily, in dark-blue, bell-shaped, waistless uniform, he would control boys as they crossed the Bath Road at mid-morning break, for the PT started by Norwood. 'There came a day when the surge of pupils was too great and when the crowd thinned he was seen to be on his back in the middle of the road, and his shape decreed that he might stay there indefinitely ... the incident did not pass unnoticed by the authorities although it was never possible to fix the blame.'

When Turner went on sabbatical in 1937 Harold Cresswell Brentnall became Acting Master. Brentnall, together with Clement Carter (both appointed by Fletcher) were responsible at Marlborough for a major expansion of geography into human and economic areas, which set a pattern that was widely followed. It was not until after the Second World War, for example, that geography was considered a subject worth teaching at all at Winchester. Together Brentnall and Carter wrote *The Marlborough Country*, Brentnall supplying the historical, Carter the geographical material. Brentnall was also co-author of the 1923 history of Marlborough, a disappointing book since it was for the most part merely an updated version of Bradley's 1893 history.

Turner had a clear idea of his duties as a headmaster. In 1954 he told the Headmasters' Conference of Australia:

> Beyond all directive and administrative duties, our obligation is one of friendship and encouragement. We must discover and use in our colleagues many gifts and aptitudes which we lack ourselves. We must be about the place, not with a censorious but with an observant eye: and we must use every convenient chance for a casual word with the boys and others whom we happen to meet in our potterings. We must sometimes address the school as a whole: let it not be too often or for too long, lest our voice becomes soporific.

His own evening potterings would take the form of calling unannounced on some housemaster with a bottle of whisky in his pocket.

Turner's real achievement was to influence the whole tone of life at Marlborough. By the time he left, for example, many of the more barbaric practices in A House had been abolished. If Marlborough in 1926 had been one of the rougher and more old-fashioned schools, by 1939 he had made it one of the more civilised.

To parents and boys Turner seemed an assured and self-sufficient character. His letters from Uganda (where he turned the high school for African boys which Makerere had been when he arrived into a university with a world reputation) show how much he had depended at Marlborough on a few senior masters, in particular on Charles Matthews, chaplain from 1930 to 1938. To Matthews he wrote, 'when you had left and Davenport and Sargeaunt were gone I had no older ... man who could give me support similar to that which I got from you three. For dearly as I love Robbie [Alan Robson] and Brentnall and Becher, Gidney too (I think), they have all such deep reserve that friendship with them is always a little lop-sided.'

Even as a boy, Turner had liked to sing. 'My only memory of him as Senior Prefect', Arthur Pelly wrote, 'was his persistence in singing 'I shot an arrow into the air/It fell to earth I know not where.' He had a good voice, but ... I thought he might occasionally sing something else.'

As an assistant master he sang the lead in the school's operetta, *The Headmistress*. His favourite song was 'Lord Randall', though significantly he sang the American version in which the boy is fed poisoned fish by his sweetheart, *not* his mother.

At the conclusion of Turner's last concert as Master he was persuaded to go on to the stage alone and sing the school song, 'Sweats'. 'This he sang most feelingly, with the school supplying the chorus. At the end when he left, with his party, along the ambulatory of the Memorial Hall, ... the whole school, on their feet, spontaneously broke into waves and waves of unrestrained cheering.'

Old Marlburian bishops at the Lambeth Conference, 1930, including St J. B. Wynne Willson (seated far left), Bishop of Bath and Wells and former Master; A. F. Winnington-Ingram (seated 2nd from right), Bishop of London, Dean of Chapels Royal (1901–59); and J. O. Feetham (standing 3rd from right), Bush Brother, Bishop of North Queensland (1913–47) and former pupil – Marlborough's only Saint.

11

A DIFFERENT WAR

1939–1952

By 1938 Turner, like many other people, expected war. Marlborough, he realised, with its extensive and not over-used buildings, in one of the safer parts of southern England, was certain to be required in any evacuation from London. Rather than leave to chance the guests whom the school would have to receive he decided to encourage a suitable institution and on 16 December that year wrote to Francis Dale, headmaster of the City of London School, with a provisional offer.

'The most important point seems to me to be that you should have some clear understanding with the Home Office, that you would have first claim upon billets in Marlborough. If that were guaranteed I think that we for our part ought to go ahead and see what we can do for you.'

Francis Richard Dale, DSO, a tall, scholarly man in his mid-fifties, had been the City of London's headmaster for some ten years. One of his boys, Kingsley Amis, wrote of him that he was 'a classical scholar in the best old style.... When the BBC ... wanted someone to read Homer aloud on the Third Programme, they chose him. He was human, too. If ever a kind of man vanished for good, his did.' Dale's school, an ancient foundation, at this time 'occupied a large, rather oppressively dignified building on the Victoria Embankment. It had lots of corridors and a vast agrophobic playground filled with self-possessed boys in black coats and striped trousers.'

As Turner's letter made clear, accommodating Dale's boys was the problem. On the same day, he wrote to the Mayor of Marlborough 'we could not possibly arrange for the boarding of some 700 extra boys, and that is where my acceptance of the Headmaster's proposal must depend upon your own arrangements in the borough and your consent.'

Three weeks later the Mayor, James Duck, told Turner that the members of his General Purpose Committee 'were all quite in accord to fall into line with any arrangement which could be come to ... on the matter of billeting the boys'. During the following months the two schools reached agreement, and as war became increasingly likely, Dale explained the plan to his parents:

The Master and Governors of Marlborough Collge have agreed to admit this School to the use of their buildings and grounds in a time of emergency.

The buildings – class-rooms, laboratories etc. – will admit both Schools to work almost as usual.

Boys would sleep in billets in or near the Town – all visited already by the second master.... Camp-beds and blankets will be provided at Marlborough where necessary.

The Marlborough scheme seems as good as possible, and though parents have every right to stand out and make their own arrangements I hope none will.

Meanwhile Marlborough's new Master had been appointed. F. M. ('George') Heywood, son of the Bishop of Ely, a Cambridge Rugby blue and since then a master at Haileybury, was still aged only 29. His senior master, Brentnall, the historian and geographer, had been appointed seven years before Heywood was born. Arriving in April 1939, Heywood had had just one term in office before, in the middle of the summer holidays, the evacuation of London was ordered.

In London the boys of the City of London School were told what to bring with them, top of the list that symbol of the early war years, their civilian gas-mask in its little cardboard box. Next came 'a haversack ration', sufficient for a day. They would travel by train, starting at Blackfriars Station, changing at Ealing Broadway. In Wiltshire the Master and his staff waited for them at Savernake. They almost missed them. Just as their train was leaving, one of the London masters checked that it would stop at Savernake. Its first stop, he was told, was 'somewhere like Taunton or Exeter. So the resourceful enquirer', Heywood remembered (in his unpublished recollections of the war years) 'wrote out a message that the train must stop at Savernake Junction, attached it firmly to one of his shoes, and, as the train went through Reading Station, flung shoe and message accurately at a railway official on the nearest platform.'

The official contacted Savernake where the train was successfully stopped – but not before an earlier train had arrived there.

We had assembled a fleet of coaches and cars to meet the train [Heywood continued] and were waiting on the platform, outwardly calm, at the time when it was hoped that the train would arrive. We had not waited long when a train approached from the London direction. We braced ourselves as the train halted, and then were horrified to see several hundred mothers, with babies in arms, getting out. They had come from the Isle of Dogs and had no intention of going any further. We had no idea whether anyone was expecting them or where they were supposed to go: no one had come to meet them. Urgent telephone calls from the station to billeting officers eventually succeeded in establishing that the mothers and babies were to be housed in the Marlborough area but had not been expected that day.

Three days later war was declared. Like many other people, Heywood

City of London School notices. *Courtesy of The City of London School.*

City of London School.

BILLET RULES

1. TIMES.

SENIORS (14 years or over) except Prefects and Sub-Prefects :

In billets by 8 p.m.

Lights out 10 p.m.

(A limited number of VI. Form boys may need to work late. They must have the written permission of their Form Master.)

JUNIORS (under 14 years) :

In billets by 7 p.m.

(On Tuesday, Thursday, Saturday when tea is at 6.30, and on Sunday when tea is at 6.45, juniors must return to their billets immediately after tea.)

Lights out by 9 p.m. at latest.

(Young boys are expected to go to bed earlier at the discretion of the hostess.)

2. RETURNING TO BILLETS.

(a) Facilities are provided at the College for games, reading, writing, etc., and no boys need return to their billets in the morning except possibly to change for games.

They are forbidden to return except with the full approval of their hostesses, who are asked to let the Visiting Master know at once if this rule is broken.

(b) It is possible for nearly all boys to do preparation at school till 6.30 on Monday, Wednesday and Friday evenings if it is inconvenient for them to return to their billets earlier.

(c) No boy may visit another billet at any time except with the permission of the hostess in the house where the visit is made.

Sixth Form boys are allowed to visit another billet for work with another boy if the hostesses agree and if the Visiting Master has given written permission stating address and times.

Boys are not allowed to visit houses at any time where no boys or masters are billeted, except with the Visiting Master's written permission.

3. MEALS.

Meals are provided in College for all except Day Boys.

Hostesses are not asked to provide more than a hot drink, morning and evening, except when special arrangements have been made with parents.

4. GENERAL.

Boys are expected to look after themselves as much as possible. They should clean their own shoes and keep their rooms tidy.

They are expected to do what is asked of them in the houses in which they live. In bad weather they should change their outdoor shoes immediately they return.

It is important that boys should never miss Assembly at 8, or breakfast on Saturday or Sunday, unless they are sick. In case of sickness, a visit will be made without delay. If they are not visited, hostesses are asked to let the Visiting Master or the School Office at the College Tel. M. 367, know as soon as they can.

Smoking is not allowed in billets or anywhere else in term time. The Cinema is out of bounds.

Any complaints should be made to the Visiting Master as quickly as possible.

F. R. DALE,

Headmaster.

Visiting Master.....J. N. Wheeler............

Address......The Red House Cardigan Rd

MARLBOROUGH, 1940.

CITY OF LONDON SCHOOL

A.R.P.

INSTRUCTIONS TO BOYS
in the event of an Air-Raid Warning

A. IN SCHOOL HOURS

School hours—when whole school is together under the control of Masters. This includes **Meal** times, **Prayers** and **Chapel.**

SENIORS (*i.e.* Third Forms and above, excluding M 3B) :—

To Trenches. Follow your Master. Move in single file. Exit by **Main Gate** only.

Third and Fourth Forms enter Trenches at **lower end.**

Fifth and Sixth Forms enter Trenches at **top end.**

Move along till you reach the half-way flag.

Leaf Block.—Occupants of upper rooms leave by Masters' door and "C" **House** steps, and steps between "C" and "B" Houses.

Occupants of lower rooms leave by Boys' doors, path between Mound and Hall, and steps between "A" House and Chapel.

Science Blocks and Memorial Hall.—Move via Main Chapel steps to Main Gate.

JUNIORS (*i.e.* M 3 B, Second Forms, and below) :—

To North Block lower corridor. Move in **Silence.**

If **outside** North Block, enter by middle door.

If **inside** North Block, occupants of all rooms except 5 and 6, turn right and fill up the corridor, two deep, in order as Forms arrive ; 5 and 6 turn left. Keep together as Forms.

B. OUT OF SCHOOL HOURS

SENIORS AND JUNIORS ALIKE :—

If on the Games Field or on the School premises.—Go to Trenches or Hyde Lane.

If at Preshute.—Go to Preshute Sunken Lane.

If in the Town.—Go to nearest Public or Private Shelter.

If in Billets.—Do as your Hosts tell you.

C. IF A RAID TAKES PLACE WITHOUT WARNING go to ground floor of the building you are in. Keep away from windows.

D. AFTER AN ACTUAL RAID commencing between the beginning and the end of the School day, report back at School.

F. R. DALE,

Headmaster.

Boys of the City of London School working in the Adderley Library in 1941. *Courtesy of The City of London School.*

remembered what he was doing at 11 o'clock that Sunday morning when Chamberlain broadcast to the country that it was at war. He was standing in the uncarpeted, uncurtained drawing-room of the Master's Lodge, surrounded by packing-cases. When he had arrived five months earlier he had found a cook, five living-in maids, two gardeners and a chauffeur to attend to him, but also Turner's furniture, and this had only finally been removed a few days before.

Though it seemed at the time inconvenient that war had begun in the school holidays, Heywood later concluded that it was lucky. It was easier to obey police orders to have the whole college blacked out within 24 hours; and it gave the boys of the City of London School three weeks with the college to themselves to find their way about and establish a routine before they saw a Marlborough boy. The essence of this routine was simple: while the London school used the classrooms, Marlborough used the playing-fields and vice versa. The details were complicated and it was only the eighth version of the timetable that proved satisfactory. At lunch-time Marlborough ate first, then, after an interval the London boys. Here there was a difficulty of a different sort: the kitchen staff which the CLS had promised to bring never appeared and Marlborough's had to feed both schools.

For four years these arrangements worked surprisingly well – in some ways too well. The boys of the two schools took curiously little notice

163

of each other. It would be possible to read some Marlborough letters and diaries of the time without learning that the CLS was any nearer than the Thames Embankment. Heywood admitted that 'joint activities' were limited to 'debates, society meetings, concerts and of course inter-school matches'. Amis did not even remember these. 'After a time some host-like gesture, in the form of joint debates or even individual invitations to tea, might have been expected. None were made to my knowledge in the five terms I was at school at Marlborough.' Marlburians confirm this. John Loch remembered that until he left in 1941 'we had hardly anything to do with the School, indeed, we entirely ignored the London boys. To this day I am ashamed that we were not more hospitable.' In spite of this, many of the London boys developed a permanent affection for Marlborough and the Wiltshire countryside.

Some of the changes which war brought to the school were similar to those brought by the First World War. At once most of the young masters left, to be replaced by older, often inexperienced ones. Among those who came was the German Jew, Richard Fuchs, a distinguished expert in international law. Fuchs had been helped to escape from Germany by Kurt Hahn, headmaster of Gordonstoun, and Hahn persuaded Heywood to employ him. He had barely arrived at Marlborough when he was interned as an enemy alien. Old Marlburians helped to have him released and he taught German at Marlborough throughout the war.

Another who came briefly was the 50-year-old Hugh Lunn, better known as the writer Hugh Kingsmill. About the school Kingsmill wrote to his friend, Malcolm Muggeridge:

> The boys are so extraordinarily pleasant. I have never met such good manners, not in the least sophisticated and perfectly natural.... Several masters tell me that it is peculiar to this place, though I think it must in some degree be connected with the general change from the vulgar opulence and security of England thirty years ago to the dangers and uncertainties of the present. This change may not be felt much at Eton and Harrow, but it is probably felt here, at least by the older boys.

Later Kingsmill wrote, 'I like the boys as much as ever.... At the end of term concert the hundred and twenty ... who were leaving went on to the stage and sang the school songs and *Auld Lang Syne*. There was none of the emotionalism I have been accustomed to on these occasions. They all sang very cheerfully, no wallowing, or self-love.'

Other temporary masters included a Lithuanian, and a Yugoslav, Pavel

Popovic (who, as his credentials, produced a diplomatic passport signed by the King of Montenegro, complete with dangling seals on ribbons, and a degree from the University of Zurich in the design and construction of fortifications). When Popovic was called away to join the Yugoslav government-in-exile, his wife, Ida Elizabeth, took his place as a language teacher. She was the second woman ever to teach at Marlborough. Celia Stoner, who had arrived a year earlier, had been persuaded to come from the Royal School at Bath to teach French, which Heywood considered she did with great success – though he added enigmatically that she was also 'a bit of a surprise'.

In 1939, as in 1914, few boys over 18 stayed on. At the beginning of one Michaelmas term the head of the school was only 16. In spite of this it was only briefly, in 1940, when some boys had been shipped by their parents to America, that the school's numbers fell below 700.

When Germany invaded France in 1940, however, the school was affected in ways it had never been between 1914 and 1918. Boys recorded these in diaries, alongside the disastrous events of that year. On 10 May Bruce Hayllar wrote, 'Chamberlain resigns ... and a coalition government is being formed. Coalition a good thing, Churchill ??' On 16 May, 'We had a terrific argument in form about conscientious objectors ... we all got pretty het up.' On 29 May, 'Evacuation is in the air. Our LDV [Home Guard] has been allotted positions on the roof to defend Field House.' On 31 May, 'In spite of the gloom of this diary it must be definitely understood that we are going to win the war and

Local Defence Volunteers (later Home Guard), all members of C2 House. *Courtesy of the Revd B. S. Hayllar.*

that the British Empire is unbeatable!'; and on 3 July, 'There was a scare early this morning that the Germans were going to land near Tidworth and all day half the LDV have been going about in uniform with rifles on their backs.... Never before have boys been into school with rifles.'

Hayllar's personal contribution was to dig (and hoe) for vicotry, usually at Church Farm, Mildenhall. David West, future commander of the Corps, joined the LDV. On 2 June he wrote to his mother, 'Everything has been at a complete standstill this week while the LDV have been getting organised.' By 7 July he had been put in charge of a platoon and was spending three nights a week guarding road-blocks or the Armoury.

During that summer term Loch remembered spending nights on duty in the countryside around the road-block on the Bath Road which Littlefield boys were required to guard. 'I had never before slept out of doors, nor enjoyed the noises and smells of a hot summer night, and the experience, together with prospects of martial glory, was exhilarating.... I was disappointed that no Germans descended upon us. I remember lying in a hedge in Littlefield garden with my rifle pointing westwards down the Bath Road absolutely confident that successfully I could hold up a German advance towards the town.' Loch later joined the Parachute Regiment. Other boys found the experience of being 'totally alone on dark windy nights, as black as pitch' disagreeably 'eerie', and Peter Brown almost shot a cow which gave a Teutonic cough close ahead of him.

Alongside the Home Guard, the OTC continued to function, as it had throughout the years of peace. Perhaps strangely, at a time when there had been much pacifism in the country, it had become more or less compulsory, and even Betjeman had been a member – although he could not decide whether he disliked Corps or compulsory games more, and dreaded especially the 'awful days ... when there was a Corps parade first and then games afterwards'. He achieved an unexpected victory. 'I decided to join the Signal Section in order to avoid carrying a heavy rifle. By sheer long service I rose to the rank of 2nd Lieutenant and thus had higher rank than any captains or prefects in my house. At camp, which I could not avoid, the head of my house tried to have the tents commanded by house ranks, so that I was put under one of my own L/Cpls. But the CO over-ruled him on my appeal. This was my only success of note at Marlborough.'

Others enjoyed the Corps, even if they never considered it 'a military institution'. Michael Birley remembered the countryside around Marlborough to which field-days took him: 'The Downs near Rockley in the sun, festooned on one occasion by my neighbour's puttees:

The winners of the Ashburton Shield in 1935. A rare smile on E. H. Dodwell's face (right).

bracken in the forest, with figures creeping through it to avoid the umpires and to fraternise illegally with Wykehamists: shadows chasing over the Downs beyond Fyfield, as an irregular line of troops swept across to the Avebury – Kennet road . . . the great fusillade that always went off when "Cease Fire" sounded.' Birley also remembered an 'Inspection Day when a lot of us agreed to say "Going into the Church, sir" if the inspecting officer asked about our future careers. He seemed surprised, but could hardly show annoyance.'

Field-days, the annual camp, shooting and Certificate A were the central features of the Corps in those years. Cert A still ensured a commission in the Territorials without further examination and still involved passing tests in drill, weapon-training and map-reading, but these were less nominal than Sorley had found them in 1912, giving a boy training which was sometimes useful in surprising circumstances. In 1936 an Old Marlburian, fighting on the government side in the Spanish Civil War, 'found he was one of the only three men in Spain who knew how to work the Lewis guns supplied by the Russians – relics of the North Russia intervention of 1919'.

Shooting had remained important, and finally in 1935 the school repeated its success of 1874 by again winning the Ashburton Shield. Thomas Davison, Captain of the Eight, remembered mainly 'the *silence* in the bus coming back to Marlborough'; and 'the warm greetings from

The only other Marlborough shooting-team to win the Ashburton Shield, in 1874.

the Mayor when he received us on the Town Hall steps and from the townspeople as our open bus went slowly down the High Street behind the Town Band playing "See the conquering heroes come".' Davison received a letter of congratulations from a member of the 1873 eight, and many other Marlburians in Britain and all over the world sent messages.

The summer camps, in which as many as 3,000 cadets from different schools would take part, were sometimes at distant places. In 1929, 309 Marlburians went to Strensall in Yorkshire, travelling there in a train consisting only of dining-cars in which they ate a special meal with specially printed menu cards. An Old Marlburian, William Platt, was the camp's Commandant. Later, as General Platt, he was to command the allied troops which drove the Italians from their East African colonies. When war seemed close in 1939, there was no joint camp, but 200 of the Marlborough Corps marched the 27 miles to camp at Newbury, the band playing all the way, sleeping one night on straw in wayside barns.

Field-days against other schools, begun in 1885, had continued (except during the First World War), and until 1929 had always been followed by the Corps Brew in the town hall. Some were against Cheltenham, and some with Winchester, Wellington and Bradfield, but from 1933 onwards they were against Winchester only. In 1939 Marlborough captured Winchester's battalion headquarters. Marlborough's successes were often the result of its superior Signal Section, and though this had been founded in the same year as the first inter-school field-day and had always been effective, in the 1930s it became outstanding, largely as a result of the contribution made to it by the master, Arthur Raymond Pepin.

Pepin was by nature an enthusiast and from the mid-1920s his enthusiasm was especially directed towards wireless. In his classroom, where he taught geography, French, Latin, scripture and English, he had two huge sets and would suddenly look at his watch and stop the class because it was time to make contact with the far side of the world. His interest broadened into communication of every kind – passing messages across Court or the Memorial Hall by nose-tapping; using barbed wire, suitably insulated, as telephone cable – but wireless remained his passion; and in 1934 he was mainly responsible for founding the school's wireless society. It used a large hut on the site of the later physics laboratories, and obtained GPO licences to operate from both stationary and moving equipment. Two years later Pepin and the society produced their most famous apparatus; the 5-metre walkie-talkie set, the first of its kind.

That year it was tested on field-days (Mrs Pepin would bring the equipment in the Pepin MG), and the British army, to its credit, took

A. R. Pepin (arms folded) demonstrates his walkie-talkies. The boy with the wireless set is drilling a squad on the Eleven receiving their orders on their sets.

an almost instant interest, buying sets made at Marlborough for one of the battalions which took part in the 1936 Palestine Campaign. Later it sent a section of the Tank Corps to Marlborough to be shown how to communicate on the move. By 1938, 14 sets were being used by Marlborough on field-days. That year Pepin was awarded the MBE for his wireless work, and on 13 June the school had a half holiday in his honour.

When war broke out Pepin became the local Home Guard battalion's communications officer, and at the college led miles of telephone wire between buildings which were inside the 'tank island' that the town of Marlborough was supposed to form – part of the college lay outside this. Pepin's sets also used in 1940 when the Corps took part in a special wartime exercise: the driving of the deer of Savernake Forest into a deer park at Tottenham House. The plan was to form a gradually contracting human ring which would force the deer to go in the right direction, but the orders of the day included the reservation: 'No boy will resist the onslaught of a stag.' Heywood, who took a keen interest in the operation, admitted that some deer escaped by leaping over the advancing circle, but claimed that these were soon shot. In 1946, however, the boys of Hawtreys School had to make a second drive.

In the sketch (labels): RELIEF SLEEPING · RIFLE · CARTRIDGES (6) · ELECTRIC FIRE

A boy's sketch of the Home Guard Signals Room in the 'Royal Oak', frequently manned by College boys.

After the war Marlborough's signal section was granted the unique honour of being renamed the Royal Signals Troop. On this occasion (12 May 1967) an Old Marlburian, Maj.-Gen. P. E. M. Bradley CBE, DSO, performed the inauguration and among other Old Marlburians present were five Brigadiers, two Colonels and one Lieut.-Colonel, all serving with the Royal Corps of Signals. Alas, Pepin could not be there, and he died two years later.

From 1938 the Corps underwent significant changes. That year the Air Training Corps was formed, and in 1943 the RN Section. In 1940 the OTC itself became the JTC; and before the war ended the JTC had finally abandoned its knee-breeches and puttees in favour of battledress.

Meanwhile a total of 4,200 Old Marlburians served in the Second World War. And though there were never the same long, black-edged lists in *The Marlburian*, giving boys the sense that school was leading inevitably to death, it soon began to carry casualty lists, and a total of 415 Marlburians died. From the summer of 1940 it also carried tales of heroism. Again a few must stand for many. The action in which Eric Wilson earned his VC was part of the campaign to eject the Italians from Somalia. On 11 August 1940 his Somali machine-gunners 'inflicted such heavy casualties that the enemy, determined to put his guns out of action, brought up a pack battery to within 700 yards, and scored two direct hits through the loopholes of his defences, which, bursting within the post, wounded Captain Wilson in the right shoulder and in the left eye, several of his team being also wounded. His guns were blown off their stands, but he repaired and replaced them, and, regardless of his wounds, carried on, while his Somali Sergeant was killed beside him.

'On August 12th and 14th the enemy again concentrated field-artillery on Captain Wilson's guns, but he continued, with his wounds untended, to man them.

'On August 15th two of his machine-gunned posts were blown to pieces, yet Captain Wilson, now suffering from malaria in addition to wounds, still kept his post in action.'

Next day the Italians finally overran his post and he was reported dead, but two months later his parents learned that he had only been captured. He survived to send a son to Marlborough.

As in earlier wars, some Marlburians distinguished themselves in ways which required a special sort of adventurousness. Lieut.-Cdr. Nigel Clogstoun-Willmott, an RN navigation officer, had the idea for Combined Operations Pilotage Parties (COPP). In early days, before the value of these parties was recognised, they were forced to waterproof their equipment with naval-issue condoms, and to soak their sweaters and long-johns in periscope grease. The first beaches they reconnoitred were those of Rhodes, but the Rhodes landings were cancelled and it was only in November 1942 that Willmott was asked by Combined Operations Head Quarters to reconnoitre and mark beaches around Algiers and Oran for the invasion of North Africa. Two years later COPP units numbered 174 officers and men, most of them trained by Willmott, who would encourage them with slogans like 'People would rather die than think. Many of them do.' COPP parties played their most important part in the war by reconnoitring the Normandy beaches, using midget submarines in these heavily mined waters. In January 1944 members of one of Willmott's parties spent several days in France, marking and measuring landing beaches, though he was not allowed ashore himself because he knew too much about D-day plans. Willmott was awarded the DSO and the DSC and bar.

Patrick O'Regan (third son of Pat O'Regan) had an equally original war. He was always a nonconformist and at first as a pacifist served in the Royal Army Medical Corps, but by D-day he had joined SOE and was parachuted soon afterwards into southern France to help the French and Italian Resistance. High in the Alpes-Maritimes, he remembered leading 150 partisans 'rather effectively, I thought' in a defence of their position, then waking next morning to find that all but three had decided it was safer at home. 'After one or two attempts to get them to come up again by long-range insults I climbed down after them.' In April 1945 he and another officer accepted the surrender of the German armoured division based at the Castle of Stupinigi, Turin. Later his CO wrote of him, 'There are literally thousands of Italians and Frenchmen whose friendship and estimation of this country are built on the admirable image which Patrick O'Regan created for them.'

The boys at school had less severe problems to face, of which food was inevitably one. This caused a bizarre episode in the autumn of 1941 when A-House boys took part in an academic study of their diet. 'It coincided', according to one of them, Denys Hodson, 'with a particularly nasty run of porage [sic] made from oats which had started to foment, and ... potatoes ... which were black, and some very repulsive sausages.' Unfortunately the master who had organised the project, 'Bolly' Lamb, had forgotten to inform the school steward who resigned in protest and was replaced by a qualified dietician. 'There was an immediate improvement, and although no one could claim the food was marvellous during the war we were never again in danger of starvation or poisoning.'

There were other wartime discomforts. To one of his boys who had just left, Hubert Wylie wrote in May 1942:

> Then the college well went wrong, and for some days all drinking-water had to be boiled. We got on the town mains ... but ... the pressure is nearly twice as heavy as ours, and within a week both boilers had burst; so that there has been for ten days now no hot water for baths and washing up. I have had one bath in that time. We take turns to get into Field House baths which have their own heating system.

School uniform was affected when clothes were rationed. The black jacket and black cap disappeared, together with stiff collars on Sundays. Uniform was not restored until several years after the war, when the lovat tweed jackets were introduced, with matching trousers to make a Sunday suit.

The life of the school was more seriously dislocated by air-raid precautions and alarms. The precautions took the form of a school ARP with the Master at its head, and of designating the basements below A,

B and C houses and their connecting passages as shelters. These were to be used by the whole school in daytime and by in-college boys at night. The alarms were given by the public siren, but at night the boys were allowed to sleep on until the two duty ARP wardens decided that there was real danger and blew their whistles. Nevertheless, in-college boys spent many uncomfortable nights below ground, especially in the early war years.

And a number of night-time bombs did fall in the neighbourhood, including a stick of them which failed to explode in a field behind the school houses on the Bath Road. Next morning Heywood received an angry phone call from the farmer of the land: 'Tell your boys to come away from my bomb 'oles.' But the occasion on which the boys were in serious danger was in daytime.

> We were finishing lunch in the Dining Hall [Heywood remembered] and the CLS were waiting in Court to go in for their lunch. The sirens sounded and everyone was immediately ordered to go to their shelters. . . . As the last Marlburian emerged from Hall and Court was packed with hundreds of boys moving in various directions to their shelters, a solitary Heinkel, hardly more than two hundred feet up, lumbered slowly into view from the direction of Barton Farm and flew over Court with a gunner clearly visible at his weapon. Amid frantic yells from the staff, 'Get under cover', the crowds of boys stopped and gazed incredulously at this intruder, with a few loud guffaws, shouts and whistles let off towards it. For a dreadful second or two I had a vision of Court littered with corpses and wounded, but the gunner did not fire and the plane skimmed over the roof of C House and was gone. There were two sequels: the plane was shot down not much later (so I was told) and a member of Common Room earned a sort of immortality by asking a colleague what it meant when a plane had black crosses on it.

There was danger of another sort. Savernake Forest became an ammunition dump, and the Downs were used for military exercises with live ammunition. This left interesting souvenirs for enterprising boys to collect, and one brought home a live mortar-bomb which he proceeded to dismantle with a hacksaw in a classroom at the Priory, while some ten of his friends watched. Luckily only the detonator exploded, pitting his face with fragments but harming no one else. At once the Master told the assembled school that every souvenir of this sort was to be deposited at the Lodge by a given time, and that the owner of any found in a subsequent search 'would be expelled without any argument. By the stated time', Heywood continued, 'the floor of my secretary's office was covered with cartons and boxes full of rifle ammunition, grenades, mortar-bombs, anti-tank shells, sticks of high explosive and flares: it was horrifying. I rang up the police officer whose special job it was to deal with explosives and asked him to come at once with a van: he did so, and when I showed him what I had for him, he went white and visibly recoiled!' A boy found later with 100 rounds of rifle ammunition (which he claimed he needed for shooting rabbits in the holidays) was expelled, but taken, as a result of Heywood's intercession, by Sherborne.

The most memorable wartime intrusion on the school occurred when the Guards Armoured Division arrived unannounced one evening and asked to be accommodated. The Master protested that the school's buildings were in full use, but the liaison officer was unimpressed. Court soon filled with jeeps and armoured personnel carriers, and the Memorial Hall became the officers' mess. Here, next morning, when hymn practice was due to take place, Heywood found many officers still asleep on camp-beds in the aisles while others were being served breakfast on the stage. He was told later by an observer that 'as I said prayers knives and forks were motionless and mastication ceased', but during the hymn-singing the officers continued to eat heartily. Meanwhile other ranks were sleeping or waking in the school's classrooms where many remained during early lessons, but by the middle of the morning the last jeep had gone.

In 1941 the outcome of the war still seemed disturbingly uncertain. On 22 June Marcus Wheeler, a boy in Leslie Coggin's house, remembered '"Cogs" inviting us into his study to hear Winston Churchill's address to the nation following the Nazi invasion of USSR.... We sat on his floor in our dressing-gowns listening with rapt attention and wondering how it would all end.' Wheeler added that Coggin, who was housemaster of A House from 1938 to 1941, 'by his own attitudes and by the interest which he fostered in us in both domestic politics and world affairs, gave the lie utterly to the widespread notion that the public schools are divorced from the "real" world'. In other ways Cogs was less than worldly, indeed notoriously absent-minded. According to a story of the time, he once left his car at Reading station and, finding it gone when he returned, reported it stolen. When the police told him it was at Reading station he set out to fetch it but forgot to leave the train at Reading and was carried back to London.

In April 1942 the school received the most serious threat to its survival since the financial crisis in the 1850s. On the 14th of that month the Master was visited by representatives of the Ministry of Aircraft Production. A day or two later he received a demand from the Ministry for plans of the premises. They were needed because the Ministry intended to evict the school and commandeer the buildings. At once Heywood set about rallying influential Old Marlburians and others to defend it. He received various answers. The Bishop of Salisbury wrote guardedly, 'I have received an extremely confidential communication from him to whom I wrote upon the disturbing subject which you put before me.' Next day the Bishop wrote to Churchill, beginning with a flattering paragraph about Churchill's biography of the Duke of Marlborough. Cyril Norwood, by this time President of St John's College, Oxford, advised Heywood to get questions asked in the House of Commons, which were 'about the only thing the Air Ministry really fears'. Sir William Jowitt, later Earl Jowitt and Lord Chancellor, went to see the Minister of Aircraft Production and was 'hopeful that what I have said has not been without influence'. He had such 'very happy recollections of Marlborough' that he was glad now 'perhaps to be of some use'. Otto Niemeyer, the well-known banker, father of three Marlburians and a member of Council, wrote to Lord Portal, at the Ministry of Works, pointing out, as others did, that the CLS would also be displaced. But the Old Marlburian with most influence was R. A. Butler, by this time Minister of Education.

Butler had not been happy at Marlborough, partly because a riding accident in India had prevented him from playing games with success, but he came to the school's defence. On 20 April he told Heywood that he would fight 'this threat . . . to the last ditch'. The same day he wrote to Sir Percy Hurd, MP for Newbury, that 'the school's circumstances' made 'eviction unthinkable'. If the idea was pressed he would take it to the War Cabinet. Next day he spoke to Churchill.

Within five days the Bishop of London told Heywood that although Attlee had informed him that 'the issue was still in doubt', Butler thought that all was well. Meanwhile, with so many people involved, it was hardly surprising that on 24 April the *Evening Standard* reported the story (getting its numbers reversed).

'I understand that Marlborough College, the Wiltshire public school, may be seeking a new home shortly. The school celebrates its foundation next year: there are about 500 boys.

'But very many more than this will be concerned in the move. For the City of London School, with nearly 700 boys, is evacuated to Marlborough.'

The acting editor who answered Heywood's protest that the story was mischievous and irresponsible was Michael Foot. Foot claimed that he had in fact helped Marlburians in the House of Commons to fight 'what to them appeared to be an iniquitous decision'. Four days later Hurd telegraphed Heywood, 'MINISTER AUTHORISES ME TO SAY COLLEGE WILL NOT BE TAKEN OVER'.

Memorable teachers of Heywood's time included Reginald Jennings. When Jennings eventually retired, after a spell as Registrar, the Master of the time, John Dancy, said that he had long looked for the essence of Jennings's genius but eventually put it down to 'a simple and relaxed love of people'. 'A great man,' wrote Dr F. P. Willis (great-great-grandson of one of Marlborough's founders, Christopher Hodgson). Boys of his time remember in particular his ability to share and encourage their enthusiasms. His own were wide and included the bassoon.

A master of longer standing was Alexander Brown, a distinguished classicist and editor of classical texts. 'Sweaty B' would wear trousers so short that they revealed boot-tags at the back. Heywood remembered visiting parents telling him that they had been talking to 'such an educated tramp' in Court. At Common Room breakfasts Brown would tap the bone of the ham on the sideboard with his knife before cutting a slice. 'Why?' John Maples asked him. 'I watch the little holes at the end', Brown said, 'and if something pokes its head out I don't have any.'

It was certain older masters who precipitated a crisis at Marlborough unlike any before. This had been maturing for several years. In October 1943 Turner wrote to Charles Matthews from Makerere:

> I'm rather troubled by some of my recent news from M.C. Several of the best of my staff can't feel happy with Heywood – notably Wylie, who was not long ago on the pt. of resigning. That wd. have been a disaster and I hope to goodness it has been averted. I think he's the best housemaster (not omitting Reginald J.) and a quite remarkable teacher. But he's very sensitive and anxiously dependent on support and encouragement.... He gave me more affection and regard than I deserve and I don't think he's happy unless he can feel so towards his boss, which he doesn't at present. A pity, because Heywood is a very nice and a very able man.

Heywood saw things rather differently, believing that the 'deeply underlying reason for some senior masters' opposition to and even dislike of me was that they suddenly ceased to have the special relationship which they'd enjoyed with George Turner'. He believed that under Turner they formed 'a kind of inner cabinet' and that when he became Master, unknown to him, they continued 'to discuss school affairs together as they had done in the past'.

If this was the underlying cause, the crisis of 1946–7 was precipitated by two of Heywood's actions. The first was to reduce from 15 to 12 years the time for which a housemaster could hold an in-college house. 'It had to be done', Heywood considered, 'to prevent able and valuable young masters leaving in frustration at far too distant prospects of being housemasters.' The second was to introduce formal sex education to replace those ludicrous occasions when housemasters, as part of preparation for confirmation, would murmur with embarrassment about the reproductive arrangements of the flowers and bees. A visiting instructor (Edward Griffiths) was recruited to explain the facts of life to new boys. At the same time a psychologist (Livie Noble) was employed occasionally to counsel boys with problems.

By the time the Council met on 18 September 1946 it had received a protest from some of the school's housemasters, about the new tenure rule. A Council member, Sir Ernest Harvey, had at once visited Marlborough, where various masters had explained their grievances. These he summarised to the Council as 'the Master's alleged failure to co-operate with his staff and particularly with housemasters; his alleged tendency to side with boys against assistant masters; his alleged lack of interest in the scholarship side of the school's work'; and the introduction of formal sex education, together with a visiting psychologist.

'The Master then attended', the minutes continued, 'and replied in detail to the specific criticisms made, some of which were shown to be trivial or completely misconceived. In his opinion only four or five senior assistant masters were at all consistently critical of his methods; and his relations with the great majority were entirely satisfactory.'

The Council concluded:

1. Although a large part of the trouble might be attributed to the overstrain of the past seven years, felt particularly at the end of the school year, the gravity of the situation should not be minimised, particularly as rumours of a lack of confidence between the Master and his staff had been heard outside Marlborough.

2. A real effort to banish misunderstanding was therefore needed; and as such criticism as appeared to be justly levelled at the Master concerned the manner rather than the substance of his actions, the Council welcomed his assurances that he had succeeded in divesting himself of some of his extraordinary duties.

3. Irrespective of any local criticism, the Council were very doubtful of the wisdom of employing Dr Griffith (for sex instruction) and Mr Livie Noble (for psychological treatment) and hoped that it would be possible to terminate their existing engagements on the appointment of a new School medical officer, or even earlier.

By November the sex education problem had been resolved. Dr Griffiths had given up his work at the school because of illness and the new medical officer had taken it over. The Council, however, had been persuaded by Heywood that, since housemasters were co-operating with Mr Livie Noble, and since it was expected of Local Education Authorities that they employ a psychologist, his work should be allowed to continue. The same month the Council adopted a compromise about housemasters' tenure: the new rule would not come into force until 1951.

This did not end the affair. The following term – Lent 1947 – was the term of the great freeze. Coal as well as food was rationed, and there was yet another scarlet fever epidemic, started by Michael Coates (he claimed). (He escaped to spend four warm weeks in Marlborough Isolation Hospital.) It was also the term of Heywood's sabbatical, during which Alan Robson, Head of Mathematics, became Acting Master. Robson thus had direct access to the Council and made a determined effort to persuade it to dismiss Heywood. He failed, and as a result informed Council on 13 March that 'in view of what had happened last July and what was likely to happen when he [Heywood] returned next term' he wished to retire on 16 April, the day before Heywood resumed office.

On his return Heywood, who had heard from the Bishop of Salisbury of the attempt to unseat him, told a staff meeting that anyone 'who felt unable to work loyally under me should send me their resignations by the evening of the next day. I did not get any resignations, and thereafter normal service was resumed, so to speak.'

On 19 July the Council minutes made a final reference to the affair, and concluded that the testimony it had 'paid at its meeting of 13th March last to Mr Robson's great educational services to the school in no way detracted from the strong sense of disapproval with which it viewed the action taken by him in opposition to the Master during the latter's absence'.

Tommy Hunter was the doctor who took over sex-education. He was the school's last full-time doctor and a worthy one to end the tradition established by Dr Fergus. At Marlborough he made an important contribution to general medicine by pioneering 'circuit weight-training' as a remedial treatment. Hunter applied this technique, first devised for athletes and servicemen, to weak and undersized boys, those suffering from defects of posture and those recovering from operations. The films which he and Gerald Murray, director of physical education, made on the subject were shown at medical conferences throughout the world. Hunter had a brusqueness which endeared him to housemasters rather than certain boys. 'Just a case of LMF', was his common diagnosis (Lacking Moral Fibre).

In 1943 it was not possible to celebrate the school's centenary, nor to hold the planned meeting to decide how to use the Centenary Fund. In 1946, when this had reached £40,000, it was finally closed and the Council and the Marlburian Club then agreed that it should become an endowment fund which would have an income of about £1,200, to be spent on buying for the school items which it needed but were not strictly essential. In a typical year some of the money went on library books, some on colour slides for the Art Room, some on the upkeep of the Common Room garden and the balance on the new band room.

Two years later it was decided to consider a planned visit by King George VI and Queen Elizabeth as a substitute centenary celebration. The year was appropriate. One Old Marlburian, Dr Geoffrey Fisher, was Archbishop of Canterbury, another, Lord Jowitt, was Lord Chancellor, another, Sir Alan Lascelles, was the King's private secretary. Lascelles suggested that yet another – Lord Chief Justice Goddard – should be invited, but Heywood replied: if Goddard, why not Sir William Platt,

King George VI and Queen Elizabeth arrive in Court on the occasion of their Majesties' visit in 1948 – a belated centenary celebration.

George Haywood and Mrs Heywood with the King and Queen on the occasion of the Royal Visit.

conqueror of Italian East Africa, or R. A. Butler, one-time Minister of Education, so although Goddard and Platt came, only Fisher, Jowitt and Lascelles were official guests. The royal party toured the school from gymnasium to sanatorium, the only disruption being that it stayed 20 minutes instead of seven with the Marlborough College Press. *The Marlburian* published a supplement to commemorate the visit.

By the end of Heywood's time, life, even for small boys at

Marlborough, had become more civilised. In 1951, in his second term, Peter Ryde remembered that when he was in a miscellaneous crowd waiting for the swimming-pool to open, 'two senior boys, both with tough reputations, were having an energetic punch-up, during the course of which they accidentally knocked me flying – a fact which you might have thought they would scarcely deign to notice. To my amazement, they apologised with evident sincerity, dusted me down, and then proceeded to go on slogging each other.'

On the other hand there were barbaric survivals. John Maples, housemaster of A House, would 'tour the dormitories armed with a cricket stump; anyone out of bed or larking about was made to lie on their bed whilst he walloped them on the bare soles of their feet ... quoting statistics from *Wisden* as he did so.' A-House dormitories were still overcrowded. In C Dorm beds were actually touching, separated at the head only by thin wooden partitions sticking out about three feet from the wall. It was said to be a practice for the occupants to tunnel under the bedclothes at the foot end, and visit each other or change places without ever getting out of bed.

During the War it was not possible to eliminate this sort of overcrowding; indeed, by the time it ended many of the school's buildings seemed more and more to belong to the previous century. To Heywood the old dining-hall when in use suggested Frith's 'The Railway Station'. Soon afterwards, however, improvements were made to the Chapel when Lieut-Col. Thomas Wright, father of two Marlborough boys who had died, made possible the redecoration of the east-end as a memorial to his sons. The work was done by Sir Ninian Comper, Bodley's old pupil, and included the elaborate repainting of Bodley's fine stone reredos. For several years afterwards there was said to be a country-wide shortage of gold leaf.

As a general war memorial the Council decided on a fund to provide scholarships for the education at Marlborough of the sons of Marlburians who had died, and launched an appeal for £100,000, to be raised over ten years. As soon as the appeal had been sent out Heywood was telephoned by the grandfather of two Marlborough boys to express his disapproval. Wouldn't the money be needed much sooner? Heywood agreed that it would. 'All right,' the grandfather said, 'I'll let you have it.' When a cheque for £100,000 duly arrived, the appeal was revised, now asking for the same amount to provide assistance to daughters as well as sons, thus in effect extending this to prep school education.

In 1952 Heywood resigned to take on what he later saw as his life's most important work at Lord Mayor Treloar College, Alton, a school for the disabled. When asked why he left Marlborough, though still in his mid-forties, he said that he believed no Master should stay more than 15 years. His own 13 years had not always been easy. Apart from the problem of the War, which had demanded a high degree of personal leadership, and the attempted coup of 1946–7, he had had to contend with at first three, later four, ex-Masters on the Council, any one of whom might say that some proposal was not the way things had been done in *his* day. It is a tribute to Heywood that he managed nevertheless to civilise the school in many ways. When asked which of these he remembered with most satisfaction, he would say: making the Master, he hoped, a less remote and Olympian figure.

12

BRIDGES AND BEAGLES

1952–1961

WHEN THOMAS GARNETT heard he had been chosen to be Marlborough's new Master he was 'walking down Racquets Court Hill at Charterhouse carrying a pail of milk ... from the evening milking'. The incident foreshadowed the special contribution he was to make to his new school.

Garnett (universally known as 'Tommy') had previously been a master at Westminster, before going back to Charterhouse (where he had been a boy under Frank Fletcher and where George Turner was now headmaster) to teach classics. During the War he had joined the RAF Regiment, serving in India and Burma, and becoming a Squadron-Leader. It was after his return to Charterhouse in 1946 that he had taken over the school farm there – at a time when more boys claimed that they wanted to become farmers than do anything else in life. Garnett considered that 'cleaning out pigsties on a December morning was a good way of sorting out the sentimentalists'. But the Charterhouse farm had also convinced him that there were 'valuable skills', apart from intellectual and athletic ones, which a school could teach, and that many boys 'especially the younger ones, found contact with animals comforting and satisfying'.

At Marlborough other matters initially preoccupied him. He believed that the character of any school was 'largely determined by three factors in this order: the sort of parents who send their children to it; the quality of the staff; and the physical surroundings'. About the first and the third he could do little – though it was they which had attracted him. While Charterhouse was city-based, Marlborough was 'a country school': and while Charterhouse parents were mostly 'stockbrokers, lawyers and doctors', those of Marlborough were 'less affluent, particularly those who served overseas'. So it was to the staff that he gave his attention. Choosing good masters, he believed to be 'the most important of a headmaster's tasks'.

He appointed Donald Wright to the staff before coming to the school, and five years later made him housemaster of Littlefield, the first out-college housemaster not previously to have held an in-college house. Garnett knew that Wright was likely to be offered the headmastership of his old school, Bryanston, and they made a bargain; if Wright accepted Littlefield he would refuse Bryanston. 'The offer duly came and I had to convince the Bryanston Council that Donald could not, in conscience, accept.... They were very cross. Wright was the sort of constructive rebel that I was looking for ... an obvious person to teach History-for-Scientists when we had persuaded the authorities to accept that as a valid A-level course.'

In 1955 came Dennis Silk and Ian Beer, both selected by Garnett while still undergraduates, on a single visit to Cambridge where one was Captain of Cricket, the other of Rugby. Garnett interviewed and appointed Silk when he was 'clad only in a towel.... Both men continued to play a part in the administration of their favourite games,' Garnett wrote, but kept these activities in proportion, believing that 'to someone actually playing a game, it should matter more than anything else in the world, but that when it is over it should come low down on the scale of importance.'

For other appointments he went outside the public school world,

Garnett's Common Room in 1957 includes ten future headmasters.

Tommy Garnett with the Captain of Cricket, P. R. H. Anderson, in 1953. Frank Fletcher, headmaster at Charterhouse when Garnett was a boy there, recorded that in 1933 Garnett made 1023 runs in 11 completed innings, with centuries against every school except Winchester.

which he believed to be too inward-looking, and chose men with wider backgrounds: Ernest Sabben-Clare, who had been in the Civil Service in Nigeria, Gerald Goodban, a headmaster in Hong Kong, Kenneth Keast, head of Frensham Heights, an experimental school in Surrey, and Barrie Hammond, a chemist from Western Australia. A photograph of Marlborough's Common Room in 1957 demonstrates Garnett's success in his choices. No fewer than ten of those shown subsequently became headmasters, including Silk at Radley, Wright at Shrewsbury, Beer at Lancing and Harrow, and John Sharp at Rossall.

Unfortunately Common Room remained 'very much divided' between Garnett's appointments and those of Heywood. One way in which he tried to unify it was by providing a better place for morning tea or coffee, a time when much important business was done. The room previously used in the Mansion had been 'absurdly crowded, and the difficulty of making easy contact led to misunderstandings and the magnification of petty incidents, such as the upsetting of a man's cup over his trousers, into lasting animosities'. By concentrating the school's three libraries in the present one he freed the Adderley to become, amongst other things, the staff's morning-coffee room. Before Garnett's time, the Master had not been a member of Common Room and he believed it 'an important step forward' when he was invited to join. It was at this time that the Adderley received its principal ornament, the Gainsborough, given to it by Henry Hony.

Garnett also abolished the practice of masters sending each other notes, believing that these lay in people's desks, ready when rediscovered to re-arouse old passions. In future contact should be face to face.

His appointment of married housemasters to in-college as well as out-college houses was a more significant reform. When he arrived 'a man who became a housemaster had to choose between marrying his house or a wife', because there was no proper accommodation for wives at in-college houses. There were married quarters for out-college houses, but by the time masters succeeded to one of these 'many had become confirmed bachelors'. In 1952 only three out of a total of 15 housemasters were married. Garnett provided married flats for B1 and B2 by moving the Registrar's and Bursar's offices into the Master's Lodge. In the Mansion the use of the Adderley by Common Room had freed space for a flat in C1 House. Married quarters were also created close to Field House. By 1961, when he left the ratio of married to unmarried housemasters had been reversed – he remembered Louis MacNeice being astonished when he saw a pram in Court. Garnett's wife, Penelope, contributed to the integration of the transformed community which Common Room now became by starting a nursery school in the attic of the Lodge – and to the school's integration with the outside world by opening this to children from the town.

Not all Garnett's reforms were readily accepted, in particular his decision to reward staff equally at all levels of teaching. When he arrived Sixth Form teachers received extra pay 'of apparently arbitrary amounts'. He maintained that 'it was fair enough for extra money to be paid for extra responsibility such as running a department but that ... those teaching the cleverest boys and those teaching the least clever were equally valuable'. He remembered vividly 'the argument as we sat in deck-chairs on the lawn. We lost Allan Ramsay, Head of Maths Department, to New Zealand as a result of the disagreement.'

Garnett's establishment of a school pack of beagles was also opposed,

in particular by one master, William Rutland, who wrote in protest to the *Marlborough Times*, but others deplored this public airing of a school matter and supported Garnett. The pack was intended to put into practice Garnett's belief in the benefits of contact with animals. Unlike those of Eton, Radley, Stowe and Ampleforth, it was run by the boys without a professional kennel-huntsman. The hounds were at first kept in the backyard of the Lodge. ('On one occasion an errant bitch produced an illegitimate litter in our meat safe.') Today it is kennelled north of the Eleven. By 1963 it was meeting twice a week in season, at places within 20 miles of Marlborough, to which hounds were transported by some outside subscriber. Alastair Jackson, Joint Master, was an example of the sort of boy whose interests it had expanded. He was the son of a London surgeon, and before he came to the school had never seen a beagle. Another boy, William Everett, had recently taken the whole pack of twenty couple home with him for the Christmas holidays. A by-product of the pack, Alan Del Mar remembered, was that the school biology labs had a useful source of hound corpses for dissection.

It was Gerald Fox and friends who started another activity of the sort Garnett encouraged: bridge-building. In total they built five, all crossing

Beagles at exercise on the Downs.

187

Bridge-builders preparing the foundations for Fox's Bridge. John Isaacson, left, and behind him sarsen stones awaiting splitting up with fire and water.

various channels of the Kennet which separated the school and the water meadows from the tennis-courts. Though the first three are now invisible below soil and concrete, the fourth, of brick (designed by William Sommerville, who subsequently became a bridge-builder for the construction firm, NRM) is still in use. So is the fifth, Fox's masterpiece, a magnificent double-span bridge of stone over the Kennet itself. Before the work could start permission had to be obtained from the Thames Water Authority, whose idea of a proper bridge began with a couple of steel girders. But the official sent to see Fox was so impressed with his plans that he recommended permission. Fox and his friends obtained virtually all the materials for nothing, begging stone from farmers with derelict buildings, and, in William Morris fashion, using traditional building methods, splitting sarsens with fire and water. In only one way was the bridge not Fox's concept. He wanted it to be wide enough for cars, but Garnett insisted that it should be too narrow. On the far side of the bridge Fox's initials are carved.

Another group which Garnett encouraged, known as Payne's Poppets after the master, Ivo Richard Payne, became eventually the 'Works Group', an alternative to the Corps. Its most notable achievement was the building of the new Music School, called at first the Band Room. In this the chaplain, Perceval Hayman, took a lead. Garnett would lend a hand, pausing as he passed to climb a ladder and lay an armful of tiles, or pull on the end of a cross-cut saw for a spell.

The restoring of Castle Farm in the Black Mountains of Wales was an equally ambitious project, undertaken partly to provide worth-while occupation for boys in the final weeks of the summer term after they had taken their public examinations. The money to finance it came from an unusual source. Shortly before the War, an ancient local farmer had arrived in the Bursar's office with a cheque to the college for £869. 16s. 9d. It was to repay what he owed, he explained, for overcharging over many years by a penny a pound for butter.

When the farmer died, his son and heir claimed the money on the grounds that his father had been in his dotage. The school's lawyers, however, discovered that the son had inherited almost £40,000 from the old man, under a will signed *after* he had made his gift to the college, and pointed out that the same argument would render the son's inheritance invalid.

'New headmasters,' Garnett wrote, 'like new Prime Ministers, have a honeymoon period when they can get away with things that might be impossible later. So it was not too difficult for me, three months into the job, to persuade the college council that it would be appropriate to use a windfall [by now grown to £1,100] for some unusual purpose.'

At a meeting in 1952 Garnett suggested that a possible project would be the sending of a party of boys to 'some distant and preferably uncivilised place. Their activities should involve a good deal of sustained physical effort – and their comfort should depend largely on their own exertions.' Garnett asked Guy Barton, the Art Master, to pursue the idea, his brief to 'find a derelict farmhouse in mountains within a day's bicycle range' of the college. Barton found Castle Farm, near Llanthony Abbey. It had 40 acres of land but the crop its paddock produced was 'nettles supported by old bedsteads variegated with docks. It appeared that all meals for some time had come out of tins, which had been used for mulch.'

The farm was bought and the money left over was used to employ a professional builder to repair its roof, but the rest of the restoration was left to the boys. Partly this was done by groups of 12 who would cycle there and stay for ten days at a time, partly by boys at the college who made new window-frames and furniture and wove new curtains. Castle Farm was also meant to be a base for the exploration of the mountains, and from the start members of the working parties, two or three at a time, began to make expeditions. After three years the restoration was complete, the farm was sold, to become Capel-y-fynn youth hostel, and another derelict house was bought, this one closer to Marlborough.

Guy Barton, who supervised the Castle Farm project, has slipped sideways into this history, responsible for activities like hill-walking and

Guy Barton in the old Art
Room (now Garnett Room).

the design of furnishings which were typical, but by no means his central
contribution to Marlborough. This was as the true founder of its Art
Department. He came from the Yorkshire Pennines and was eventually
to retire there, to walk and paint their hills. In the 1930s, with no formal
art qualifications, he had been appointed Bedford School's art master.
Back from the War, in which he became a captain in the Royal Corps
of Signals, he arrived at Marlborough in 1946. At this time the Art
Department consisted of a single classroom for drawing which was 'not
disgraced by a sink or any painter's clutter'.

> I was offered in rapid succession [he later wrote] the possibility of
> converting the Mount House, a racquets court, the laundry . . . and
> the armoury. In each case it required only a superficial investigation
> to show that a very expensive conversion would merely add to the
> menagerie of white elephants already possessed by the school. It was

Mr Garnett who suddenly came up with the bright idea of a studio under the cloister separating the Norwood Hall [the new dining-hall then being planned] from A House.... Mr Roberts, the architect, produced an engaging idea – based presumably on the basement of B House – of a studio overlooked by galleries from which the world of admiring passers-by could enjoy – or otherwise react to – operations going on below. Not wishing to be disclosed as the keeper of a Zoo I managed to persuade the powers that be to cage us in more effectively, and the idea of the pretty (and highly non-waterproof) lantern was born.

Other extensions to what became known as the old art room followed, but it was not until 1963 that the whole area was transformed into the New Art School. The college then recognised that it was impossible for Barton alone to teach art history to the Sixth Form and at the same time supervise boys of the Shell 'coming to enjoy splashing paint about', and he was given an assistant. By 1992 there were seven art teachers.

Barton also professionalised, in the best sense, the school's drama. His first production, the Victorian melodrama, *Sweeny Todd the Barber*, was followed by *The Importance of being Earnest*, *Hamlet*, and two home-made operas *Circe* and *Daniel*. For the Chapel he designed stall-cushions (embroidered by his wife's working-parties) of such distinction that he was later commissioned to design kneelers at Winchester Cathedral to

Circe, a home-made opera (libretto: Mike Davis, music: Tony Smith-Masters) was performed in 1956 and involved a principal lady and chorus of priestesses – all played by boys.

A group of Common Room wives, many of them embroidresses of cushions for the Chapel. Organiser Mrs Garnett seated sixth from the left and trainer Mrs Barton second row, second from the right, in the 1950s.

span the 45 feet in front of the nave altar. His wartime signalling experience enabled him to supervise the re-equipping of the Corps with modern sets to replace Pepin's now ancient walkie-talkies and to install field telephones in the college during an Asian flu epidemic, at a time when Marlborough had no internal telephone system and when on a single day 400 boys were in bed in different sick-bays.

In his Prize Day speech of 1953 Garnett announced an unequalled Marlburian achievement: the successful climbing of Everest by members of an expedition led by Colonel (as he then was) John Hunt. Hunt was not the only Marlburian on the expedition. A month earlier a press report had read,

> News has just been received of an Old Marlburian Mount Everest expedition dinner. It was held at Camp IV on May 2.
>   OMs present were Col. Hunt, Dr Ward and Major Wylie. Dr Evans and Mr Bourdillon were guests.
>   Owing to a blizzard, dinner had to be eaten in the diners' respective tents. The menu was lean pemmican soup à la Bovril, luncheon meat à la WD with carrots, and coffee.
>   No speeches were made owing to the circumstances.

Marlborough had produced earlier mountaineers – Geoffrey Winthrop Young, for example, at the college in the 1890s. 'Forty-five years ago,' Young wrote, 'I opened Whymper's *Scrambles* in the VI Form Library and found my own new world.' Though Young lost a leg in the First World War, he continued to break climbing records for mountaineers with two legs. But it was Edwin Garnett Kempson (known as 'G') who, from 1925 onwards, brought mountaineering to a generation of Marlborough boys, Hunt one of the earliest of them.

Kempson and Hunt first skied together, then in 1933 had 'an excellent season' in the Alps. Next year Kempson founded the Marlborough College Mountaineering Club.

Kempson was as remarkable a master as Barton. Son of the Bishop of Sodor and Man, he had become interested in mountaineering at Cambridge, where he obtained a first in Mathematics. As a teacher and housemaster he favoured academic boys. Others found him less sympathetic. 'I wish he would beat me', one said, 'instead of understanding me.' But he could encourage enthusiasm in any boy. 'You had only to show some sort of spark about something, and he would fan it into a flame.' Among his own many interests were madrigals,

Members of the 1953 Everest team. Old Marlburians John Hunt (front row, centre), Charles Wylie (front row, far right) and Michael Ward (middle row, far left). Others include Edmund Hilary, behind John Hunt, and Sherpa Tensing. *Courtesy of The Royal Geographical Scoiety.*

printing, natural history, bird-watching and above all local history. His most remarkable historical discovery was the Vicar's Library: the diary and 750 books of the seventeenth-century vicar, William White, who left them to the Mayor and Corporation of Marlborough for the use of a young colleague, the Vicar of St Mary's, Marlborough. 'In 1942', Kempson wrote, 'the Town Council had to organise a campaign for the salvage of wastepaper and ... the senior alderman said he believed that there were some old books in the attic: would they do? I was lucky enough to be on the Town Council at that time and offered to inspect them.' Kempson was allowed to bring them to the College, where he spent the next 40 years cataloguing and commenting on them in a windowless cupboard at the back of a classroom in the North Block. Shortly before he died they were accepted by the Bodleian. He was also president of the Wiltshire Archaeological Society for a number of years, but rarely published because of his horror of making mistakes.

Mountaineering, however, was his true passion. In the first two years of the Marlborough Mountaineering Club he was a member of two successive Everest expeditions. When conditioning himself he would go to bed on the ground outside Field House in a sleeping-bag. On the 1936 expedition 'he had acclimatised well and, had the weather been reasonable ... would have been a strong contender for the summit party. With quick bird-like movements,' the *Alpine Journal* continued, 'he seemed to flit easily from rock to rock and from tussock to tussock, and his mind moved as phenomenally fast as did his feet. He was still going when those around him almost ceased to move or think from sheer exhaustion.'

Under his presidency, members of the Marlborough Mountaineering Club undertook winter climbs in North Wales, the Lake District and the Scottish Highlands, and in the summer went regularly to the Alps. When he died one of the other Marlburian diners on Everest, Charles Wylie, wrote of him, 'G was I think without doubt the person who had the greatest influence after my parents. He was also about the nicest and kindest person I have known. I owe my Everest connections entirely to him.'

Kempson was at Marlborough for 37 years, rejecting offers of headmasterships elsewhere, becoming in turn housemaster of B3 and Preshute House, then during the interregnum between Garnett and Dancy, Acting Master. He was also as successful as masters like Thomas, Bambridge and Leaf in forming connections with the town, becoming mayor in 1947 and at different times chairman of the Savernake Hospital and of the governors of Marlborough Grammar School.

During Garnett's time the school experienced an embarrassing form of success, the result of the post-war baby boom. By November 1956 some parents were being refused registration for their sons even though they had applied on their eighth birthday. In 1957 the school was forced to start a provisional waiting-list as well as a definite one, but in May that year there were 34 names on the latter for only ten vacancies. At this time Elmhurst, north of the Bath Road, was opened as a new house for 20 boys.

Meanwhile the school, like other public schools, was threatened by left-wing politicians with abolition, or at least transformation. If such harassment had taken the form of removing the school's charitable status it would have been serious, but this did not happen, and in practice when in office the Labour Party did nothing. Garnett took the attitude that he didn't mind whom the school educated, but someone had to pay for the extra staff a boarding-school needed. When two Labour ministers, Dick Crossman and Christopher Mayhew, visited Marlborough he bet them that the school would still exist when a sapling cedar of Lebanon which he had just planted in the Master's garden reached maturity.

In the 1950s Marlborough continued to pride itself on being a tough school, its toughness epitomised by 'HOB', the hour every afternoon when, whatever the weather, Houses were Out of Bounds. Del Mar remembered windows wide open on freezing nights, prefects' beatings, endless sweats, and worst of all the boxing bouts which every new boy was compelled to fight in front of the watching school. But the bleakness of life was redeemed by happy experiences. Soon after he arrived Jack Halliday, biology master, passing him in Court, told him,' You've got doctor's hands'. Three years later when Del Mar arrived in Halliday's class, the first thing Halliday said to him was 'I've been waiting for you'. He became a doctor – as did a number of Halliday's other pupils.

In an appreciation *The Marlburian* picked out, as Garnett's most important quality, his intense dislike of rules and regulations. When he arrived at Marlborough, Garnett himself remembered finding 'that there was a rule-book given to each new boy; and I soon learnt of one boy who was working his way through it, ticking off each one as he broke it.' He reduced the list to 12, with a final sentence reading, 'a breach of common sense may be regarded as a breach of school rules'.

Garnett was far from fluent, his conversation 'full of ums and ers', his lisp a school joke; the warm relationships he formed with masters and boys were based, in Donald Wright's opinion, on his insights. As a result the school community in his time became 'an extended family'. One mid-term, Wright remembered, 'there was a boy who hitched a lift – in a Tate and Lyle heavy tanker late one night – to London docks, in an attempt to emigrate to Canada. . . . The boy failed to emigrate –

for lack of a work permit, but when he arrived at his home in a state of collapse he found Tommy [Garnett] waiting for him.... On the way back to school, the boy told him he was fed up with school: it was so dull and nothing ever happened.' Garnett forgave him and for the last three weeks of term allowed him free time to attempt to write a novel. When Del Mar was rusticated for a term because his housemaster had found contraband substances in his room during what Del Mar considered an unfair search, Garnett told him privately, 'I have to support my housemaster'. On his return, Garnett made him a beater in his shoot.

About caning Garnett was ambivalent. He knew of no other punishment which so satisfactorily 'put a full stop' to an incident.

> On the other hand, when, in my first term, I beat the good-natured outstanding athlete of the school because he was relying on cheating to produce every bit of school work, the experience – in his eyes – did him so much good that he thought beating was a panacea and, as head of house, was disastrous. It has been on my conscience [Garnett added] that on one occasion – and I can remember only one occasion – a boy was unbendingly bitter when he left.

Such conscientiousness is uncommon in a headmaster, but was typical of a man who had, in the words of *The Marlburian*, a 'profound and sincere interest in every boy'. As one of them put it more bluntly, they felt that he was 'on the boys' side'. He not only sympathised with those in difficulties, but took trouble to understand the successful, instituting at Marlborough the equivalent of what was called 'Bunners' at Charterhouse, occasions when senior boys could come to his study, 'drink tea or cocoa, eat a bun and talk about anything under the sun. I invited the school prefects to come once a week to such a function at the Lodge; and would deliberately make outrageous statements. It took me a little time to discover that these were solemnly recorded as considered opinions.' Understanding of this sort led to remarkable successes with his Senior Prefects. The first two he chose to succeed Peter Brooke were Nicholas Goodison and Christopher Hogg, subsequently chairman of the Stock Exchange and of Courtaulds respectively.

In 1961 Garnett became headmaster of Geelong Grammar School, Victoria, Australia. While he was there he was asked whether he would accept Prince Charles as a pupil. He replied, he would need 'to see the boy and interview the parents'. Both proved satisfactory.

'The slightly tousled, tweed-clad figure,' *The Marlburian* continued, 'striding along with his twelve-bore under one arm and the ever-faithful Merlin trotting behind, will be sadly missed in the Marlborough countryside.'

13

ALL CHANGE

1961–1972

IN HIS FIRST Prize Day speech John Dancy announced two significant events at Marlborough. Littlefield had gone and Norwood Hall had come.

Littlefield, one of the school's first pair of purpose-built out-college houses, had gone on the fourth day of the 1962 Easter holidays. The housemaster had already left when the cook came downstairs, placed her case at their foot and set out to walk to the town to fetch her car. By the time she came back the building was blazing, and before the fire could be put out the boys' side had been irreparably damaged. The foot of the stairs was where the fire had started, but this was also above the house boiler and the fire's cause was never established.

Norwood Hall had taken longer to materialise. In 1959 the Council had finally decided that the old dining-hall with its antiquated kitchens, built in 1848 when the school expanded to 500, was inadequate now that it was half as large again. For a replacement the architect, David Roberts, Cambridge Professor of Architecture, produced a plan which by no means everyone liked, but the Council approved it essentially unchanged. Critics of the hall's exterior have a point. Its cubic form and large panes of glass contrast disturbingly with the elegant, tiled Queen Anne Mansion on one side and the traditional if utilitarian, slated A House on the other. But all except the most prejudiced who use the new hall will admit that it is a pleasant place in which to eat, with a remarkable quietness, freedom from smell and above all spaciousness which makes even queuing for food and scraping bones into a plastic bucket an agreeable experience.

Littlefield ablaze in 1962.

The old Hall and kitchens from across Court *c.* 1955.

With the old kitchen block went the Dames' dining-room which had been above the Steward's office and had had, Howard Lansley remembered, 'a well-defined membership'!

> The in-college Dames – Miss Wilkes from Field House, Miss Burgess from A House, Mrs Hime from B House and Miss de Chaville from C House were a formidable quartet. To these, add the housekeeper, Mrs Ellis, the School Secretary and the Accountant [men]! It was established that the carving of the daily roast was a male responsibility so if Mr Goodchild was delayed the mantle fell on me as a very young man totally ignorant in the way to carve a big joint.... Miss Wilkes stood over me and directed my hands.... It was a frightenening experience.

Dancy was the first of three Wykehamist Masters. He had also taught at Winchester before becoming headmaster of Lancing for eight years. He was a man of enormous energy. John Isaacson remembered him, as he was leaving A House one evening where Isaacson was housemaster, suggesting a climbing race up the building's central iron-pillars. Isaacson won but Dancy, though he limped from polio, also achieved the climb. It was energy of this sort which he had used to promote so much change at Lancing that it became known as Dancy's Inferno.

Why, it may be asked, was anything similar needed at Marlborough?

The school was apparently flourishing. Under both Heywood and Garnett it had continued to win an impressive number of Oxford and Cambridge scholarships: 187 between 1940 and 1951, 147 between 1952 and 1961. And by the time Garnett left it offered a remarkable variety of other activities. Apart from those the school itself promoted, there were at any given time 60 or 70 societies devoted to special pursuits which ranged from stamp-collecting to badger-watching. Though each term two or three foundered, as many new ones were launched.

Partly it was the times which made change seem necessary. The 1960s were years in which students rejected the beliefs and practices of their parents and teachers in favour of such heresies as long hair, ragged jeans, raw food and Buddhism. They were also years in which public schools felt themselves increasingly threatened by the Labour Party's hostility to private education. But Dancy was himself in large part responsible. He later claimed that he found Marlborough a far more 'powerful' school than Lancing: powerful Common Room, powerful parents with powerful connections, powerful scholarships. The amount of energy around was so colossal that he understood what George Turner meant when he compared Charterhouse with Marlborough: while being head of Charterhouse was like riding 12 powerful horses at once, being Master of Marlborough was like riding one quite enormously powerful horse. As a result Dancy maintained that he had to change the style of his rule, channelling rather than providing the impetus for change. But the more the various changes are examined the more they seem to fit into a pattern which Dancy himself was promoting.

The reforms of the curriculum were typical. In isolation they seem somewhat arbitrary. But the 1960s, Dancy believed, was the decade of 'the social gospel' as well as of protest, and he saw all Marlborough's curriculum reforms as 'designed to make [the school] an even better place into which to welcome the wider social range of pupils I wanted'.

Such pupils would clearly benefit, for example, from a modernising of mathematics teaching of the sort which a group of mathematics teachers from Marlborough, Charterhouse, Sherborne, Winchester and Southampton University were developing and which became the School Mathematics Project (SMP).

At this time, though more students than ever before were taking A-levels and going to university, a smaller proportion were studying mathematics. One of SMP's aims was to reverse this trend by making mathematics 'more exciting and enjoyable'. Another was to 'impart a knowledge of the nature of mathematics and its uses in the modern world'. But devising an improved syllabus was of little value unless

Norwood Hall from the Terrace with Leaf Block on the left.

schools allowed this to be taught. As Bryan Thwaites wrote in the book which celebrated SMP's twenty-fifth anniversary (to which Colin Goldsmith and Douglas Quadling from Marlborough contributed), 'SMP would have been stillborn if it had not been for the readiness of the headmasters of the original schools to entrust radical change to their teachers of mathematics'. It was this trust which Dancy gave.

Business studies, another revolutionary development of the curriculum pioneered at Marlborough, not only ruptured the distinction between 'academic' and 'vocational' subjects, which Dancy considered a piece of antiquated snobbery, but was even more likely to suit Dancy's wider social range of pupils. During 1965 and 1966 there had been discussions at Marlborough about setting up a vocational course to teach managerial skills. The following year Dancy received an invitation to lunch with Lord Wolfson, but when the day came he was too busy to keep the appointment. There matters rested until one midnight he was phoned by an excited Old Marlburian who was attending an Old Cliftonian dinner.

An earlier view from the Terrace showing the hotch-potch of buildings which were the former kitchens and staff quarters.

Here he had heard Wolfson tell Clifton that Marlborough was not interested in his plan to finance an experiment in the teaching of business studies, so he was looking elsewhere. That night Dancy prepared a full outline for a proposed course in managerial skills which he posted to Wolfson next morning, together with a date on which he would be in London the following week (having had his secretary check which days Wolfson would be in London).

Eventually Wolfson told Dancy that he had made two lists, one of 'top schools', the other of schools willing to promote his project. The only school to appear on both lists was Marlborough. Dancy originally insisted that a Bristol comprehensive school should take part, but it dropped out and for the first ten years the business studies project was based at Marlborough, where the central aim was to develop an A-level course in the subject. To do this Dancy brought Richard Barker from Bedales, and it was Barker who transformed the original ideas for a vocational course in managerial skills into an academic one requiring as much scholarly discipline as any other.

By 1978 the subject had become respectable and 100 schools were offering it. By the same date at Marlborough a third of the students working for A-level were taking it as one of their options. Since they usually took three subjects this meant that business studies formed about 11 per cent of A-level teaching. That year John Powell, by now Marlborough's Head of Business Studies, divided into three categories the sort of boys who chose it: those who wanted to go into business or commerce, those who thought it would be a broadening addition to their studies of mathematics or science, and those who were 'weak at everything else'. Interestingly, the third group did well, and by the end of the course a notably larger number of those originally in groups two and three were considering business or commercial careers.

For scientists to take business studies, or indeed any subject other than the required three (mathematics, physics and chemistry) was not easy. Either they had to drop one of these or add a fourth subject. To solve this problem, and give them the opportunity for a broader education, at least while they were at school, Dancy promoted an A-level course which would make physics and chemistry a single subject. If mathematics was also taken, a student would be free to take a non-scientific subject for his third, something which would be particularly valuable, he believed, for future medical students. But universities complained that science students knew less than they used to know when they arrived, and the combined course was eventually abandoned. Again Dancy had been trying to modify Marlborough's curriculum to make it more appropriate for pupils from less academic homes. He continued his attempts as a representative of the Headmasters' Conference on various committees set up by the Ministry of Education, which, ahead of their time, proposed five-subject A-level courses.

The introduction of the Technical Projects scheme at Marlborough like Business Studies, was in part designed to break down the barrier between academic and vocational learning. Dancy gave his views on technical education in a paper delivered as chairman of the British Association in 1965. His general views on public schools he had already published in his book, *Public Schools and the Future* (1963). Because their pupils suffered from 'social isolation' – and for other reasons – he believed that it would be right for those which were large enough to become state comprehensives. Some Marlburians considered the book a betrayal, but it was widely noticed, the subject of a *Times* leading article, and the Labour Party which was, in Dancy's words, 'pushed for a policy on public schools', asked him to become a member of the Public Schools' Commission. Dancy, however, dissociated himself from the Commission's recommendation that *all* public schools should become comprehensives. Comprehensives would be expected to take pupils whose education would end at 15 or 16, and while Dancy believed that most, including Marlborough, could handle these, others like Winchester and Westminster he considered should remain 'geared only to academic excellence'.

In 1962 it seemed that the sort of change which he hoped for might be about to occur. Both the Governing Bodies' Association and the Headmasters' Conference had supported the proposal made in the Fleming Report (1944) that a proportion of state schoolboys should be admitted to public schools. Now Dancy made it clear that if the party which won the forthcoming general election was to propose state bursaries at public schools, Marlborough 'would be among the first to welcome it'. But when the Labour Party established no scheme of this sort, Marlborough made an arrangement of its own, offering about 20 places to boys from Wiltshire state schools. The places were not free; parents contributed according to their means. The boys were to be seniors, and were to stay two years, working for A-levels. The only government contribution was the funding by the Ministry of Education of a reserach project, to be undertaken by Dr Royston Lambert, a Fellow of King's College, Cambridge, which would assess the scheme's success.

The Wiltshire boys did at least as well academically and at other school activities as any similar group of Marlborough boys. They also mixed amicably with their contemporaries. At home, however, the result was less desirable, because they lost their local friends and became social oddities. When Dancy explained the scheme to Labour MPs at the House of Commons they repudiated it on the grounds that it had merely produced a group of 'pseudo-middle-class sophisticates'. It had been fated from the start, they told him, when the boys had been forbidden those 'symbols of their masculinity', their motor-bikes.

Nor had the school gained as much as it had hoped. Dr Lambert gave the Wiltshire boys a standard psychological test when they arrived, asking each of them which of four ideal-types of schoolboy they would most like to become: scholar, sportsman, prefect or artist-musician. Almost all of them answered 'scholar', whereas a control group of Marlburians, asked the same question, gave an even spread of answers. When the Wiltshire boys left and were again questioned they now gave evenly spread answers. 'The visitors', Dancy concluded, 'for good or ill had conformed.' One deduction was clear. If a public school was to have a social mix which would change its nature the proportions would need to be far more even. But the economic and political state of the country by then made the chances of this happening slight. To Dancy this was 'a great disappointment'. Public schools, he believed, had two things to offer: boarding, and high-grade Sixth Form facilities. 'Both these commodities are in very short supply elsewhere. It seems absurd that we can't do business.'

A wider social mix of another sort Marlborough did now introduce. In July 1966 Dancy had reported to the Council that for the first time he had been receiving requests to admit girls. 'With one exception, which set no precedent,' he had refused these requests. In March 1968, however, he told the Council that the matter was now urgent since one member of Common Room had a daughter he was anxious to have admitted that September.

'A full debate followed,' the Council minutes recorded. But Dancy had stage-managed matters by introducing at the same time a proposal that day-pupils should be admitted. Much of the debate concerned placing stringent restrictions on this second suggestion, and the Council had exhausted its inclination to resist change by the time the admission of girls was discussed. At its next meeting in July it 'took note that 15 girls had been selected for entry'. One or two other boarding-schools had already done the same thing, but Marlborough was among the first.

Though Dancy had obtained Council permission, he had not consulted Common Room. One housemaster, David West, remembered being summoned, alarmingly, to the Master's study at 8 p.m. and not reassured when he found cognac and two glasses set out. 'David, I want you to be the first to know', Dancy told him, 'that Council has agreed to the admission of Sixth Form girls next September.' West believed that he had been identified as the principal opposition, but the brandy was wasted; he told Dancy that it was just a year earlier than he had expected and that he was entirely in favour.

Not all masters accepted the change so readily. When Hugh Weldon's class were giving him their names: 'Smith, Jones, Brown, Elizabeth Clough,' he interrupted, 'hyphenated, I presume.' There was heated argument when Janet Tanner arrived as the first female teacher (apart from Heywood's wartime appointments). Where should she have breakfast and dinner? Common Room, she remembered, was organised as a gentlemen's club, and 'a female beak with full Common Room status was an embarrassment. I gather the problem . . . was tossed from one sub-committee to another. No one was prepared to take responsibility for a decision, so the secretaries and dames, who . . . ate . . . in the adjoining small dining-room graciously invited me to share their meal. . . . When on various occasions I asked why I was excluded I was given a rich variety of answers' which included, 'I understand this is how things are organised in the Indian army.' Not until 1974 was another female teacher appointed; Alison Webb, a physicist.

The great majority of parents and Old Marlburians welcomed the change. For every letter of disapproval the Master received he had eight of approval (and eight applications for places). 'Some Old Marlburians', he reported to that year's Prize Day audience, 'have put temptation in our way by offering to subscribe heavily to the appeal if we promise to make the new house [Turner House] a girls' house. We have resisted

the temptation.' In September the girls duly arrived. All were Sixth Formers, and all either daughters of staff or sisters of boys. About a third of the eligible sisters had applied, and from these Dancy had 'easily found 13 intelligent, industrious and charming young ladies, who with two Common Room daughters made up the quorum'. One of these two was his own daughter, Nicola.

John Dancy with the first intake of Sixth Form girls in 1968.

Despite Dancy's claim, selecting girls was never easy. Simply choosing the cleverest out of a large number of clever applicants might produce a group who would make their boy contemporaries feel inferior. And it was not necessarily good for a girl to choose her just because she was clever if she was less than charming, to use Dancy's word, since she might have a miserable time at school. In the end compromise formulas were devised: the mix of girls should as nearly as possible duplicate the mix of boys: and the most essential quality required of a girl was that she would be likely to 'fit in'.

In one way the first 15 girls were a disappointment. These were years when schools (and politicians) were worried that fewer students were choosing to study science. Marlborough had hoped that a high proportion of the girls it admitted would be scientists, basing this hope on the fact that many girls' schools were finding it difficult to teach science to a high standard. This did not happen. Only three of Marlborough's first girls were scientists. But in other ways they were a success, and were soon integrated into the school. Some boarded at the Master's Lodge, some on the private sides of B1, B2, Summerfield and Littlefield. The following year (September 1969) another batch brought the total at the school to 27, and for the first time some were neither daughters of staff nor sisters of boys. The year after there were 41. The Council continued, however, to insist that Marlborough should remain a boys' school, that girls should not enter below the Sixth Form and that there should be no separate girls' house.

Apart from the reasons he gave in public, Dancy had a private reasons for wanting to introduce girls to the school. They would 'consolidate the liberal position'. Fundamentally he believed that women were more sensible than men, and that women in the school, girls and staff, would see that a lot of the things which male Marlburians stood for were obvious nonsense. His wife, Angela, was not only a keen advocate of admitting girls, and of great assistance in integrating them into the school, but provided an example of such good sense by strongly opposing uniform for girls. Instead a 'dress-code' was adopted, and this was soon extended to Sixth Form boys.

As for the girls themselves, the experiences of Ann Willis, who came in the fifth batch, were probably representative.

> Fifty of us as opposed to 800 boys made it quite hard to maintain the certain kind of poise and toughness that Dancy admitted was required. I enjoyed enormously the plays, games and social side of the school. My work record ... might perhaps have been better if there hadn't been so many distractions.... It was marvellous to have an opportunity to act in *King Lear* (Cordelia) among a tremendous cast, something no girls' school could have provided.... There was perhaps too much attention paid to the girls in general though – one does a lot of growing up between 16 and 18 and it could be quite difficult to cope with.

The year of the first girls saw the resolution of the argument about another reform to which Dancy was personally committed: the abolition or at least modification of rules compelling boys to attend chapel. A Christian himself – in 1954 he had published *Commentary on Maccabees I* – he believed that worship and compulsion were incompatible. In

March 1966 he had told the Council that he 'was planning to give boys some degree of choice in their Sunday worship' and asked for its opinion on the general principle of compulsory chapel. The following July he arranged two days of discussion by Common Room on the subject, chaired by Kenneth Carey, the Bishop of Edinburgh. After the first day he reported to the Council that 'there was no strong feeling against a change from compulsory chapel', but after the second day that 'a mainly voluntary system of chapel attendence [even] on weekdays would at present be unacceptable to a significant minority'.

As a compromise Dancy proposed for one year to make 'an act of worship' still compulsory on five weekdays, but with greater freedom in its 'form, content and location'; and on Wednesdays to hold voluntary Holy Communion or 'perhaps music or intercession'. On Sundays chapel would remain compulsory.

During this year a Common Room working party continued to discuss the question and at a staff meeting of October 1968 a large majority were in favour of voluntary worship on all weekdays. So, too, were a large majority of the clerical parents who answered a letter from the Master. Presented with these facts, the Council held 'a wide-ranging discussion on the subject'. When the final vote was taken (as Sir Henry Fisher remembered it) he and one other layman were alone in favour of continuing compulsory chapel – on the grounds that it provided a daily unifying event for the school. They were outvoted by the clerics, and the Council resolved that chapel be voluntary on all weekdays and only compulsory on Sundays for boys in their first two years and for the whole school on about half a dozen Sundays a term, at special services like the annual carol service or at 'university sermon-type services in the Memorial Hall'. Though Fisher had favoured its retention, he admitted that compulsory chapel had by this time become 'almost a dead duck' because of the disciplinary problem of forcing something they did not want on '900 boys largely from heathen homes'. Dancy, in fact, modified the Council resolution, and only retained compulsory chapel on Sundays for pupils in their first year. Some staff told him that if they were forced to go to chapel for two years they would never go again. In March 1969 Dancy told the Council that 80 to 100 boys and 20 staff were on average attending weekday services.

Underlying all that Dancy did was a belief in encouragement rather than compulsion. 'It is of course a good deal more difficult to run a school on these (as I call them) more liberal principles,' he told a school audience, 'but ... I am convinced that the liberal principle is a sound one: the most important part of education is training people in responsible choice.'

How difficult it was to run a school on liberal principles became increasingly clear as student protest rose to the climax it reached in 1968. During a sabbatical that year Dancy thought hard about that symbol of Flower-Folk times, long hair, and decided that it must be cropped. The following term he announced that boys' hair should no longer cover the ears or overlap the collar. Though this was his decision, he was prepared to argue about it with anyone who cared to meet him afterwards in the Adderley. To his astonishment, when he reached the door of this very large room he could barely force his way in. His back to the entrance door in the only space he could find, he explained that, whether rightly or wrongly, it was a fact that long hair caused the school's reputation to slip, and as a result the reputations of every one of them as individuals. Presently a boy from the back, who claimed to have just had a £10 styling, asked 'Is the Master aware that the human ear is the second ugliest part of the male anatomy?'

Such authoritarianism on Dancy's part was unusual, and it was more typical that he abolished beating by prefects. The liberalism of his regime probably explains why the 1960s passed without dramatic incident at Marlborough. In 1966 the main complaint of the editorial of *The Marlburian* centenary number was that there was nothing to protest about. 'If the young people of today ... are going to rebel ... it is essential that they are given something to rebel against. When the brick wall which they had imagined they were attacking turns out to be a cotton-wool curtain, then they are completely lost.' The editor actually complained about the reduction in corporal punishment. 'No longer is a boy punished for breaking a minor rule, he is only admonished verbally; his psychology might be upset by the cane.' On the other hand 1968 was a year in which Nicholas Milner-Gulland, a young classics master, felt that 'the lid was only just kept on the boiling pot'. Every day some fresh radical broadsheet was being distributed around Court.

Alongside a general loosening of discipline in favour of trust, Dancy made a positive attempt to defuse protest by establishing staff–pupil discussions, known as Dialogues. In 1968, 40 members of Common Room and 90 students volunteered to take part in these. They were divided into 13 groups, approximately three staff and seven students to each, and were asked to consider specific school problems, the first being how pupils should spend the hours on Wednesday afternoons which they were required to devote to some form of community service. 'The ultimate decision will still remain with the Master and the Council,' the Acting Master explained (during Dancy's sabbatical). 'In fact what we really have is democracy presided over by a benevolent dictatorship.' Two years later (October 1970) Dialogues were taking place about three

Plate 5.
Museum Block and Bradleian Arches.

Plate 6.
The Master's Lodge with St Peter's Church behind.

times a term; the subject of the most recent had been: 'What is Marlborough for?' The conclusion was unexpected: not for obtaining A-levels, which might have been the parents' view, but for forming personal relationships.

It would have been surprising if the Corps had survived the 1960s without some parallel, liberalising reform. In 1960 it was 100 years old. At its centenary parade on Level Broadleaze, 640 cadets advanced in review order, band playing. When they halted the spectators felt the ground tremble. But it was rapidly losing numbers to the works group or to various other permitted 'community service' alternatives. In these years there was a general feeling among the boys that they did not want to be trained to kill people.

The Corps' CO, David West, then devised a scheme sometimes called the Compulsory Corps Demilitarisation, but which he preferred to describe as its transformation into 'state-sponsored youth service'. Boys in the year in which the Corps had been compulsory (their second at the school) were to be put into non-military uniform and trained for a range of non-aggressive activities (map-reading, vehicle maintenance, first aid etc.) which were nevertheless sufficiently military to satisfy the War Office that they were appropriate for future members of the Combined Cadet Force (as the Corps was by then named). Only in their subsequent years would they be able to choose, if they wished, to go into the army, navy, air force or civil defence sections of the Corps itself. War Office permision had to be obtained to create a civil defence uniform by dyeing

Corps Centenary Parade on Level Broadleaze in 1960. Inspecting Officer General Sir Charles Keightley (OM), Governor and C-in-C Gibraltar. On either side of him, C.O. David West and Tommy Garnett.

CCF Band during the
Centenary Parade, Beating
Retreat in the Master's
Garden.

battledress blue. The scheme was a success, and it could now be said that
anyone wearing a military uniform was doing so of his own free will.
Numbers fell below 200 at one time, but are now around 250.

A reform which was precipitated from the outside began in 1963. That
year external inspectors visited the school and instead of reserving all
comment until they left, one of them came to Dancy to tell him about
something so important that it should not wait. Why did he preserve
a feature of the school which, more than any other, prevented boys from
reading books? He referred to Upper School which still survived in New
Court. When Dancy closed it, finding junior boys day-rooms or studies
in their houses, George Turner congratulated him on extinguishing the
last relic of tribalism at Marlborough, a word Dancy took to refer to East
African tribalism, but Turner may have meant to refer also to those tribes
formed by the boys of the school in its early anarchic years.

Dancy would have liked to make one further reform: to abolish the
school's junior houses. By this time they consisted of A house in college
and Barton Hill, Elmhurst, Upcot and Priory out of college. But there
was so much opposition to the proposal that he was only able to close
the last two, and junior houses as an institution survived for another 20
years.

Near the end of Dancy's time the Council made an internal change
which, despite its own protestations, somewhat loosened the school's
direct connections with the Church of England. Until then the ex-officio

Chairman and President of the Council had been the Bishop of Salisbury. But Bishop Fison was not a natural chairman. In 1964 when the Master received a letter from the National Society against Cruel Sports about Marlborough's beagle pack, Fison let the discussion continue until all members of Council had expressed their opinions a great many times, then concluded, 'I find this a very difficult question. Shall we pray?' He was also in poor health and in July 1970 told the Council that although he thought that the Bishop of Salisbury should still be a Council *member*, he was no longer sure that he need be chairman. That October the clerics of the Council submitted a memorandum which suggested that the Council 'should take immediate steps (*a*) to relieve you and your successors of an obligatory chairmanship [and] (*b*) to ensure that this change is not misinterpreted as implying any weakening of the Marlborough commitment to a Christian vocation.' The Council agreed, retaining the Bishop as its President who would officiate on Prize Day, but deciding in future to have a non-clerical chairman. For the first of these it chose Lord Brooke of Cumnor.

Henry Brooke, who had arrived at the school as a boy in 1916, and become the first Senior Prefect from an out-college house, had been elected to Parliament as Conservative member for West Lewisham in 1938. He had joined the Council in 1945 and been chairman of its finance committee from 1948 to 1954, but had given up this position when he became a government minister. From 1962 to 1964 he was Home Secretary, and in 1966 became a life peer. The Council, in his opinion, was not an ideal governing body. It was too large, its members were on average too old and it never met at Marlborough. He failed to have it reduced from 24 to 16 or 18, which he believed desirable, but he did persuade it to hold an annual meeting at Marlborough, and did gradually reduce its average age. Though Brooke had been a member of Council when it approved many of the reforms of the 1960s, he was essentially conservative. About Dancy he once said, 'John Dancy does have ideas. They aren't all equally good but he goes on having them.'

In 1973 he told a Marlborough audience, 'Behind every successful man there stands an astonished woman.' He referred to Lady Brooke, a peeress in her own right. Both their sons were at the school, and Peter Brooke, Garnett's first Senior Prefect and now also a politician, was the Minister for Northern Ireland who recently made as realistic an attempt to solve the Irish problem as anyone this century.

During his time Dancy considered that there was an important swing of influence in the school. Though Marlborough's housemasters had never been able to form so-called baronies, because their periods at particular houses were limited, they were powerful men when Dancy arrived, and he admitted that he 'led them a bit of a dance'. His habit was to enliven meetings by setting people arguing, or with provocative suggestions. One master remembered an occasion on which, by accident, a vote was almost passed entirely to abolish PE. Dancy's aim was to transfer some of the housemasters' powers to heads of departments. Gradually he did so, gaining for them, for example, the right to give boys advice about the courses they should follow and their future careers. Meetings of heads of departments he found 'pure joy', and remembered as an example a discussion about how to find more time for music and art. Unasked, Goldsmith, head of mathematics, suggested giving up certain mathematics periods. It might even be good for boys to do less mathematics.

Common Room also contained an entrenched body of evangelicals, who would proselytise at evangelical summer camps where the uncommitted would be encouraged to 'take the step'. Dancy remembered being stopped in Court by one of these enthusiasts and asked loudly, in the hearing of boys and other staff, 'Master, do you believe that Jesus Christ is the Son of God?' But such embarrassments were untypical and on the whole Dancy believed that he had the firm support of the great majority of the staff. 'We did feel (and I think the plural is justified) that we were in the lead among schools, that the changes we were making were (i) important, (ii) inevitable or at least necessary, (iii) effectively irrevocable.'

As for his feelings about Marlburians, they were quite simply 'splendid people'. He would quote the school's architect, David Roberts's pleasure at having Marlburians come to him to study architecture at Cambridge. While a Wykehamist, when shown the reading-list, would say of some book, 'I simply must glance at that again,' the typical Marlburian would read the list with unsophisticated enthusiasm.

Whatever the final verdict on Dancy, he was a Master to whom it was impossible to be neutral. When he went in 1972 to become Principal of St Luke's College of Education, Exeter, some considered this appropriate because he was an educationalist rather than a headmaster, others were dismayed to lose the most exciting and inspiring Master of the century.

14

AFTER THE STORM

1972–1986

I F THE COUNCIL wanted a period of calm for Marlborough after the
many changes of the 1960s, it chose wisely when it appointed Roger
Ellis, headmaster of Rossall, to succeed Dancy. Ellis approved of
Dancy's reforms; he considered that the Council's most important
decisions had been, time after time, to appoint Masters who would
support liberal policies. But he was essentially more conservative than
Dancy.

This did not prevent him from being apprehensive when summoned
to the House of Lords to meet the Council's new chairman, Lord
Brooke. Was he to be told that the Council considered the experiment
with girls a failure, or ordered to reimpose compulsory chapel? 'We have
one worry,' Lord Brooke told him. 'A number of Old Marlburians are
not happy about the entertainment provided at Penny Readings.'

Ellis considered that the liberalism for which Marlborough by this time
stood, led to a paradox. Whereas most Marlburians took a pride in the
individuality which the school encouraged, the school itself was highly
centralised and collegiate in style. Not only did the majority of boys live
close together at its centre, but they spent their first year in a junior
house, and there formed friendships which lasted when they moved to
other, often different houses. In this way it was, for example, quite
unlike his own school, Winchester. And though he felt at first that the
junior house system need not be totally abolished, gradually he came to
believe, like Dancy, that it should go. While the 13-year-olds of the early
1970s were still 'bright-eyed and bushy-tailed', ten years later they were
far more sophisticated and quite ready for an all-age house. But all he

could do was modify the system and reduce its centralisation by transforming Barton Hill, the only surviving out-college junior house (since it had absorbed Elmhurst), into an all-age house, and reopening Elmhurst as a junior house to take some of the boys from A House.

Ellis was prevented from doing more by the other main feature of Marlborough, its poverty. When he arrived in 1972 he was shocked by the living conditions of in-college houses. At this time it seemed possible that the school's finances might be transformed by selling the valuable 40 acres of Barton Farm which it still owned. George Turner, with much foresight, had bought Barton Farm and Granham Hill in 1930, with the intention of protecting the school's environment. The greater part of the farms had been sold in 1968, but these 40 acres now seemed about to prove even more important to the school's future. At the last minute, however, the Victorian Society intervened – disastrously, as it seemed at the time – to prevent the destruction of Upcot which the scheme involved, on the grounds that it was an important example of the work of Norman Shaw.

The Computer Centre. An ingenious use of roof-space in the Leaf Classroom Block.

Devising and getting permission for alternative access to the Bath Road which would avoid Upcot took many months and by then Heath's Conservative government had fallen and there had been a dramatic drop in property values. As a result the Council postponed the sale, which was not effectively revived until the 1980s. Then a first 20 acres were sold for a modest half million pounds, the idea being to allow environmentalists to become accustomed to the new houses and to increase the value of the land which remained. One of the conditions for the first sale was that the rest should not be sold for five years. When this was eventually offered, six bids were received. Five ranged from £4 to £6½ million, but the accepted bid was of over £8 million.

This deal, which hugely improved the school's finances (and which made possible the enormous changes of the last few years) was only signed, however, a week after Ellis left. And the money raised by the earlier deal was used mostly for a more urgently needed purpose: the building of the Dene – Pudmore block (these ancient names supplied by Kempson) to provide studies and bedsits for the boys of the nearby Field Houses. (B3 and C2), thus leaving space in New Court for additional studies for the houses around Court. At other times Ellis had to discover extra space within existing buildings, for example by creating attic bedsitters in the old B House, and by making room for a computer department out of the roof space of Leaf Block classrooms.

Of all Dancy's changes, the introduction of girls was undoubtedly the most important. But from the start it was Ellis's opinion that the arrangement for Sixth Form girls could not be permanent. For one thing,

214

they compounded a feature of the school which, he believed, put it out of balance: its top-heaviness. In the autumn when boys and girls stayed for what was known as the Oxbridge term there could be as many as 400 in the Sixth Form; and even when Oxford and Cambridge set their exams earlier, some stayed on to make use of the Art Department's excellent facilities. This made the Michaelmas term exciting but distorted the shape of the school, something which admitting younger girls would correct.

By 1977 there were 91 girls, all Sixth Formers, constituting 10 per cent of the school. The experiment was widely considered to have been a success, not only by those involved but by other schools who came to see how it had been done. Wellington College, Charterhouse, and St Edmund's, Oxford among others, soon followed Marlborough's example. It was the attaching of groups of about a dozen girls to various houses which had led to their quick and virtually complete integration into the school. The following year one of them, Tori Holt, began her report on a survey she had carried out: 'There have now been girls at Marlborough for about ten years, and like parasites, they have become well adapted to their situation.' The overwhelming majority were contented parasites. Eighty-three per cent considered that they had 'gained confidence from being in a minority at such a large school', only 15 per cent had ever wanted to return to their old school, 79 per cent felt the teaching to be better at Marlborough. On average during their two years each girl had had 3.1 boyfriends. One hundred per cent felt that Marlborough had overall 'been a success for them'.

There had, of course, been problems, most of them handled by the housemasters' wives who were given special responsibility (and a small payment) for attending to the girls, or by Mrs Ellis, who still liked to accommodate a few at the Lodge so that, at the 'grizzly Monday evenings' when once a term these ladies all met, she could share their worries. She also perpetuated an occasion known as 'girls' break', which coincided with the general morning break, during which the girls could, if they wanted, gather at the Lodge.

Selecting girls for entry remained difficult especially for the ten years while Marlborough was ahead of other major schools in offering girls places, and when, as a result, there was enormous demand. The same general criteria were applied: that they should be the sort of girls who would 'fit in' and 'be able to cope', but Mrs Ellis remembered that she would be surprised later to find how well some had done who had been admitted as borderline cases. The pressure eased when more schools began to take girls.

A number of members of Common Room, however, considered, as

Ellis did, that the experiment was incomplete and in January 1978 Richard Barker, Head of Business Studies, prepared a paper on the subject. He argued that remaining a single-sex school even between 13 and 16 would make Marlborough look 'increasingly anachronistic'. Preparatory schools were now beginning to admit girls, and universities were soon to become entirely co-educational. It would be absurd that boys should come from one co-ed community and go to another, and in between spend a few years in sexual isolation. The weaknesses of all-boy schools were well known, and so were those of all-girl schools. In today's changed society boys needed 'to learn to live with, lead and be led by girls'. And girls, he claimed, would get a 'more serious work atmosphere' at a boys' school.

There were also economic arguments for change. He foresaw a swing away from boarding-schools to day-schools, something which Marlborough must lose from, because of the smallness of the town. As a result its intake would either decline or 'weaken in calibre'. Girls could fill the gap and help to maintain academic standards.

'So clearly do I see the need for co-education', Barker ended, 'that I feel the onus of maintaining the status quo should rest with any who feel that way.'

When the Master soon afterwards submitted a list of possibilities for the school's future to the Council, it responded by setting up two planning committees, one of its own members, one of staff. Though these committees also considered enlarging the Sixth Form, opening the school to day-boys, recruiting more students from overseas and dividing Marlborough into junior and senior schools, they eventually recommended pursuing Ellis's first proposal: the admission of 13-year-old girls.

The Council itself agreed. In November 1978 it wrote to parents telling them so, and set up a working party to consider how the change could be made. Where the girls should live was the most difficult problem. Though the working party favoured mixed boy and girl houses at all ages, it reluctantly rejected this because adapting the houses would be too expensive, and suggested instead all-girl houses up to O-level and mixed houses thereafter.

Meanwhile Old Marlburians, parents and the boys of the school, showed themselves less than enthusiastic. After the AGM of the Marlburian Club there were what Barker called 'rumblings'. The parents at a meeting on Prize Day were mostly against change. So were the majority of boys when the plan was explained to them at an assembly.

As for Common Room, like many a common room, it turned out to have almost as many opinions as members. Attempting to summarise these, Barker wrote that although a majority hoped eventually for full co-education, some believed that this would never be successful in the 'essentially artificial' circumstances of a boarding-school, some that the college was not yet ready for the change, some that the working-party's plans were too expensive and some that they would produce too slow a change. Though a small majority were in favour of the scheme despite its drawbacks, 'most senior members of Common Room, including housemasters and heads of departments, were against it'.

Ellis remained in favour. On 10 March 1979 he concluded a long submission to Council by reminding it that the previous November it had agreed that 'while there were at present no compelling reasons for going co-educational, if the step was to be taken ... the least advantageous time would be if it was forced upon the college for economic reasons'. The Council was persuaded in principle, but not that the particular plan proposed was satisfactory. Sir Henry Fisher, by now chairman, was against it on financial grounds, and the scheme indeed foundered on lack of money. In Ellis's words, 'there was not enough pressure for change to move the financial mountain which blocked the way'.

Barker was not convinced by this explanation. It was, he believed, an outcome of allowing past members of the school to rule its future – not a wise policy – and was a great missed opportunity for Marlborough, which set back the cause of co-education by ten years, in particular at prep schools. But Barker, in Ellis's opinion, represented the most radical wing of a divided Common Room.

The decision against further change can be seen as symptomatic of the 1970s and 1980s. On the one hand pupils became less radical, on the other schools reimposed some of the restraints of earlier times. At Marlborough Ellis found that New Court on a Saturday night had become a 'no-go' area, something which he courageously refused to accept. There was more drug-taking than he had expected, and during his first 18 months he dismissed a larger number of pupils than during the whole of the rest of his time. He also discontinued the Dialogues which Dancy had started, believing that boys and girls were 'tired of being endlessly consulted about everything'. On the other hand in 1973, when the sale of land along the Bath Road seemed imminent, he thought this a good opportunity to start a new consultative process with a discussion in which boys and girls participated about how the money should be spent. And in 1978 he estabished the School Council, consisting of three elected members of Common Room, an elected member from each house and the Senior Prefect. With slightly altered constitution, this survives today as the School Forum.

The modest conservatism of Ellis's regime was good for Marlborough. Dancy's innovations, most of which now seem desirable if not inevitable, had given the school a reputation which discouraged conservative parents and, equally important, prep-school headmasters, with the result that numbers had fallen. Slowly Ellis increased the school's size to around 900. Much of the credit for this should go to J. R. Thompson, the school's first full-time Registrar. Thompson had an effective personal touch. When shy boys first came to see the school with their parents he would tell them 'this is *your* visit, not *theirs*. But you don't have to speak, just nod or shake your head. Cricket? Science?' Much was also done by Ellis himself to persuade preparatory school headmasters of Marlborough's merits by inviting small groups of them to dinner-parties. Maintaining numbers was more of a problem towards the end of Ellis's time, when the market became a buyer's one, and parents no longer needed to register their children with a particular school many years ahead.

Like Dancy, Ellis was impressed by the strength of Common Room. There was an academic liveliness which he believed unequalled except perhaps at Winchester. Other masters besides the mathematician, Goldsmith, whom he considered outstanding were the biologist Michael Roberts, the English master Andrew Davis and the two history masters, Oliver Ramsbotham and Peter Carter. At Carter's memorial service in 1983 the historian Richard Southern said:

> The perspicacity, learning and labour which he lavished on reading and commenting on pupils' essays and examination papers of a single term would have produced a substantial review for the *English Historical Review*; his notes for a term, a long article; those for a couple of years, a long book – an original and notable one moreover. He made a conscious choice to renounce all these things, because he believed that he could do more for the people and things he valued simply by speaking to a handful of people each day, and preparing to speak to them for much of the night. In the world's eyes it was a fantastic renunciation.

Outstanding, too, was Robin Child, who, after a brief interval, had succeeded Guy Barton as Art Master. Boys and girls would come to Marlborough solely because of the reputation of its Art Department, and after A-levels be able to pursue a one-term course considered the equivalent of their art 'foundation year'. Under Christopher Joseph geography also acquired again some of its pre-war standing. Appointed by Dancy in 1967, Joseph had found the department 'very quiet', subsidiary in standing to history which dominated the modern side.

The print room in the Art School. Note its central position, looking out on to the main court. The press pictured is older than the College!

There was a Geography Society, but it was, in one boy's words, 'not the kind of society which goes up to the downs and picks up stones – more social'. Joseph disbanded it.

The so-called blocking system was a great help to the department in gaining an increased number of A-level candidates. This system, devised by Laurence Ellis, the mathematics master and author of many SMP books, divided Sixth Form subjects into four blocks. Some subjects could appear in more than one block. Provided a pupil chose subjects in different blocks he would be able to construct a personal timetable. The general effect of this was that pupils could choose a more varied group of subjects, of which geography was more often one. From 1970 onwards Marlborough, helped by its Sixth Form girls, began to win Cambridge awards in the subject.

The geography department and outdoor activities overlapped at the Kirkpatrick Centre, the property in Snowdonia acquired by the school in Dancy's time. It consisted of an old stone building, with outbuildings, and would sleep about 25. Here parties would go on week-long field-trips. Under Pat Heffron the Outdoor Activities department took under its control other school groups like the Mountaineering Club, and many different groups regularly use the Kirkpatrick Centre. The department has also organised holiday expeditions to places as distant as the East Indies. At the school it has extended its influence by providing one compulsory day a term of outdoor activities for every lower-school boy.

By comparison with heads of departments, Ellis found good

Evocative of the Marlborough countryside. A 30-mile charity walk on the Ridgeway Path.

housemasters difficult to discover. He remembered discussing the problem with Frank Fisher, head of Wellington College, who had precisely the opposite problem. If only they could have arranged swaps. Housemasters of the time remembered that Ellis gave them exceptional support, perhaps because, unlike Dancy, he had been one himself (at Harrow), and understood their problems. One of his reforms was related. Dancy had introduced a system under which pupils could choose their own personal tutors. This, Ellis believed, meant that those most in need of good advice chose tutors who were known to be unlikely to interfere with their way of life. It was also a system which took out of the house something which should belong there, and Ellis abandoned it, expanding instead house tutor arrangements.

One of Dancy's introductions which did now begin to flourish was the Technical Projects scheme. The original idea had been that of a

220

Sevenoaks master, Gert Summerhoff; science masters from Marlborough who visited Sevenoaks were impressed by the variety of ingenious projects which the boys had supposedly conceived, but somewhat less so when they asked whose idea each had been and were invariably told 'Mr Summerhoff, sir'. Nevertheless a Technical Projects laboratory was established at Marlborough in a hut near the Mound. But it was difficult to find a master who would inspire boys to undertake such work, and, because the subject was non-curricular, it remained a hobby activity.

In the 1970s its computing side gathered momentum under the mathematics master, Marcus Gray, but only when its 'design and make' side was made a curricular subject did the project as a whole become a success. One problem was to decide whether it was more a science or an art; eventually the decision was in favour of science and the new laboratory was attached to the science block. Ellis believed that this was justified by the way in which its ideas soon permeated the attitudes of the school's scientists. But the Art Department remained interested. One of his most gratifying memories was of a three-hour period during which science and arts masters together became increasingly excited as they watched boys trying to turn piles of wood into chairs of their own design.

One of Ellis's influential appointments was Robin Nelson who came in 1982 to be Director of Music. It was Ellis's view that the music of 900 boys and girls was being performed by 100 of them. He chose Nelson, who was director of music at a large comprehensive school, as the man to involve the whole school, even if the great majority would never be musical. Nelson's aim was to make music fun. He revived the 'House Shout', once the inter-house singing competition, but in a liberated form. Each house, under its own music director, would now choose and stage its own pieces. The day when these were performed on the Memorial Hall stage came to resemble the last night of the Proms.

'Brasser' in the Queen Elizabeth Hall, London, in 1980, when they gave the first western world premiere of Khachaturian's *The Battle of Stalingrad*. Robert Peel, conductor, far right.

Nelson also began to stage musicals (the first *Oh What a Lovely War*) and was amazed when hundreds of boys and girls would come for auditions. He arranged large trips to musical events (100 to a West End *Guys and Dolls*) 'to give the feeling of going in a group'. And he organised tours by the choir, now in cassocks again, of France and the USA. Music teaching he broadened, by adding for example the harp, jazz piano and jazz violin, and by increasing to about three dozen the number of pupils taking singing. As for the orchestra, he believed that it was important for it to perform adult music, even if at the top end of its abilities; 'the more adult the music the more like musical adults the performers will behave'.

It was the Director of Physical Education, Brian Ashley, who, in June 1975, promoted an entirely new development at Marlborough when he persuaded the college to allow its premises to be used during the summer holidays for what has been described as an 'intellectual Butlins'. The description is too narrow for the activities of the Marlborough College Summer School, a limited company which, for the last 18 years, has offered courses in over 70 subjects, from squash, fly-fishing and karate, to caligraphy, yoga and 'human destiny'.

Jack Asbury, who became Bursar in 1976, deserves special credit for turning a first-year loss of £375 into a regular profit. This is covenanted to the college. There were various reasons for the Summer School's rapid success. It was unique at the time in offering a deal for the whole family.

A Summer School concert in Adderley.

And in 1978 it was filmed by the BBC, the result shown the following January as 'Holiday 79'. That year it received 30,000 letters of enquiry. Clearly it had devised the sort of self-improvement holiday for which there was a wide, unsatisfied demand. It quickly expanded to an annual three-week event for 500 students each week; courses could last one, two or three weeks. Such numbers have been maintained ever since. More students could have been taken if there had been more accommodation, but, as *The Marlburian* commented, 'you can't put adults into A House or the old Field House dormitories'. The bedsitters, however, which were being introduced, were ideal and the Summer School gave the college an incentive for increasing these.

Marlborough has benefited in other ways. Since the Summer School is run *by the college* the visitors experience the personality of the college – as they would not if it merely let its buildings to some other organisation. Over the years it has engendered much goodwill, and even if some who come could never afford to use the College for their children, a significant number of future parents and students first discovered Marlborough at the Summer School. It also provides holiday work for staff if they want it. The cost of a week's course with private room in 1991 was £295 – little if anything more than the price of a hotel room – and for non-resident students less than half as much. Each course runs from Sunday afternoon to Saturday morning and though this may seem short it is enough to produce an ocean-liner-style community, welcomed with a sherry party, celebrating its break-up with an entertainment based on the songs of student children. There are so many regular customers that the operation takes on the flavour of an annual reunion.

On 14 July 1984 the Marlburian Club celebrated the hundredth anniversary of its foundation with a Centenary Ball. For this well over 200 Old Marlburians (with partners) came to the school. The two most senior were the surgeon, B. L. Williams, FRCS, and Capt. G. H. Stanning DSO, RN (Bursar from 1963 to 1976) who arrived at the school in 1924 and 1925 respectively. At 9 p.m. the centenary cake was cut and when darkness fell there were visits to the observatory. Throughout its life the Marlburian Club has had two principal functions. To maintain and strengthen connections between Old Marlburians and the College; and to administer the various funds established as a result of appeals or bequests. Most important have been those which followed the two world wars, and which resulted in the building of the Memorial Hall, and in the awarding, since 1946, of numerous bursaries. Today this fund has an annual distributable income of £50,000.

Other funds help Marlburians at university or between school and university with travel, so that they can undertake worth-while projects for example work at a Cheshire home in India. The club also administers the Centenary Fund, which contributes to extra but not essential school items. While the club has been the body which has administered these funds, the funds themselves are the result of the contributions of individual Old Marlburians, which, during the last 70 years, have not only been impressive in amount but provided impressive evidence of the loyalty of Marlburians to their old school. Nor should the generosity of parents be forgotten. Today the Club has a nominal membership of 10,000, but its secretary admits that living members number closer to 8,000.

Though games in post-war Marlborough were no longer the obsession they had once been, they were still keenly played and watched. Ellis remembered that, 'until the 1980s the crowds watching the First Fifteen were sometimes embarrassingly enthusiastic in the way in which they expressed their support'. The annual Rugby match against Radley was now an occasion, as was the annual cricket match against Cheltenham. In both games the school continued to do well, as it did at cross-country and long-distance running and at tennis, but it was at hockey that it was outstanding. David Whitaker, briefly the team's coach, went on to coach the British side which won an Olympic Gold Medal.

Before Ellis came to Marlborough, as well as throughout his time there, he was actively concerned with the problems of preparatory schools in general. While at Rossall he had been asked by the ex-Marlborough master, Donald Wright (then headmaster of Shrewsbury, and chairman of the Headmasters' Conference) to chair a committee of public and preparatory-school masters on the problems boys experienced when moving from one to the other. Because the subject was a large one, Ellis persuaded Wright to allow the committee to discuss only the making of teaching at the top of prep schools lead naturally to what they would be taught at public schools. The committee's report was accepted and the country divided into regions in which the masters of both sorts of schools teaching the same subjects would meet. Ellis remembered 'having an entertaining afternoon crawling round the floor of the study in the Lodge at Marlborough sticking coloured pins into a large map of Britain in order to get the most convenient regional boundaries'. These meetings became known as Ellis Committees and later, because of their concern, Curriculum Committees. Ellis considered that as a result preparatory schools could claim 'to have anticipated by nearly 20 years the DES approach to a National Curriculum'.

In 1983 Ellis himself became chairman of the Headmasters' Conference and here he worked closely with his predecessor, Warwick Hele, to establish the Independent Schools Joint Council, a central body for all

Plate 7.
Left: A corner of Fountain Court.
Below: New Court. Behind a familiar façade has been created a house for girls.

Plate 8.
Leaf Block, with paths through the Wilderness leading to the new developments
(Language Centre and two new houses for C3 and Mill Mead) beyond.

sorts of independent schools, their governors as well as heads. The ISJC now incorporates an equally important body which Ellis also helped to establish, the Independent Schools Information Service. In 1984 his contribution to education was recognised when he was awarded the CBE.

When Ellis was asked in 1986 for his reflections on Marlborough's strengths and weaknesses he said he was sorry that promotion from form to form was now almost entirely by age or seniority. Though 'double jumping', as it was called, had produced a somewhat immature Sixth Form, it had given the school an academic élite which it now lacked. As a strength he picked out the Lower Sixth intake (predominantly the girls). They came to the school intending to make good use of their two years, not 'stuck in lower-school habits'.

That year it had surprised Ellis to discover that his regime had lasted longer than any other Master's except Canon Bell's. He left, not to go to some other school or university, like so many of his predecessors, but to join Barclays Bank, but he retained his connections with education by becoming the bank's graduate recruitment officer.

Roger Ellis with Princess Anne on the occasion of her visit in 1978.

The Memorial Hall today.

It is possible to find those who would criticise Ellis during his later years as Master, when they would claim that he let the behaviour of boys and girls slip out of strict control. Some would say that he allowed too much drinking and was too liberal about late night hours, dangerous policies in a partly co-educational school. In Ellis's opinion criticisms of this sort from outsiders often reflected 'the natural hostility towards Marlborough of the headmistresses, who sedulously spread rumours that all the girls in the College were advised to be on "the pill", which was the opposite of the truth'.

Some members of staff were also exasperated by the time he would take to make up his mind. But it is impossible to find a single person, master, pupil or parent, who did not like and trust him. As a headmaster he admitted that he was not comfortable, and had 'always felt bad about being in the middle of a mass of boys and girls that I don't really know'. It was in relationships with individuals – staff and pupils – that he *was* comfortable. If the ability to understand and sympathise deprived him of the ruthlessness required of a reformer, it made him the right Master for the time.

15

A NEW START

1986–1993

AVID COPE, who came to Marlborough as the new Master in 1986, had held two headmasterships before, one at Dover College, the other at the British School in Paris. He was given no specific brief by the Council, but he believed he was chosen because his record in these posts showed that he was the sort of man who would make changes. If so, the Council should be well satisfied with the seven years of his regime.

At Marlborough he did not like what he found and said so in public, inevitably disturbing those who had been happily loyal under his predecessor. He was 'shaken', to use his own word, by the slackness, the number of boys who broke the rules, the macho atmosphere, a certain cynicism among staff and pupils and above all by a sense that no one any longer knew what Marlborough stood for. There was a pleasant atmosphere, and there were pockets of excellence, but the emphasis was on the right of everyone to do his own thing. The Sixth Form entry, the Oxbridge term and the artbridge term (the term in which art students stayed on) made the school top-heavy and as a result it had more of a university than a school atmosphere. There was also a marked difference in the amount of liberty allowed by different housemasters. In sum he felt that 'central direction needed to be reasserted'.

The most obvious change he made was the introduction of girls from the age of 13. At Dover he had found an all-boy school and left a fully co-educational one. The various effects, both social and academic, this had brought he believed to have been 'wholly beneficial'. At Marlborough he found that Common Room attitudes had changed so that there was now a great swell of opinion which expected the same good results, and which considered it appropriate that, just as Marlborough had been one of the leaders in admitting Sixth Form girls, so it should now lead the way in introducing full co-education.

As in Ellis's time the financing of the change was the principal obstacle, but now all was altered by the £8 million from the sale of the final 20 acres of Barton Farm. An important problem remained: should the new houses be mixed or single sex? The decision Cope favoured was a compromise, but with the emphasis on separate houses, his main argument that parents of girls aged 13 would not want their daughters to be in mixed houses. He was also influenced by the problem the school would have faced in finding the number of housemaster-and-wife partnerships which would have been needed to run a school made up entirely of mixed houses. The pattern as it finally emerged had five girl and five boy in-college houses. The compromise was to allow out-college houses each to retain about a dozen Sixth Form girls.

Important for the new layout around Court which this required was a second change which Cope considered almost as important, though it is less often seen to be so: the final abolition in 1989 (after almost 130 years) of the junior house system. This had been started by Cotton, following Wilkinson's advice, at a time when many new boys were only aged eight or nine, and needed segregation, something they did not need when they were over 13. Boys and girls would now go at once into their permanent houses. As a result A House, greatly reconstructed inside and gaily redecorated, could become a girls' house and was renamed Morris House. Other girls' houses were made out of New Court, Elmhurst, Field House and one of the new houses on Mill Mead. Boys' in-college houses were B House, C1, C2 in Dene–Pudmore, Barton Hill and C3 in the second new house on Mill Mead. The majority of these changes were made by the start of the 1991 autumn term, and the conversion of Field House and Dene–Pudmore during the following two years. An important consequence has been that every house now has 'territorial integrity', i.e. its own and not a shared building.

Two problems, connected with the school's buildings, remained. In 1991 the school consisted one-third of girls, two-thirds of boys, once considered the right proportions to maintain. But fixed proportions of any sort are not acceptable to the Equal Opportunities Commission. On the one hand the school has assured the Commission that in principle it is committed to an open entry in which neither sex has a fixed proportion of places allotted to it. On the other hand the Commission has told the school that it understands the problem it would face if from one year to the next it had to convert girls' or boys' houses into the opposite, in

High summer – the view across to the running-track and tennis courts.

order to house different proportions of the sexes. Unisex (easily converted) accommodation has been discussed.

The second problem – whether to admit day-pupils – had been considered by Council at least from Dancy's time. There were, in fact, a few so-called home boarders in the 1930s. The strongest argument in favour of the change today is that throughout the country parents as a whole are tending to want day-schools for their children, partly because these are less expensive, partly because they prefer to keep their children at home. When Cope spoke to a meeting of Wiltshire parents with the aim of justifying co-education at Marlborough, he was soon told that this was unnecessary – what they wanted to hear about was the possibility of the school admitting day-pupils. The argument often used in the past that Marlborough town is too small to provide the school with a significant number of day-pupils no longer applies now that Swindon is so close by car and has a large monied class. Admitting day-pupils, however, would be a break with Marlborough's tradition which many Marlburians are reluctant to accept and in 1992 the matter was still being discussed.

Just as important as these transformations of the school's structure were reforms which Cope set about making in order to improve its academic standards. The underlying change required, he believed, was to the work ethic. He detected a feeling that it was not the done thing to work hard. A change in something so basic would not be easy, but certain reforms were possible. It was one of Marlborough's great

David and Gill Cope in the
Master's Garden on Prize Day.

strengths that it had always encouraged a huge variety of extra-curricular activities. Cope believed that this had got out of hand. Pupils could, for example, be excused 7.30 to 9.15 prep for any number of reasons, all worthy in themselves but cumulatively damaging to their school work. Term-time field trips, though of benefit to pupils studying a particular subject, would take them away for as much as a week from their classes in other subjects. Restraints on extra-curricular activities inevitably caused dismay to Common Room empire builders; the aim of the new Director of Studies, James Rothwell, was not to destroy their empires but to prevent them interfering with the proper teaching of school subjects.

To implement these reforms, the school was given an expanded senior management team, consisting of two Deputy Heads (one a woman appointed in January 1992), Senior Master, Senior Mistress, Director of Studies, Bursar and Registrar. The Master intended this inner cabinet to free him from a mass of paperwork and allow him to be in direct contact with pupils and staff.

The school's academic achievements, measured in terms of A-level results, showed a steady improvement over these years. Between 1986 and 1991 the number of A and B grades has remained steady but the percentage of passes has risen from 92.5 to 97 and the grade average from 3.13 to 3.4. Sceptics may have suspected that the goal-posts had been moved and the pass-level lowered, but alternative ways of assessing academic success, for example by league-tables, have their own inbuilt distortions.

The money from the sale of Barton Farm land also contributed to the building of the new Language Centre, formally opened in 1991 by Peter Brooke, and an expansion of language teaching at the school. This had been a feature at Marlborough for many years. In Dancy's time, for example, Chinese was briefly introduced. Today courses in nine languages are regularly offered and two more occasionally. Included for the last few years have been Arabic and Japanese, as well as Chinese, the courses in each of these oriental languages incorporating the study of the cultures and histories of the countries where they are spoken. Acquiring teachers of exotic languages has not been easy and some have been sent abroad to study them. Just as Charles Bull was given 50 guineas in 1872 to spend a month in Germany, so in 1937, George Turner sent Coggin to Russia. Recently staff have been sent for training in Chinese to Oxford and to Taiwan, in Arabic to Exeter University and in Japanese to Sheffield University. Though it might seem that courses in exotic languages must be extravagant in teachers' time since the classes are likely to be small, in fact such teachers usually teach other languages and have other duties.

Alongside classroom and language laboratory teaching, the school has a long tradition of organising foreign visits and exchanges for language students. The first of these was arranged in the 1930s when boys from Marlborough went to Salem, at Birklehof, Germany. Robin Swann remembered the return visit.

> At the start of one Summer Term, maybe 1935, there appeared a handful of blonde Adonises with little English but great presence. Turned out they were sixth-formers from Salem – founded by Kurt Hahn before he fled Hitler and came over here to make Gordonstoun and ... the whole Outward Bound Movement. His boys made an impact, academically as well as athletically, I ... would dearly like to know whether in due course they shot down Spitfires or set my M.T.Bs alight in the Med.

Today there are also term-long exchanges with two other German schools, and exchanges of half a term with King's College, Madrid. Marlborough requires every A-level language candidate to spend at least four weeks 'fully immersed' in a country which speaks the language.

For lower-school pupils there are four-week exchanges with Le Caousou school, Toulouse, and ten-day Easter holiday exchanges with Heidenheim, Germany. In 1988 a group of Marlburians made a two-week summer visit to a school in Jordan, which was returned by Jordanian boys and girls the following year. There have also been visits to Russia for a number of years, for example a joint visit with St Paul's of 35 pupils in 1987, the year in which Marlborough celebrated 50 years of Russian teaching with a Russian Day. In 1990 exchanges began with Kiev School No 57. Exchanges with a school in Japan and another in Oman are being planned. The Modern Language Department has been commended by the *Times Educational Supplement* for its exchange arrangements.

In recent years many other departments of the school have flourished and it would be invidious to select. It does, however, seem appropriate, because of the aims of Marlborough's founders, to mention the work of recent school chaplains. Peter Hardman, who came to the school in 1972, had, in Ellis's opinion, a gift for chapel's big occasions: confirmation Sunday or the Advent carol service, for example.

By contrast, Laurence Gunner, who arrived at almost the same time as Cope, has aimed to reduce 'mass occasions' by offering four or five Sunday alternatives, each with a different character, from which boys and girls can choose. There are also voluntary services on Tuesdays and Thursdays, organised and conducted by pupils known as House Sacristans.

His creation of these (housemasters believed that Marlburians would be too laid back) was based on a view with wider relevance: that during the last 20 or 30 years the school's most serious failure has been to neglect to promote the notion and practice of leadership. It was Gunner's idea that new House Captains should attend a rigorous training day, consisting of much self-examination, mutual examination and discussion of typical problems (three Lower Sixth pupils found smoking behind the bike-shed).

Gunner believes that his third role is to be available to pupils who have personal problems they need to discuss. It is essential, if they are to bring these to him that they shall know that what they tell him is confidential, and to reassure them that he is in this way to be distinguished from other members of Common Room he likes to be called Father Gunner.

In addition to these internal matters, he has re-established Marlborough's contacts with the outside world, believing that 'schools like Marlborough can only justify their privileges by what they give back to society as a whole'. Marlburians are now working again in various impoverished Swindon estates; there are exchange visits with a Birmingham comprehensive school, Sir Wilfrid Martineau; and there are again lively contacts and interchanges with Tottenham, where the parish which the school supported until 1920 lies on the edge of the notorious Broadwater Estate, and now has a largely coloured population.

In one way the character of the school has undergone an important change during the last 10 or 20 years: the home backgrounds of its pupils are no longer what they were. The school has become too expensive for

'Brad Arches': a favourite
meeting place.

the sort of professional middle-class parents who at one time formed the
overwhelming majority. Today many are newly rich, in business, while
others are foreign. There is a danger, as some see it, that schools like
Marlborough will acquire the character of a Swiss finishing-school, and
become exclusively patronised by the world's very rich. On the other
hand it could be argued that the wave of new public schools founded
after 1840, of which Marlborough was one, were required to do
something very similar: turn the children of the self-made manufacturers
of the Industrial Revolution into English gentlemen.

Whatever its aims, Marlborough in its first 150 years has made a contribution to the life of the nation which is as remarkable for its variety as for its
importance. To name just a few Old Marlburians who have not already been
mentioned, they include the yachtsman, Francis Chichester; the saint, Oliver
Feetham, Head of Bush Brotherhood, Australia; Sir Nicholas Goodison,
Chairman of the TSB Group, formerly Chairman of the Stock Exchange; Sir
Nigel Gresley, designer of the LNER engine which still holds the world speed
record for steam; Norris McWhirter, originator of the *Guinness Book of
Records*; Captain Mark Phillips, the horseman; Simon Verity, stone carver;
Mark Tully, BBC foreign correspondent; and J. Z. Young, Linnean gold
medal winner. During the 1991 Gulf War the Armilla Patrol which cleared
Iraqi mines was commanded by Rear-Admiral Colin Cooke-Priest.

The future is unpredictable, the recession of the early 1990s is giving all independent schools problems, and Marlborough is not escaping. The new
Master who will succeed David Cope after his early retirement in 1993 will not
find his task easy. But the cedar of Lebanon which Thomas Garnett planted in
the Master's garden and against which he backed the school is still many years
from maturity, and most Old Marlburians would make a similar bet today.

233

CHRONOLOGY

1702–25	Mansion built.
1751	Mansion becomes Castle Inn.
1838	Aug: First known mention of Revd Charles Plater's school proposal.
1840	Jan: Plater's first prospectus.
1841	Dec: Committee formed to promote school.
1842	July: Public meeting chaired by Archbishop of Canterbury, Castle Inn chosen.
1842–3	Lower School built.
1843	August: School opens. **Revd Matthew Wilkinson first Master**.
1845–48	Dining Hall, Master's Lodge, Upper School, first chapel, A House and B House are built.
1851	First *Marlburian* published. Nov–Dec: Rebellion.
1852	**Revd George Edward Lynch Cotton Master**.
1852	Lower School established in A house.
1853	Cotton circulated parents about games.
1853–4	Financial crisis.
1854	Modern School established.
1855	First inter-school cricket match (against Rugby).
1858	**Revd George Granville Bradley Master**.
1860	Sanatorium built.
1860	Rifle Volunteer Corps formed.
1862	Preshute House opened. College wins both Balliol open scholarships.
1864	Natural History Society formed. First inter-school Rugby match (against Clifton). Clarendon Commission reports on Marlborough. Railway reaches Marlborough.
1865	*The Marlburian* refounded.
1870	Scarlet fever epidemic. School closed for first Easter holiday. Foundation scholarships established. Reduced fees for sons of the clergy suspended.
1871	**Revd Frederick William Farrar Master**. First science master appointed.
1872	First two purpose-built out-college houses, Cotton and Littlefield, opened. Bradleian opened.
1874	First Penny Reading. Marlborough wins Ashburton Shield.
1875	*Lancet* reports on Marlborough.
1876	**Rev George Charles Bell Master**.
1877	Porter's Lodge built.
1881	Marlborough mission at Tottenham founded.
1882–3	Museum block built.
1886	Consecration of new Chapel.
1893	North Block built. Jubilee celebrated. A. G. Bradley's history published.
1894	The Marlburian Club founded.
1902	Boer War ends: 43 Marlburians dead.
1903	**Frank Fletcher Master**.
1908	Rifle Volunteer Corps becomes Officers Training Corps. Gymnasium built.

1910–11	Field House and bridge built.
1911	**Revd St John Basil Wynne Willson Master.**
1914	August: War declared. First Marlburian casualties.
1916	**Cyril Norwood Master.**
1918	War ends: 742 Marlburians dead.
1923	Electric light installed.
1924	*The Heretick* published. First Marlborough–Swindon Camp-Club camp.
1925	Memorial Hall opened.
1926	**George Charlewood Turner Master.**
1933	Science block built. Centenary Fund appeal launched.
1934	The Marlborough Press founded. Marlborough Mountaineering Club founded.
1936	Corps Signal Section develops first walkie-talkie sets. Leaf Block built.
1939	**Francis Melville Heywood Master.** Sept: War starts. City of London School evacuated to Marlborough.
1942	Marlborough threatened with occupation by Ministry of Aircraft Production.
1945–6	War ends: 415 Marlburians dead.
1946–7	Attempt by several masters to have Heywood replaced.
1948	Visit of George VI and Queen Elizabeth.
1952	**Thomas Ronald Garnett Master.**
1952–3	Castle Farm bought and restored.
1953	Everest climbed by Lord Hunt's expedition.
1961	Development of School Mathematics Project at Marlborough.

1962	**John Christopher Dancy Master.** Littlefield fire. Norwood Hall, new dining-hall, opened. Art School built. New Upper school abolished.
1965–7	Swindon boys at Marlborough.
1968	Business Studies started at Marlborough. First Sixth Form girls admitted. Compulsory chapel rules modified. New Music School finished.
1969	Kirkpatrick centre established in Snowdonia.
1972	**Roger Wykeham Ellis Master.**
1974	Barton Hill extended and converted to all-age house with Sixth Form girls.
1975	Marlborough Summer School established.
1978–9	Debate about entry of girls at 13.
1984	Technology building opened.
1984	First sale of Barton Farm land for *c.* £1/2m.
1986	**David Robert Cope Master.**
1987	Second sale of Barton Farm land for *c.* £8m.
1987–8	Sports Hall built.
1989	Junior houses abolished. 13-year-old girls admitted.
1989–91	New girls' houses created in New Court, Elmhurst and A house (renamed Morris House). New Houses built, one each for boys and girls on Mill Mead.
1991	Language Centre opened.
1992	Dene-Pudmore extended for boys and Field House for girls.

INDEX

Afghanistan 96
After Many Days 110
Ailesbury, Marquis of 20, 25, 65, 90
Aldershot 96
Algiers 80
Alpine Journal 194
Amis, Kingsley 160, 164
Ampleforth College 187
Anderson, Peter Ralph Hendry 185
Anne, Princess 225
Arnold, Matthew 79
Arnold, Thomas 12–4, 51, 122
Asbury, Jack 222
Ashanti War 93
Ashburton Shield 96, 167–8
Ashley, Brian Gordon 222
Attlee, Clement 175
Australia 16, 70
Avebury 140

Badbury 55
Bain, John 9, 100
Balliol College 66, 109
Bambridge, William Samuel 107, 117–18, 120
Barker, Richard 201, 216–17
Barton, Guy Gunliffe 189–92, 193, 218
Bath 23, 24
Becher, Godfrey George 159
Bedales School 201
Bedford School 109, 190
Beer, Ian David Stafford 184, 185
Bell, Arthur Capel Herbert 154
Bell, George Charles 86–108, 140, 142, 155, 225
Bell, John 116
Belloc, Hilaire 124
Bennett, Robert Douglas 121, 122, 123, 124–5, 129, 133
Benson, Edward Frederic 92, 105, 118–20, 136
Benson, Edward White 64, 68, 101, 111
Bere, Charles Sandford 55, 102
Betjeman, John 123, 134–6, 144, 148, 156, 166
Biden, John 94
Bird, Arthur Leyland 134

Birkbeck College 155
Birley, Michael Pellew 166–7
Birley, Robert 148
Blackfriars Station 160
Black Mountains 189
Bloemfontein 97
Blore, Edward 32–3, 53, 84, 88, 89, 140, 151
Bodley, George 89–90, 181
Bompas, Gate-Sergeant 31–2, 38
Booth, William 124
Boughey, Charles Lovell Fletcher 140
Bowers, George Hull 18, 19, 20, 21, 25, 27–8, 29, 30
Bowle, John Edward 135, 136, 137
Bowood Park 96
Bowra, Maurice 137
Boyle, John Archibald, 103
Boys, Charles Vernon, 81
Bradbury, Edward Kinder 130
Bradfield College 168
Bradley, Arthur Granville 15, 16, 18, 25, 30, 34, 38, 42, 44, 45, 46, 57, 64–5, 70, 99, 101–3, 105, 117–18, 158
Bradley, George Granville, 63–76, 78, 81, 86–7, 90–1, 96, 99, 103, 109, 110, 111
Bradley, Peter Edward Moore 170
Bredgar 43
Brentnall, Harold Cresswell 158, 159, 161
Bright, James Franck 55, 69, 70, 104
Bristol Grammar School 134
British School in Paris 227
Broadwater Estate 232
Brooke, Henry 144, 211, 213
Brooke, Peter Leonard 196, 211, 231
Broughton, William 16
Brown, Alexander 176
Brown, Lancelot 'Capability' 22
Brown, Peter Brindley, 166
Browning, Robert 79
Bruce, Lord 20
Bryanston School 184
Buckingham Palace 32
Buchanan, Robert 53
Budd, E. H. 56
Bull, Charles Musgrave 55, 69, 72, 94,

95, 100, 104, 117, 231
Bullock, A. E. 144
Burn, Thomas Harris 55
Butcher, Samuel 67–8, 75, 109
Butler, Richard Austen 156, 175, 180
Butler, Samuel 12
Butterworth, Charles Henry 94, 95

Callendar, Hugh Longborne 80
Cambridge University 14, 62, 66, 102, 155, 161, 184, 193, 197, 199, 212, 215
Cameron, Julia Margaret 69
Camps, Francis Edward 154–5
Canning, Clifford Brooke 136
Canterbury 15–16
Caousou School 231
Capel-y-fynn 189
Cardigan Bay 72
Carey, Kenneth Moir 146–7, 207
Carlisle 106
Carroll, Lewis 14
Carter, Clement Cyril 158
Carter, Peter Noël 218
Castle Farm 144, 189
Castle Inn, Marlborough 20, 21, 22, 23, 24, 25, 28, 29
Cator, Susan 93
Cattley, Stephen 16
Cawnpore 93
Chamberlain, Neville 163, 165
Channel, English 106
Charles, Prince 196
Charterhouse 11, 41, 120, 183–4, 199, 215
Cheltenham College, 14, 56, 87, 102, 109, 125, 139, 168, 224
Chichester, Francis Charles 233
Child, Robin 218
China 96
Chippenham 55
Christ Church (Oxford) 86
Christ's Hospital 87
Church Family Newspaper 122
Churchill, E. Bailey 142
Churchill, Winston 165, 175
Circe 191
City of London School 16, 160–4
Clarendon Commission 68–9

Clayton, Harold 100
Clayston, Jonathan Page 59, 60
Clifton College 61, 70, 102–3, 201
Clogstoun-Willmott, Herbert Nigel 171
Cloudsley-Thompson, John Leonard 155
Coates, James Michael Campbell 178
Cobb, Clement Francis 27–9, 30, 33, 34, 99
Coggin, Frederick Leslie 174, 231
Commentary on Maccabees I 206
Compton, Daniel Goddard 37
Concise British Flora in Colour, The 92
Congreve, Walter 59
Connaught, Duke of 138
Cooke-Priest, Colin Herbert Dickinson 233
Cope, David Robert 226–33
Cope, Gill, wife of David 230
Corfield, Mrs, Matron 27
Cornish, Thomas Brooking 47
Cotton, George Edward Lynch 13, 29, 40–65, 76, 100, 101–2, 115, 117, 122, 228
Cranbrook School, Sidney 156
Crimean War 62, 93
Croft 14
Crossman, Richard 195

Daily Mail 135
Dale, Francis Richard 160–1
Dancy, Angela, wife of John 206
Dancy, John Christopher 176, 194, 197–212, 213, 218, 220, 229, 231
Dancy, Nicola, daughter of John 205
Daniel 191
Daresbury 14
Darwin, Charles 76
Davenport, John Archibald 159
David Blaize 92
Davidson, Miss 81
Davidson, Thomas Arthur 167–8
Davies, Sergeant 95
Davis, Andrew Hellier 218
Davis, Michael Justin 191
Delafosse, Henry George 93
Delhi 93
Del Mar, Alan Richard 187, 195, 196
Devizes 126
Dictionary of National Biography, 18, 93
Dodgson, Charles 14
Dodwell, E. H. 167
Dover College 227
Duck, James 161

Dyson, George 139

Eagle House School 11
Ealing Broadway 161
Ecclesiologist 32–3
Eden rapids 106
Edinburgh, Duke of 92
Edwards, Francis Drewe 53
Elder, Harry Montagu 80
Elizabeth, George VI's queen 179, 180
Ellis, Laurence Edward 219
Ellis, Margaret, wife of Roger 215
Ellis, Roger 212–26, 228
Ellis Committees 224
Elverson, Hamilton James, 155
Enfield 141
English Historical Review 218
English Tradition of Education, The 134
Eothen 11–12
Epsom 130
Equal Opportunities Commission 228–9
Eric or Little by Little 76, 85
Etna 80
Eton College 11, 20, 40, 41, 61, 85, 94, 106, 125, 141, 152, 158, 187
Evans, Geoffrey Maynard 143
Evening Standard 175
Everest, George John 52
Everest, Mount 192–4
Everett, William Marriott 187
Exeter 161

Farrar, Frederick William 27, 75–86, 87, 91, 99, 106, 117
Fearon, W. 86–7
Feetham, John Oliver 159, 233
Fergus, Walter 35, 52–4, 70, 73, 80, 83–4, 100, 117
Fergusson, Gilbert Charles Dalrymple 97
Few, Robert 21, 38, 47–8
Fiennes, Celia 22
Filkins Hall 20
First World War 128–34, 164, 168
Fisher, Frank 220
Fisher, Geoffrey Francis 112, 124, 125, 150, 156, 179
Fisher, Henry Arthur Pears 207, 217
Fisher, Robert 143
Fison, Joseph Edward 211
Flecker, Henry Lael Oswald 144
Flecker, James Elroy 144
Fleming Report 203
Fletcher, Frank 108–20, 122, 136, 158,

183, 185
Fleus, H. J. 27, 36–7
Florence 90
Foch, Marshal 138
Foot, Michael 175
Fox, Gerald Daukes 187–8
Fra Angelico 79
Francis, John 16
Frensham Heights School 185
Freshwater 69
Fuchs, Richard 164
Fyfield Downs 167

Gardiner, John 53
Garner, Thomas 89–90
Garnett, Penelope, wife of Thomas 186, 192
Garnett, Thomas Ronald 120, 183–96, 199, 209, 233
Garrod, Archibald Edward 79–80
Geelong Grammar School 196
Genus Micraster around Marlborough, The 155
George VI 114, 179, 180
Gidney, Alec Ralph 135–6, 144, 159
Gilbert, George 16
Gildea, William 34, 47
Gill, Albert
Gilmore, James Boyd 73–4, 107
Gladstone, William Ewart 15, 18, 19, 20
Glennie, Alfred Henry 94–5
Gloucester 49
Goddard, Rayner 179, 180
Goldschmidt, John Herman Thorburn 114
Goodban, Gerald Archer 185
Goodison, Nicholas Proctor 196
Gordonstoun 164, 231
Gould, Marius Herbert 105, 122
Granham 71, 214
Graves, Robert 132, 134
Gray, John Marcus 221
Great Bedwyn and East Grafton 21
Gresley, Nigel 233
Griffiths, Edward 177–8
Gunner, Laurence 232
Guys and Dolls 222

Hahn, Kurt 164, 231
Haileybury College 18, 61, 70, 77, 161
Halcomb, Charles Henry 20–1, 29
Haldane, Richard Burdon 126
Halliday, John Harrison 195
Hamilton, Niall 89

Hamlet 191
Hammond, Barrie Rees 185
Harding, Thomas Oliver 107
Hardman, Peter 232
Harrison, John William Drinkwater 61, 68, 96
Harrow School 11, 41, 76, 79, 85, 86, 91, 145, 148, 185, 220
Hart, Reginald Clare 96
Harvey, Edward Robinson or Herbert 56
Harvey, Ernest Musgrave 177
Hawtreys School 169
Hayllar, Bruce Sherwill 165, 166
Hayman, Perceval Ecroyd Cobham 188
Hayward, Maurice John 135, 139–40, 141
Headmasters' Conference 202, 203, 224
Headmistress, The 140, 158
Heath, Edward 214
Heberden, Arthur Clement 139
Heffron, Patrick 219
Hele, Warwick 224
Herbert, Sydney 21
Heretick, The 136, 148
Hessey, J. A. 30
Heywood, Francis Melville 161–82, 185, 199, 204
Hilary, Edmund 193
Hilton, John Robert 136
Hodgson, Christopher 19–20, 30, 59, 176
Hodgson, George Edgerton 36–7
Hodson, Denys Frazer 172
Hogg, Christopher Anthony 196
Holt, Tori 215
Holy Angels, Hoar Cross 89
Hone, Brian William 155, 156
Hony, Henry 186
Hooghly 62
Hort, Arthur 109
How, Henry Walsham 141
Huddersfield School 30
Hughes, Christopher Wyndham 8, 136
Hughes, George Hill 134
Hughes, John Bickley 50
Hughes, Thomas 12
Hulloch 131
Hungerford 54
Hunt, Henry Cecil John 192–3
Hunter, Thomas Alexander Alfred 178
Hurd, Percy 175–6
Hutchesson, Henry 16

Iceland 80

Ilbert, Courtenay Peregrine 66, 68, 99, 109
Illustrated London News 26–7
Importance of being Earnest, The 191
Independent Schools Information Service 225
Independent Schools Joint Council 225
Indian Mutiny 93, 94
Ingles, Henry 41
Ingoldsby Legends 100
Inkerman 93
Irving, Henry (jnr.) 100
Isaacson, John Hugh 198
Isle of Dogs 162
Isle of Wight 63, 69
Ivimey, John William 139–40

Jackson, Alastair Ian 187
James, Herbert Armitage 109
James, Leonard Warwick 16, 57
Japan 105
Jennings, Reginald Angus Unwin 176
Joseph, Christopher Ariaratnam 218–9
Jowitt, William Allen 175, 179, 180

Keate, John 11–12, 41
Keightley, Charles Frederick 209
Kempson, Edwin Garnett Hone 192–4, 214
Kennet, river 38, 50, 148, 189
Kensington Grammar School 30
Kiev School No. 57 232
Kingham, 28
Kinglake, A. W. 11–12
King's College, Cambridge 203
King's College, Madrid 231
King's School, Canterbury 16, 41
King's School, Parramatta 16
Kirk, John William Karnegie 97–8
Kirkpatrick Centre 219
Kitson, Robert 95
Kooshtea 62

Ladysmith 97
Lambert, Royston 203
Lancet 53, 73, 83
Lancing College 185, 198, 199
Land's End 106
Lansley, Howard 140–1, 198
Lascelles, Alan Frederick 114, 179, 180
Leaf, Herbert 140–1
Lechlade 20
Leeds 49
Lidell and Scott 14
Life of Christ 85

Lindfield 106
Lipari Islands 80
Llanthony Abbey 189
Lockesley Hall 114
Lockwood, Edward Dodswell 28, 30, 33, 35, 38, 44–5, 46, 117
Lord Mayor Treloar College 181
Lords 128
Lowndes, Ashley Gordon 154–5
Lowndes, George Alfred Norman 133
Luckington 14
Lucknow 93
Lunn, Hugh Kingsmill 164
Lupton, Joseph MacDougal 122

McAlpine, Michael Scott 153
McGeachy, Clara, wife of Foster 86
MacNeice, Frederick Louis 123, 135, 136, 148, 156, 186
McWhirter, Norris Dewar 233
Mafeking 98
Makerere College 146, 158, 159
Manchester Grammar School 61
Maples, John 176, 181
Marlborough Anthology, The 156
Marlborough College (School):
Academic achievements and standards 66, 101, 113, 230
Aesthetes 134–7, 148–9
Art department 190–1, 221
Athleticism 92, 100, 104–6, 112, 115, 122–3, 135, 137, 148–9
Beagles 186–7
Blocking system 219
Biology 154–5
Bridge building 187–8
Buildings, construction, changes of use etc., of college buildings at Marlborough: Adderley Library 32, 186; A House 30, 60, 88, 150–3, 210, 228; Band Room 188; Barton Farm 214, 216, 228, 230; Barton Hill 210, 214, 228; B House 30, 88, 214, 228; Bradleian 81–2, 140; Chapel (first) 30–1, 32–3, 84, 88–9; Chapel (new) 88–90, 181; Cotton House 73–4, 81; Dene-Pudmore 214, 228; D House 53; Dining-hall 30, 32, 88; Elmhurst 195, 210, 214; Field House 115, 119, 120, 214, 228; Green, The 83; Gymnasium 70; Hermitage 70; Language Centre 231; Leaf Block 141, 214; Littlefield 73–4, 81, 197; Lower

Marlborough College cont.

(Modern) School 29–30, 61, 73, 80;
Mansion (C House) 23, 29, 32,
42; Master's Lodge 32; Memorial
Hall 137–40, 226; Memorial
Reading Room 90; Mill Mead
houses 228; Morris House *see* A
House; Museum Block 90; New
Court (New Upper School) 29,
70, 151, 228; North Block 90;
Norwood Hall 191, 197; Pavilion
102; Porter's Lodge 31, 42, 81–2,
88; Preshute 70; Priory, The 123,
210; Sanatorium 53, 70; Science
Block 154; Stables 29;
Summerfields 83; Tin Tabernacle
89; Turner House 204; Upcot
123, 210, 214; Upper School 30,
89, 123–5, 135, 150–1; White
House 21, 29, 53; Wiamate 118.
Bullying 37, 68, 101, 151–3
Bursaries 223
Business Studies 200–2
Centenary Fund 154, 179, 224
Chapel attendance 206–7, 232
Circuit weight-training 178
Colbeck Reading Prize 69
College servants 157–8
Common Room 199, 216–17, 218,
227–8, 230
Corporal punishment 34–6, 40, 44–5,
84–5, 113, 124, 196, 208
Corps (Rifle Volunteer, OTC, JTC,
CCF) 94–6, 125–9, 130, 146,
166–70, 192, 209–10
Council 19, 24, 29, 30–1, 32, 33, 39,
40, 47–8, 50, 51, 58–60, 62–3,
66, 73, 74, 78, 80, 81, 87, 89,
108, 121, 140, 146, 181–2, 197,
203–4, 207, 210–1, 213, 216, 226
Curriculum 17, 19, 50, 61, 67–9, 77,
79, 135, 137, 199–202
Day-boys 204, 216, 229
Debates 62
Dialogues 208–9
Discipline 207–8, 217
Drama 191
Electricity 140
Epidemics 72–3, 74, 192
Fagging 150
Fees 17, 18, 19, 20, 39, 58, 70, 74,
153–4
Fights 34, 26–7, 39
Finances 18, 39–40, 56–60, 70, 74,
214, 229

Marlborough College cont.

Fines 36, 52, 57
Food 33–4, 36, 52, 53–4, 57, 68, 100,
122, 153, 172
Foundation 12, 13, 15–23
Foundation scholarships 74
Games 33, 55–8, 99, 100–5, 115, 125,
156, 224
Gating 36, 42, 47, 48
Geography 158, 218–19
Girls 203–6, 214–17, 227–9
Governors 18–19, 58, 74
Health 83–4
History teaching 114
Home Guard (LDV) 165–6, 169
Homosexuality 85
Hostel system 64, 68, 111–12, 121
Housemasters 176–8, 186, 211–12,
219–20, 227
Jubilee (50th) 98–100, 106
Language teaching 107, 231–2
Marlborough–Swindon Camp-Club
143–4
Marlborough College Press 155–6, 180
Mission at Tottenham 141–3, 144, 232
Modern School 60–1, 68–9, 79, 100,
107
Mountaineering 192–4
Music 33, 117–20, 139–40, 221–2
Natural History Society 80, 90–2
Numbers 18, 19, 30, 33, 36, 48, 60,
68, 88, 137, 165, 218
Opening 13, 24–9
Outdoor activities 219
Parents 73, 74, 153, 184, 199, 207,
232–3
Payne Poppets 188
Penny Readings 118–20, 213
Prefects 34, 51, 52, 61, 112, 124, 151
Rebellion 15, 40–8
Red Book 107, 113
Review 67, 68, 108, 109, 113
Scholarships at Marlborough 81
School Council 217
School Forum 217
School Mathematics Project 199–200
Science 79–81
Sex education 177–8
Staff 33, 52–3, 55, 68, 88, 107,
144–5, 176–8, 184–7, 212, 218
Summer School 222–3
Swedish drill 121
Technical Projects 202, 220–1
Tutors 220
Uniform 115–17, 172, 206

Marlborough College cont.

University scholarships 66, 115, 137,
189
Wiltshire (Swindon) boys 202–5
Works Group 188, 209

Marlborough, Duke of 143, 175
Marlborough Country, The 158
Marlborough Grammar School 21, 194
Marlborough Litany, The 156
Marlborough Magazine 33, 72
Marlborough Struwwelpeter, The 115–17
Marlborough Times 71, 96, 187
Marlburian, The 33, 54, 56, 71–2, 77,
96, 104–5, 106, 114, 115, 129,
130, 132–3, 141, 156, 167, 170,
180, 195, 196, 208, 223
Marlburian Club 138, 179, 216, 223–4
Martin, F. P. Brounker 20
Martin, William Keble 92
Martinsell 56, 85, 98
Mason, James Neville 149–50
Matthews, Charles Henry Selfe 158,
176
Maurice, J. B. 92
Maurice, Thomas Richardson ('Dick')
155
Maurice, Walter Byron 92
Mayhew, Christopher 195
Medawar, Peter Brian 154
Melbourne Grammar School 156
Merchant Taylors' School 68
Mildenhall 166
Miles, Ernest Henry 105
Milner-Gulland, Nicholas James 208
Milton, John 78
Mons, Battle of 129
Montenegro, King of 165
Montgomery, Mr 21
Montmorency, Raymond Hervey
Lodge de 97
Moore, Mark 152, 158
Moore, Peter Fitzgerald 155
Morris, William 39, 188
Morshead, Owen Henry 52
Moseley, Edward Nicholas 62
Muggeridge, Malcolm 164
Mullins, Joel Francis 52
Murray, Gerald Walker 178

Napoleon III 94
Nash, John 32
National Service League 126
Navy League 126
Naylor, Christopher 16

Nelson, Robin 221–2
Nelson, T. M. 28
Néry 130
Nettlestead 27
Newbury 168
Newcastle, Duke of 20
New College, Oxford 66
New Quarterly Review 87
Newton, William Godfrey 138, 140, 154
New Zealand 186
Nichold, John Beverley 114
Nicolson, Harold 108
Niemeyer, Otto 175
Nisbet, Hugh Ulric Swinscow 115, 123–4, 128–9
Noble, Livie 177–8
Nonsense Rhymes 124
Normandy 171
North, William 94–5
Norwood, Cyril 134–45, 158, 175
Nunns, Robert Augustine Luke 49–50, 51, 52, 56, 117

Ogbourn St Mary 43
Oh What a Lovely War 222
Omdurman 97
O'Regan, John Rowan-Hamilton ('Pat') 113–15, 171
O'Regan, Michael Lionel Victor Rowan-Hamilton 148
O'Regan, Patrick Valentine Rowan-Hamilton 171–2
Oxford University 14, 66, 89, 102, 158, 199, 215

Packe, Edward 59
Palermo 81
Pall Mall Gazette 107–8
Palmer, Henry 55, 61–2
Palmer, Henry George 90, 99
Palmer, John 24
Palmerston, Lord 62, 94
Papillon, John 66
Papillon, Thomas Leslie 66, 99, 109
Pattison, college editor 88–9
Payne, Ivo Richard 188
Peel, Robert 221
Pelly, Arthur Roland 132
Pennines 190
Penny, Edward 115
Pepin, Arthur Raymond 168–70
Peviar, T. 38, 42–3, 44
Phillips, Mark Anthony Peter 233
Pigott, Samuel James 43

Pigott, S. R. 43
Pitt, William, Earl of Chatham 23–4
Plater, Charles Eaton 15–9, 20, 59
Platt, William 168, 179, 180
Pole, Reginald Carolus, 61–2
Ponsonby, Noel Edward
Popovic, Ida Elizabeth, wife of Pavel 165
Popovic, Pavel 164–5
Portal, Lord 175
Powell, William John 201
Poynton, Frederick John 88, 110
Prelude 114
Preshute village 20, 84
Preston, Thomas Arthur 91, 92
Proctor, George Henry 93
Public Schools and the Future 202
Purton village, match 56–7

Quadling, Douglas Arthur 200
Queen Anne's Bounty 19

Radley College 185, 187, 224
Railway, arrival at Marlborough 70–1
Ramsay, Alan Richard Dalhousie 186
Ramsbotham, Oliver Peter 218
Randle, Leslie John 155–6
Reading 28, 161, 174
Recollections of School Days at Marlborough College 1848–1851 34
Reeve, Jonah 70
Repton School 125
Rhodes 171
Rice, Richard 20
Richardson, Henry 92, 97, 99, 103, 110, 113
Richmond Grammar School 11, 14
River 15, 16
Roberts, David 197, 212
Roberts, Lord 126
Roberts, Michael Bliss Vaughan 218
Robson, Alan 159, 178
Rochester 85
Rockley 166
Rodwell, George Farrar 79–81, 107
Rogers, butler 28
Rogers, Cecil Denis 150–1
Rogers, Horace Mordaunt 104, 118
Rogers, John Davenport 78, 117
Romola 110
Roseveare, Harold William 129
Rossall School 18, 40, 61, 72, 94, 109, 185, 224
Rothwell, James 230
Royal Institution 77

Royal School at Bath 159
Rugby School 11, 12–13, 29, 51, 56, 63, 64, 86, 101–2, 109, 110, 120
Ruskin, John 79
Russell, Richard Squire 156
Rutland, William Rutland 187
Ryde, Peter John 181

Sabben-Clare, Ernest Elwin 185
St Augustine's, Pendlebury 89
St Columbus College 144
St Edmund's School, Oxford 215
St John's College, Oxford 175
St Mary's, Marlborough 194
St Paul's School 68, 231
St Peter's, Marlborough 23, 30, 40
Salem 231
Salisbury Journal and Devizes Mercury 23
Salisbury Plain 63, 129
Salmon, Nowell 93, 99
Sandford, Temple Charles Gabriel 115
Sargeaunt, George Montague 144–5, 159
Sassoon, Siegfried 105, 113, 132, 134, 156
Savernake Forest 20, 21, 34–5, 38, 50, 65, 90, 93, 169, 173
Savernake station 70–1, 161–2
Savory, Douglas Lloyd 101, 105
Scott, Edward Ashley 55
Scrambles 192
Scutari Hospital 93
Sebastopol 62, 93
Second World War 158, 160–6, 168–75
Sellick, W. P. 54–5, 81, 100, 117
Sevenoaks School 221
Shakespeare, William 79
Sharpe, William Charles 56
Shaw, Norman 214
Sheen, Samuel 17
Sheppard, Percy 156–8
Sheppard, second wife of Percy, subsequently Mrs Hulbert 156–8
Sharpe, John 185
Sherborne School 109, 174, 199
Shrewsbury School 11, 12, 41, 94, 185, 224
Silbury Hill 22, 39, 55, 140
Silk, Dennis Raoul Whitehall 184, 185
Simpkinson, Henry Walrond 69–70
Sindhara 93
Sir Wilfred Martineau School 232
Sketches from Marlborough 92
Smith, Edward Floyer Noel 142, 143

Smith, George 23
Smith, Reginald Boswell 86–7, 100–1, 142
Smith, William Saumarez 47, 59
Smith-Dorien, H. 129
Smith-Masters, Anthony Bruce 191
Sodor and Man 193
Somaliland 96, 171
Somerset, sixth Duke of 22, 23
Somerset, Boscawen Thomas George Henry 38, 44, 50, 56, 117
Somme, Battle of 132
Sommerville, William 188
Sorley, Charles Hamilton 8, 9, 126, 127–8, 131–2, 135, 143, 156, 167
South African Wars 93, 96–8, 125–6
Southerton, Thomas Henry Sutton 59
Southampton University 199
Southern, Richard 218
Spanish Civil War 167
Spencer, Charles Bernard 148
Spencer-Stanhope, John Roddam 89–90
Stalland, Dr 73
Stanley, Arthur 12, 69, 78, 86, 117
Stanning, Geoffrey Heaton 223
Stonehenge 63
Stoner, Celia 165
Stowe School 186
Street, A. E. 90
Street, George Edmund 73–4, 81–2, 90
Strensall 168
Studdy, Henry William 36–7
Stukeley, William 23
Stupinigi castle 172
Summerhoff, Gert 221
Swann, Robin David Sidney 153, 231
Swann, Sidney 105–6, 153
Sweeny Todd the Barber 191
Swinburne, Algernon 84–5
Swindon 27, 54, 56, 71, 143–4, 153, 232
Syria 106

Talmadge, Charles William 52
Tanner, Janet 204
Tate, James 11
Taunton 161
Tayler, Charles William 60–1
Taylor, Alfred Waterhouse Somerset 85
Teesdale, Thomas 14
Tennyson, Alfred, Lord 69
Tennyson, Hallam 69–70
Tensing, Sherpa 193
Thackeray, Edward Talbot 93
Thomas, Arthur Frederick Wolferstan

143–4
Thomas, John Shearme 33–4, 35–7, 38–9, 40, 42, 44, 46, 51, 55, 57, 72, 80–1, 85, 86–7, 99, 100–1, 117, 143
Thompson, Francis Edward 73–4, 97
Thompson, H. L. 86–7
Thompson J. R. 218
Thorpe, Charles Edward 92
Thwaites, Bryan 200
Tidworth 166
Times, The 109, 202
Times Educational Supplement 232
Tom Brown's Schooldays 12, 51
Tomkinson, Col. H. 62
Tomkinson, Henry R. 60, 94
Tonbridge School 153
Tottenham House 169
'Trebla' 104–5, 106
Trinity College, Cambridge 51, 76
Tully, William Mark 233
Turner, George Charlewood 115–16, 136, 146–59, 160–1, 176, 183, 199, 210, 214, 231
Tweed, Robert (called Henry by Canon Gildea) 34
Twyford, Augustus Samuel 44, 47, 56

University College, Oxford 70, 74, 132
Uppingham School 72, 84

Vailly 129
Vaughan, Charles James 85
Vere, Lady 23
Verity, Simon 233
Vesuvius 80
Victoria, Queen 76, 85, 98
Voss, W. 43

Waddy, Lawrence Heber 153
Wall, Arthur Henry 122
Walpole, Horace 24
Walters, Edward Henry Seymour 156
Ward, John
Ward, Michael Phelps 192–3
Waterloo, Battle of 31, 95, 96
Webb, Alison M. 204
Weldon, Hugh de Weldon 204
Wellington College 64, 70, 72, 101, 111, 125, 168, 215, 220
West, David Ramsay Courtenay 166, 204, 209
Westcott, Frederick 109
West Lavington 50
Westminster Abbey 76, 85, 99

Westminster School 11
Wheeler, Marcus Christopher Corbet 174
Whitaker, David 224
White, George Kirkpatrick 144, 148, 148
White, William 73
White, Revd William 194
Whitehead-Smith, James 117
Whitstable and Seasalter 16
Whittington Press 156
Who's Who 105
Whymper 192
Wilde, Oscar 85
Wilkinson, Matthew 21, 25–50, 53, 57, 60, 70, 115, 228
Williams, Arthur de Coëtlogon 115–16
Williams, Bernard Lewis 223
Willis, Ann Caroline 206
Willis, Francis Peter 176
Willson, John Basil Wynne 121–33, 135, 159
Wilson, Eric Charles Twelves 171
Wiltshire Archaeological Society 194
Winchester Cathedral 41, 191
Winchester College 11, 12, 41, 61, 86, 94, 141, 152, 158, 167, 185, 198, 199, 212, 213, 218
Winnington-Ingram, Arthur Foley 159
Wisden 181
Wolfson, Lord 200–1
Wood, Henry Evelyn 45–6, 93–4
Wood, W. S. 30
Woodroffe, Leslie and Kenneth Herbert Clayton 130
Woodroffe, Sidney Clayton 130–1
Woodward (Robert, Thomas or Samuel) 52
Woolwich Academy 69, 79
Wordsworth, Charles 12
Wordsworth, John 109
Wordsworth, Matthew Charles 136
Worksop Manor 20
Wright, Arthur Robert Donald 184, 185, 195, 224
Wright, Thomas 181
Writtle 66
Wylie, Charles Geoffrey 192–4
Wylie, Hubert 172, 176

Young, Edward 86–7
Young, Geoffrey Winthrop 192
Young, John Zachary 233

Zurich, University of 159